Whistleblowing

The Law of Retaliatory Discharge

Whistleblowing

The Law of Retaliatory Discharge

Daniel P. Westman

BNA BOOKS

The Bureau of National Affairs, Inc., Washington, DC

Library of Congress Cataloging-in-Publication Data

Westman, Daniel P.
Whistleblowing: the law of retaliatory discharge/Daniel P. Westman.
p. cm.
Includes index.
ISBN 0-87179-661-9
1. Employees—Dismissal of—Law and legislation—United States.
2. Discrimination in employment—Law and legislation—United States.
3. Whistle blowing—Law and legislation—United States. I. Title.
KF3471.W47 1991
344.73′012596—dc20
[347.30412596] 90-23947
CIP

Published by BNA Books, 1231 25th St., N.W., Washington, D.C. 20037
International Standard Book Number: 0-87179-661-9
Printed in the United States of America

For Alison and Peter
my joy and inspiration

Preface

Thirty years ago virtually no legal protections existed for whistleblowers. Today the majority of states have created legal protection for whistleblowers either by statute or by judicial decision, and numerous federal statutes contain whistleblower protections as well. However, until now there has not been any compilation of these various legal protections. This book is an attempt to collect the numerous different legal protections for whistleblowers in one place so that any interested persons—employees, human resources managers, business executives, corporate counsel, and legal practitioners—may have easy access to them.

This book is also a response to the fact that the mere mention of the word "whistleblowing" often provokes extreme reactions. To their supporters, whistleblowers are viewed as "citizen crime-fighters," "ethical resisters," or similar figures of heroic proportion who risk their lives or careers for the public good. Their supporters argue that whistleblowers are necessary in a world governed by large bureaucracies which are not accountable to the people whose lives are affected by bureaucratic decisions. To their detractors, whistleblowers are viewed as "snitches," "stool pigeons," or "industrial spies" who are willing to publicly embarrass their co-workers and their companies in order to satisfy their political, ethical, moral, or personal agendas. Such employees not only wish to hurt their companies, their detractors argue, but also wish to keep their jobs.

This book arises out of the belief that, more often than not, the truth lies somewhere between these extreme views. Many whistleblowers may not be as noble as their supporters would make them out to be, but they also may not be as noxious as they are portrayed by their detractors. This book attempts to take a balanced view of the phenomenon of whistleblowing by discussing both the positive and negative aspects of whistleblowing. At this point I would like to mention that most of my litigation experience has been on the side of employers rather than on the side of whistleblowers. It would be less than forthcoming if I did not admit the possibility that this advocacy on behalf of companies may have colored my perceptions of whistleblowing. Mindful of this possibility, I have made an effort to discuss the topic of whistleblowing in neutral terms so as to avoid value judgments which may be inappropriate in a general legal discussion of this nature. The readers will judge whether I have succeeded.

This book also arises out of the belief that whistleblowing may be appropriate in public sector employment in circumstances under which whistleblowing may be inappropriate in the private sector. The book is organized so as to compare and contrast the legal protections for whistleblowers in the public and private sectors in order to highlight the differences between the two. Chapter 1 provides an historical overview of the evolution of whistleblower protections, discussing their origins in the public sector and the related area of government contracts. Chapter 2 then discusses the tensions between the competing legal duties owed by employees to their employers, and to the community at large, which help to explain the extreme reactions caused by whistleblowing. The chapter then discusses how those competing duties are balanced by the various laws protecting whistleblowers, using specific statutes or common-law doctrines as examples. Chapter 2 also discusses the different nature of employment in the government and in industry, and the different legal protections for whistleblowers in those sectors.

Chapters 3 through 6 specifically discuss different legal protections for whistleblowers in the public and private sectors. Chapter 3 addresses protections for persons employed by federal, state, and local governments; Chapter 4 addresses federal and state statutory protections for employees in the private sector; Chapter 5 addresses common-law protections for private sector employees; and Chapter 6 addresses statutes which protect persons regardless of whether they work in the public or private sectors. Chapter 7 discusses the conflicts which may arise when the various whistleblower protections overlap.

It is a measure of how far whistleblower protections have developed that the question often is no longer whether whistleblowers should be protected, but instead is whether whistleblowers should be given financial incentives to make disclosures. One of the most dramatic developments in recent years was the passage of the federal False Claims Reform Act of 1986, which is discussed in detail in Chapter 6. The Act not only protects whistleblowers who report their employers' submission of false claims in government procurement, but also provides significant financial incentives to make disclosures. Opponents of the Act argued that the law would create a class of modern bounty hunters who would abuse its provisions to obtain financial windfalls. At this writing there has not been enough experience under the Act to determine whether financial incentives, above and beyond protection from retaliation, are wise policy.

The book concludes with two chapters discussing the practical aspects of avoiding and defending whistleblower litigation. Chapter 8 discusses the litigation of whistleblower cases from the perspective of both whistleblowers and employers. As discussed in detail in that chapter, the litigation of whistleblower cases can be extremely time consuming and damaging to the reputations of individuals and of companies. In the hope of providing guidance as to how to avoid litigation of this nature, Chapter 9 offers suggestions regarding how individuals and companies may informally resolve their differences short of litigation. The intent of this chapter is to provide suggestions for protecting the public interest in a manner which preserves the dignity of individuals and companies alike. Finally, the appendices describe in detail the whistleblower protections discussed throughout the book.

Acknowledgments

The origins of this book go back to research I performed in whistleblower cases under the direction of several partners of our firm, principally William F. Hoefs, Philip R. Placier, and Steven L. Hock, and our former partner Kennedy P. Richardson. To them I am indebted for involving me in their whistleblowing cases, and for much of the practical litigation advice contained in this book. The research I performed grew into an article on the California whistleblowing statute, which I was encouraged to write by James P. Hargarten, chair of the Labor & Employment Relations Group of Thelen, Marrin, Johnson & Bridges. To him I am indebted for his enthusiastic encouragement and support as the article gradually evolved into this book. I also wish to acknowledge all of my partners, each of whom has indirectly made this book possible.

I have been fortunate to have had the able assistance of many colleagues in preparation of the manuscript. I would like to gratefully acknowledge the contributions of Theresa M. Beiner, Jennifer Black, Bryan E. Earl, Leslie E. Orr, Mark H. Wildasin, and Anne B. Wright. Special mention for their tireless assistance must be given to Bruce T. Wilson, Renee A. Roberts, Marci Kollar, Ann Borkin (and the firm's library staff), and the firm's word processing department. Further, I received thoughtful comments on various portions of the manuscript from Evan Jay Cutting and William F. Hoefs. None of the persons listed above are responsible for any matters with which readers may disagree, which of course are my responsibility alone.

My greatest thanks go to my wife, Alison L. Carlson, for her patience and understanding during the preparation of the manuscript. I would also like to thank my parents, Jack C. and Nancy K. Westman, for their invaluable encouragement and practical advice.

DANIEL P. WESTMAN

San Francisco
November 1990

Contents

1

The Evolution of Whistleblower Protections

It is generally accepted that employees owe a duty of loyalty to their employers which requires them to follow reasonable directions, and to conduct themselves in a manner in accordance with their employers' interests. However, it is also generally accepted that employees' civic or professional responsibilities may require them to take action detrimental to their employers' interests. For example, most jurisdictions require their citizens to serve on juries, or to testify as witnesses, regardless of whether acting as jurors or witnesses hampers their employers' productive efforts.

In the past century the conflict between these two generally accepted values—the employee's duty of loyalty and an individual's civic responsibility—has been heightened by statutory and common-law developments which either encourage employees to take actions detrimental to their employers' interests, or affirmatively protect employees who take actions which are contrary to their employers' interests. For example, ever since the Civil War the federal False Claims Act has encouraged citizens, including employees, to report fraudulent practices committed by companies in their business dealings with the federal government. Until recently, however, the False Claims Act did not affirmatively protect employees of federal contractors.

One of the most prominent statutes that affirmatively protects employees is the National Labor Relations Act (NLRA), which gives employees the right to participate in union activities for the purpose of collective bargaining, a development which many businesses vigorously resisted on the ground that it would seriously hamper their profit-making activities. To effectuate the right to organize, the NLRA prohibits employers from retaliating against employees for engaging in peaceful union activities, or for giving evidence in proceedings to enforce the NLRA. Thus, the NLRA protects an employee who testifies in an enforcement proceeding that his or her employer's conduct violated the NLRA. Numerous other federal and state statutes similarly encourage employee participation in proceedings to enforce such statutes, and protect participating employees from subsequent discharge.

Parallel developments have taken place in the common law of many jurisdictions. As discussed later in this chapter, the courts have long recognized that employers may not discharge employees who refuse to commit crimes at their employers' direction. More recently, several jurisdictions have protected employees who arguably have acted against their employers' interests in a variety of circumstances. For instance, as discussed in Chapter 5, many jurisdictions have held that employees may not be discharged for filing workers' compensation claims, even though such claims may cause employers to pay money even if the employees were at fault for their injuries.

Most would agree that employees should not be discharged for refusing to commit illegal acts, because employees should not be forced to choose between criminal liability and losing their jobs. It is not so clear, however, whether employees who are not legally responsible for any suspected improprieties, and who do not have first-hand knowledge of whether the employer actually committed any improprieties, should be protected from discharge if they disclose such alleged improprieties. No similar choice between a career or criminal liability is forced upon such individuals.

It is in this gray area where the boundaries between duties of loyalty and civic responsibility are unclear that most whistleblowing cases arise. As will be discussed in the following chapters, it is vigorously debated whether employees who have no responsibility for suspected improprieties, and who do not have sufficient information to determine whether the alleged improprieties actually have occurred, should be protected if they complain to their employers or to government agencies. Employers argue that encouragement of speculative whistleblower complaints, with the resulting need to exhaustively investigate and disprove such complaints, causes unnecessary expenditures of scarce resources. Employees contend that encouragement of even speculative complaints is necessary to effectively enforce the laws.

The developing modern law regarding whistleblowers is more readily understood when placed in the context of the False Claims Act, and of various labor relations statutes which have been enacted since the early 1900s, most of which make some attempt to protect employees who participate in proceedings to enforce the labor relations laws.

Historical Background

The following overview of the False Claims Act, and of labor laws enacted during the course of this century, illustrates that the concepts of encouraging employees to report their employers' wrongdoing, and of protecting employees who oppose their employers' prohibited conduct, are longstanding aspects of American labor law.

The 1863 False Claims Act

Fraud in federal government procurement programs has recently received a great deal of attention, one of the most notorious examples being the criminal convictions of persons involved in the Wedtech scandal.[1] However, federal procurement fraud is not solely a recent phenomenon, but has been a concern of the federal government since at least the time of the Civil War.

Congress enacted the False Claims Act[2] in 1863 to address the problem of unscrupulous profiteers who were taking advantage of shortages caused by the Civil War in order to extract unfair premiums from the federal government. The Act authorized private citizens to sue, in the name of the United States, any company which was engaging in fraudulent practices with respect to the federal government. In its original form, the Act did not allow the federal government to intervene in such lawsuits. The Act was amended in 1943 to permit the government to intervene.[3] However, the practical effect of private lawsuits under the original Act was to bring fraudulent practices to the attention of the federal government.

To encourage lawsuits, the Act allowed private citizens to recover for themselves a percentage of the amount that a contractor had fraudulently obtained from the federal government. The Act permitted private citizens who were employees of contractors engaging in fraud to sue their employers, but did not also prohibit retaliation by employers against such employees. As set forth in Chapter 6, the Act was amended in 1986 to prohibit retaliation against employees who sue under the Act.[4] Nevertheless, even in its original, limited form, the Act demonstrated Congress's intent to encourage all citizens to take steps which would bring federal procurement fraud to the attention of the appropriate authorities. Moreover, the Act was one of the first laws to encourage employees to challenge procurement fraud committed by their employers.

Labor Law Developments Restricting Management Discretion to Hire and Fire

At the turn of the century, employees had virtually no protection against discharge by their employers. The dominant rule in this

---

[1]*See* W. STERNBERG & M. HARRIS, JR., FEEDING FRENZY: THE INSIDE STORY OF WEDTECH (1989); J. TRAUB, TOO GOOD TO BE TRUE (1990).

[2]The False Claims Act, as amended, is codified at 31 U.S.C. §§3729-3733 (1988).

[3]The history of the False Claims Act is contained in the legislative history of the False Claims Reform Act of 1986, S. REP. NO. 99-345, 99th Cong., 2d Sess., *reprinted in* 1986 U.S. CODE CONG. & ADMIN. NEWS 5226.

[4]31 U.S.C. §3730(h)(1988).

country was that an employee without a written contract of employment for a specified term could be discharged at any time, for any reason, at the will of the employer. Conversely, an employee could leave his or her employment at any time for any reason. This "at-will" rule of employment was stated as follows in a leading employment law treatise of the 19th century:

> With us the rule is inflexible that a general or indefinite hiring is *prima facie* the hiring at-will, and if the servant seeks to make it out a yearling hiring, the burden is upon him to establish it by proof. The hiring at so much a day, week, month, or year, no time being specified, is an indefinite hiring, and no presumption attaches that it was for a day even, but only after a rate fixed for whatever time the party may serve.[5]

The unstated rationale for this rule was that employees needed freedom to seek other employment in an expanding industrial economy, while employers needed latitude to structure their work forces as required by the dictates of the constantly evolving economy. Under this at-will rule, an employee could be discharged for any reason, including an employer's desire to retaliate for complaints about the propriety of the employer's conduct.

The doctrine of employment at-will was virtually elevated to constitutional status by the Supreme Court in *Coppage v. Kansas*[6] on the ground that freedom of contract, and freedom not to enter into contracts, was a constitutional right. In that case, the Court overturned a state statute which made it a misdemeanor for employers to require employees to sign contracts, commonly known as "yellow-dog" contracts, under which they agreed to refrain from becoming a member of a labor union during the period of their employment. The Supreme Court held:

> Included in the right of personal liberty and the right of private property—partaking of the nature of each—is the right to make contracts for the acquisition of property. Chief among such contracts is that of personal employment, by which labor and other services are exchanged for money or other forms of property. If this right be struck down or arbitrarily interfered with, there is a substantial impairment of liberty in the long-established constitutional sense. The right is as essential to the laborer as to the capitalist, to the poor as to the rich; for the vast majority of persons have no other honest way to begin to acquire property, save by working for money.[7]

At the same time that the Supreme Court was placing restrictions on the rights of employees to organize, Congress was enacting legislation designed to place unions on an equal footing with employers. Prior to World War I, it was commonplace for employers to obtain federal court injunctions against strikes or picketing on the grounds

---

[5]H.G. Wood, A Treatise on the Law of Master and Servant (1877) §134, p. 272, *cited in* Feinman, *The Development of the Employment at Will Rule*, 20 Am. J. Legal Hist. 118, 125-127 (1976).

[6]236 U.S. 1 (1914).

[7]*Id.* at 14.

that unions were unlawful criminal conspiracies of workers or were monopolistic combinations in violation of the antitrust laws, and that such activities interfered with the property rights of employers. In response, Congress passed the Clayton Act that declared that labor unions were exempt from the federal antitrust laws, and prohibited federal courts from issuing injunctions restraining labor unions from peaceful picketing, or from "peacefully persuading any person to work or to abstain from working. . . ."[8] Thus, the Clayton Act was the first federal law restraining an employer's right to obtain an injunction prohibiting its employees from persuading other employees to join a labor union or to join in a strike. It is important to note that this protection was limited to restraining federal courts from issuing injunctions, and did not prevent an employer from discharging or refusing to hire individuals who engaged in organizing activities.

The next significant national development curbing the power of employers to discharge employees engaged in union activities was the passage of the Railway Labor Act (RLA) in 1926. Although limited by its terms to railroads and other common carriers, the RLA made it unlawful for any common carrier "to influence or coerce employees in an effort to induce them to join or remain or not to join or remain members of any labor organization. . . ."[9] The RLA made an employer's violation of these prohibitions a misdemeanor, and placed responsibility for enforcement with any district attorney of the United States. Although the RLA did not permit an individual employee to bring an action to enforce its provisions, and although the RLA was limited to the common carrier industry, it was the first attempt to prohibit employers from retaliating against employees for their union activities.

Due to restrictive interpretations of the Clayton Act, Congress passed the Norris-LaGuardia Act in 1932, reiterating in plain terms the principle that federal courts must not issue injunctions in labor disputes, and confirming that an injunction could not be issued to prohibit an employee from "[g]iving publicity to the existence of, or the facts involved in, any labor dispute, whether by advertising, speaking, patrolling, or by any other method not involving fraud or violence. . . ."[10] Once again, this protection was limited to prohibition of injunctions restraining the organizing activities of employees.

After several decades of labor unrest and violence, and the upheavals caused by the Great Depression, a national consensus developed that the interests of the United States would be best served by the encouragement of collective bargaining. Thus, after previous attempts had been invalidated by the Supreme Court on constitutional grounds, Congress passed the Wagner Act, which stated in its preamble:

---

[8] 15 U.S.C. §20 (1988).

[9] 45 U.S.C. §152 (1988). The Railway Labor Act is now codified at 45 U.S.C. §§151-188 (1988).

[10] The Norris-LaGuardia Act is codified at 29 U.S.C. §§101-115 (1988).

> The denial by some employers of the right of employees to organize and the refusal by some employers to accept the procedure of collective bargaining lead to strikes and other forms of industrial strife or unrest, which have the intent or the necessary effect of burdening or obstructing commerce. . . . The inequality of bargaining power between employees who do not possess full freedom of association or actual liberty of contract, and employers who are organized in the corporate or other forms of ownership association substantially burdens and affects the flow of commerce, and tends to aggravate recurrent business depressions, by depressing wage rates and the purchasing power of wage earners in industry and by preventing the stabilization of competitive wage rates and working conditions within and between industries. Experience has proved that protection by law of the right of employees to organize and bargain collectively safeguards commerce from injury, impairment, or interruption, and promotes the flow of commerce by removing certain recognized sources of industrial strife and unrest. . . . It is hereby declared to be the policy of the United States to eliminate the causes of certain substantial obstructions to the free flow of commerce and to mitigate and eliminate these obstructions when they have occurred by encouraging the practice and procedure of collective bargaining and by protecting the exercise by workers of full freedom of association, self-organization, and designation of representatives of their own choosing, for the purpose of negotiating the terms and conditions of their employment or other mutual aid or protection.[11]

The Wagner Act (which, as amended, has come to be known as the NLRA) established that the national policy in favor of collective bargaining may limit an employer's right to discharge employees. Reversing its earlier precedents elevating freedom of contract to a constitutional property right, the Supreme Court upheld the NLRA in its landmark decision in *NLRB v. Jones & Laughlin Steel Corp.*[12]

In order to protect the right to bargain collectively, Section 8(a)(3) of the NLRA prohibited "discrimination in regard to hire or tenure of employment or any term or condition of employment to discourage membership in any labor organization. . . ."[13] Moreover, the NLRA established the National Labor Relations Board (NLRB) to monitor union election campaigns, to enforce the Act's prohibitions against unfair labor practices, and to establish a uniform, nationwide body of federal labor law. In order to protect the integrity of the NLRB's monitoring and enforcement processes, Section 8(a)(4) of the NLRA also made it an unfair labor practice for an employer "to discharge or otherwise discriminate against an employee because he has filed charges or given testimony under this Act. . . ."[14] The rationale for this provision is that the NLRB could not adequately enforce the NLRA if employers were allowed to discourage their employees from participating in NLRB proceedings.

By 1940, two concepts had gained a foothold in the federal labor laws. First, the Supreme Court approved the principle that certain

---

[11]29 U.S.C. §142 (1988).
[12]301 U.S. 1, 1 LRRM 703 (1937).
[13]29 U.S.C. §158(a)(3) (1988).
[14]29 U.S.C. §158(a)(4) (1988).

national policies, as defined by Congress, could restrict the right of employers to discharge employees for any reason. Second, the NLRA recognized that employee participation in the enforcement proceedings of the NLRB was essential to implement the policies of the Act, and that discrimination by employers against employees who participate in NLRB proceedings must be prohibited so that such participation was not undermined.[15]

These labor statutes laid the doctrinal foundation for later antiretaliation statutes and common-law developments by encouraging employees to step forward to oppose unfair labor practices in violation of the NLRA, and by attempting to ensure that employees who do so are not subjected to discrimination. Enforcement of the NLRA's antiretaliation provisions, however, was limited to filing complaints within the administrative framework of the NLRB. Only under later laws would employees be able to challenge retaliation by employers by filing suit in the courts. Moreover, because only approximately 25 percent of American workers belonged to unions over the past 20 years, the vast majority of private sector, nonunion American workers had virtually no legal protection against retaliatory discharges.[16]

Increased Regulation of Business

Businesses in the United States have been subject to various forms of economic regulation by Congress since the early 1900s. For example, the Sherman Act has forbidden monopolistic and other anticompetitive business practices since the turn of this century.[17] In the aftermath of the Great Depression, the Securities Exchange Act of 1933 was enacted to prevent fraud in the offer, sale, and distribution of securities in order to protect the economic interests of the investing public.[18] For the most part, Congressional regulation of business conduct was primarily directed to the economic damage which might be caused by unfair business practices, rather than towards damage to the public health and safety or to the environment. The regulation of business conduct affecting the public health and safety was generally left to state and local authorities. The exception to this general rule is the Food, Drug and Cosmetic Act of 1938, which was aimed at protect-

---

[15]The antiretaliation provisions of the NLRA are discussed in detail in the THE DEVELOPING LABOR LAW (C. Morris, 2d ed. 1983 & Supp. 1988). A substantial body of law has developed under those provisions, with nuances which relate to provisions of the NLRA which are not found in most of the recent whistleblower protection statutes. Because the antiretaliation aspects of the NLRA are extensively treated elsewhere, and because many of the developments under the NLRA are peculiar to that statute, the body of law interpreting the NLRA's antiretaliation statute is beyond the scope of this work.

[16]Bureau of the Census, U.S. Department of Commerce, *Statistical Abstract of the United States: 1989*, Nos. 682-684, at 415-16 (109th ed. 1989).

[17]15 U.S.C. §1 (1988).

[18]15 U.S.C. §77x (1988).

ing the public welfare by prohibiting sale of adulterated or misbranded food, drugs, or cosmetics into interstate commerce.[19]

In the 1960s and 1970s the subject matter of federal regulations concerning businesses expanded dramatically to extend into the areas of civil rights, consumer protection, workplace safety, environmental pollution, and public health.[20] For instance, the Civil Rights Act of 1964 (Title VII) was enacted to combat discrimination in employment and public accommodations on the basis of race, national origin, sex, and other criteria; the Consumer Credit Protection Act was passed in the early 1970s to prevent unfair lending practices against consumers; the Occupational Safety and Health Act (OSHA) was passed to ensure the safety of the workplace; and numerous environmental protection statutes were enacted, including the Federal Water Pollution Control Act.[21]

In setting up enforcement mechanisms for these statutes, Congress grappled with some of the same issues as when it passed the NLRA. In order to encourage employees to assist in enforcing these statutes, it was necessary to prohibit businesses from discriminating against employees who aided in enforcement proceedings. Because these statutes applied to most employers in the country, whether union or nonunion, for the first time much of the private sector American work force, which previously had enjoyed no protection whatsoever against retaliatory discharge, was given limited protection against retaliation for acts in furtherance of enforcement of the civil rights, workplace safety, and environmental laws. Many of these statutes also shifted enforcement of their antiretaliation provisions from the government to individual employees, permitting employees to maintain a civil action in court on their own behalf.[22]

The range of employee conduct protected by these civil rights, safety, and environmental laws varies. For example, a narrow protection provision is contained in OSHA, which protects only employees who testify in hearings regarding employer violations. Such provisions are commonly known as "participation" clauses. Broader protections are contained in Title VII, which prohibits retaliation against employees who "oppose" an employer's improper conduct. This includes behavior as varied as indicating support of another employee's complaint at internal management meetings, engaging in activities on behalf of minorities during offhours, and refusing to

---

[19]Federal Food, Drug and Cosmetic Act of 1938, 21 U.S.C. §§301-392 (1988).

[20]Sunstein, *Interpreting Statutes in the Regulatory State,* 103 HARV. L. REV. 405, 409 (1989) ("During the 'rights revolution' of the 1960's and 1970's, the national government substantially increased its regulatory responsibilities by moving to protect the interests of consumers, the national environment, and victims of discrimination.").

[21]See Chapter 6 for a detailed discussion of Title VII and similar civil rights laws. See Chapter 4 for a detailed discussion of OSHA and the various federal environmental statutes.

[22]See Chapter 4, and Appendix C, for a discussion of the remedies provided by the federal laws protecting whistleblowers in the private sector.

falsify a minority job applicant's test score in order to disqualify the applicant.[23]

Thus, by the 1970s a substantial number of federal statutes had restricted an employer's ability to discharge employees at-will. These statutes have made familiar the notion that social policies established by state legislatures or Congress may properly limit an employer's previously inviolate right to hire and fire. It has also become a widely held notion that the numerous statutes regulating employers cannot be effectively enforced without employee participation, because employees may be the only persons with access to information which would assist in enforcing the statutes.

Perception of Increase in Improper Business Activity

At the same time as businesses were being subjected to regulation in the fields of health, safety, and the environment, numerous developments contributed to a public perception that businesses were increasingly engaging in corrupt or illicit practices. In 1970 Congress enacted the Racketeer Influenced and Corrupt Organization Act (RICO) based on a consensus that organized crime was infiltrating legitimate business enterprises to an alarming extent.[24] In response to concerns regarding the use of corporate "slush funds" to influence political campaigns, the Federal Election Campaign Act was passed in 1971, and strengthened in 1974 and 1976.[25] Further, in the early 1970s, the Securities and Exchange Commission (SEC) began a voluntary disclosure program to encourage prompt and thorough investigations by businesses into potentially illegal domestic or foreign payments, which were required to have been disclosed to the SEC. Eighty-nine corporations participated in the program, and disclosed practices which the SEC concluded could not be viewed as isolated occurrences.[26] In 1977, partially in response to the SEC's report regarding the disclosure program, Congress passed the Foreign Corrupt Practices Act to prohibit bribes and political payoffs to officials of foreign countries.[27]

These statutes reflected a loss in confidence in the integrity of business. At the same time, the American public was losing confidence in its political leaders. The publication of the Pentagon Papers in 1971 eroded support for an increasingly costly and deadly Vietnam War, and called into question the good faith of the political and military establishments. The prolonged Watergate scandal with its daily tele-

---

[23]See Chapter 6 for a detailed discussion of the "opposition" clause of Title VII.

[24]18 U.S.C. §§1961-1968 (1988). See Chapter 4 for a detailed discussion of RICO.

[25]The original Federal Election Campaign Act appears at 86 Stat. 3, the 1974 amendments appear at 88 Stat. 1263, and the 1976 amendments are codified at 2 U.S.C. §437c *et seq.* (1988).

[26]Report of the Securities and Exchange Commission on Questionable and Illegal Corporate Payments and Practices, SEC. REG. & L. REP. (BNA) No. 353 (May 12, 1976).

[27]The Foreign Corrupt Practices Act is codified at 15 U.S.C. §78dd *et seq.* (1988).

vised sessions questioning the conduct of then-President Nixon, culminating in Nixon's resignation in 1973, diminished public confidence in the highest elected officials of the country. These developments helped contribute to a climate which encouraged individuals to question the practices of highly placed persons in government and business.

In addition to these general social forces which created a climate favorable to whistleblowing, the practice of whistleblowing was publicly encouraged at the Conference on Professional Responsibility, which was organized by consumer advocate Ralph Nader, held in Washington, D.C., on January 30, 1971. The conference sought to encourage whistleblowing as a means of enforcing laws designed to prevent injuries, disease, corruption, and economic waste based on the perception that the traditional law enforcement mechanisms were not working. The conference also sought legal protection for responsible whistleblowers:

> [T]he willingness and ability of insiders to blow the whistle is the last line of defense ordinary citizens have against the denial of their rights and the destruction of their rights by secretive and powerful institutions. As organizations penetrate deeper and deeper into the lives of people—from pollution to poverty to income erosion to privacy invasion more of their rights and interests are adversely affected. This fact of contemporary life has generated an ever greater moral imperative for employees to be reasonably protected in upholding such rights regardless of their employers' policies.[28]

Eleven individual whistleblowers spoke at the conference, most of whom stated that they had been subjected to retaliation by their employers.

As mentioned previously, the regulatory statutes enacted in the 1960s and 1970s were preceded by decades of regulation of the economic behavior of businesses. Many of the earlier economic regulations not only prohibited various business practices, but also made it a crime to violate the regulations. For example, businesses could be punished as criminals for offenses such as dealing in milk or poultry without a license, or failing to keep proper stockyard records.[29] These criminal economic regulations have been criticized for over-criminalizing business behavior,[30] and as creating a disorganized body of restrictions. [31]

The combination of the earlier criminal economic regulations with the civil rights, individual rights, consumer rights, and environmental protection regulations resulted in a backlash against regula-

---

[28]R. Nader, Whistleblowing: The Report of the Conference on Professional Responsibility 7 (1972).

[29]Orland, *Reflections on Corporate Crime*, 17 Am. Crim. L. Rev. 501, 519 (1980).

[30]Kadish, *Some Observations on the Use of Criminal Sanctions in Enforcing Economic Regulations*, 30 U. Chi. L. Rev. 423 (1963).

[31]1 Working Papers of the National Commission on Reform of the Federal Criminal Law 403 (1970).

tion in the 1980s.[32] The trend of deregulation in the 1980s also tended to increase the incidence of whistleblowing. The failure of many federal agencies to issue regulations prompted numerous lawsuits in which special interest groups attempted to compel agencies to carry out their functions.[33] Accordingly, some citizens concluded that federal agencies were failing to carry out their legislative charters, that illegal activities were going unregulated, and that whistleblowing was one of the few ways of attempting to stop illegal practices.[34]

Despite these broad regulatory developments, until the mid-1970s there were no uniform statutory or common-law protections for employees who protested improper conduct under any and all statutes. For instance, as of the mid-1970s, no protection was available to employees who refused to participate in violations of the antitrust laws.[35] Rather, a patchwork of statutory protections existed only for employees who protested conduct regulated by statutes which happened to include antiretaliation provisions.

A dramatic expansion in whistleblower protections began in the late 1970s. At that time, the federal government and numerous states passed legislation protecting public sector whistleblowers. These statutes are discussed in Chapter 3. These developments were followed by the passage of several state statutes protecting private sector whistleblowers which were designed to fill in the numerous gaps left by statutes which did not contain antiretaliation provisions. These statutes are discussed in Chapter 4.

Moreover, the judiciary of many states began to carve out exceptions to the common-law at-will rule in favor of employees who complained about alleged improprieties. These common-law protections, which are discussed in Chapter 5, dramatically expanded the remedies available to employees. Under most statutes, an employee could recover backpay, reinstatement, and possibly attorneys' fees. Under the common law, however, most jurisdictions have permitted tort damages including substantial amounts for pain and suffering, and punitive damages, which may greatly exceed the amount of backpay and attorneys' fees at issue.

So that these various protections may be discussed in a practical context, the following section of this chapter discusses the efforts of two early whistleblowers, in the public and private sectors respectively, to obtain legal protection.

---

[32]Garland, *Deregulation and Judicial Review*, 98 HARV. L. REV. 505 (1985).

[33]*See, e.g.*, Public Citizen v. Steed, 733 F.2d 93 (D.C. Cir. 1984) (automobile tire safety regulations).

[34]M. GLAZER & P. GLAZER, THE WHISTLEBLOWERS: EXPOSING CORRUPTION IN GOVERNMENT AND INDUSTRY 12-20 (1989). The social and political atmosphere also gave rise to the creation of whistleblower support organizations such as the Government Accountability Project, which was founded to assist whistleblowers who complained about government waste and fraud. *Id.* at 61-63.

[35]Shaw, *Retaliatorily Discharged Employees' Standing to Sue Under the Antitrust Laws*, 67 ORE. L. REV. 331 (1988).

Two Case Histories Illustrating the Need for Whistleblower Protections

As described in the preceding sections, whistleblower protections have evolved on a case-by-case basis, whether such protections have been enacted by the federal or state legislatures, or have been created by the common-law courts. One benefit of this evolution has been that the legislatures and courts have carefully and deliberately crafted whistleblower protections to the specific facts of each case. One negative aspect of this gradual growth has been that individual whistleblowers, whose conduct was not legally protected at the time they criticized their employers' practices, have borne the burden of acting as pioneers by seeking legal protection through the legislatures or the courts.

The case histories of two such individuals are discussed in this chapter. The first individual, A. Ernest Fitzgerald, was employed by the federal government when he acted as a whistleblower. The second individual, P.E. Petermann, was employed in the private sector by a trade union. These two cases are discussed not only because the two individuals were legal pioneers, but also to illustrate the different considerations applying to whistleblowers in the public and private sectors.

Nixon v. Fitzgerald: *The Civil Service Reform Act*

Over the last 30 years, the federal government has employed an increasingly large percentage of the total work force of the United States. In 1986, the federal government employed approximately three million persons, with a total payroll exceeding $75 billion.[36] Until the enactment of the Civil Service Reform Act of 1978 (CSRA),[37] however, most of the federal work force had little or no protection against retaliation for whistleblowing activities.

Before the CSRA, there was no comprehensive federal protection for federal employees who complained about waste within the federal government, or regarding fraud committed by businesses providing goods or services to the federal government. Until recently, one of the few legal remedies available to federal employees who witnessed such abuses was the False Claims Act, which permitted individuals to prosecute lawsuits against businesses which submitted false claims for payment.[38] The Act permitted such individuals to be awarded a portion of the amount recovered. However, until it was amended in

---

[36] *Statistical Abstract of the United States, supra* note 16, No. 512, at 318 (109th ed. 1989).

[37] Pub.L. No. 95-454, 92 Stat. 1111 (1978). The CSRA is codified in various sections of 5 U.S.C. The CSRA is discussed in detail in Chapter 3 at "Statutory Protections for Federal Employees."

[38] The False Claims Act, as amended, is codified at 31 U.S.C. §§3729-3733 (1988), and is discussed in detail in Chapter 6.

1986, the False Claims Act provided no guarantee that a federal employee pursuing such a claim would not be harassed, demoted, or even dismissed for having filed such a lawsuit. The widely publicized case of *Nixon v. Fitzgerald*[39] illustrates the predicament of a federal employee who was unprotected from retaliation for his whistleblowing activities.

In September 1965, A. Ernest Fitzgerald was appointed to the position of Deputy for Management Systems in the Office of the Secretary of the Air Force.[40] Throughout his tenure, Fitzgerald was an outspoken critic of the Air Force's procurement activities, particularly of the Air Force's program to develop the C-5A aircraft. Fitzgerald was terminated from his position in November 1969, allegedly due to the elimination of his position as part of a reduction in force. Fitzgerald contended that the true reason for his termination was that his superiors were retaliating against him because of his criticism of the Air Force's programs. After more than a decade of litigation, including a lawsuit against the President of the United States, Fitzgerald finally obtained reinstatement to his position in 1982.[41] Fitzgerald's legal odyssey demonstrates the uphill battle which whistleblowers faced without effective statutory protection.

According to Fitzgerald, in 1968 the Air Force's program to develop the C-5A aircraft, the largest cargo airplane ever built, was behind schedule and over budget. The Air Force had already paid huge sums to the Lockheed Aircraft Corporation to design and build the C-5A, and it was clear that massive new funding would be required. In addition, Lockheed faced major financial difficulties in 1968, and appeared on the verge of bankruptcy unless the federal government agreed to continue to fund Lockheed's C-5A program at increasing levels. Some members of Congress, primarily Senator William Proxmire, chairman of the Joint Economic Committee, opposed further funding of the C-5A program.

In October 1968, Fitzgerald was invited to testify before the Joint Economic Committee. Fitzgerald's superiors initially refused to permit him to testify, despite a federal law making it a criminal offense to intimidate Congressional witnesses.[42] Fitzgerald was at last permitted to testify after his superiors counseled him to "stay away from the C-5A." Fitzgerald appeared before Senator Proxmire's committee on November 13, 1968, and in response to a direct inquiry from Proxmire, admitted that the costs of the C-5A contract might amount to $2 billion more than originally estimated.

---

39 Fitzgerald v. Seamans, 384 F. Supp. 688 (D.D.C. 1974), *rev'd*, 553 F.2d 220 (D.C. Cir. 1977), *rev'd sub. nom.* Nixon v. Fitzgerald, 457 U.S. 731 (1982).

40 A.E. Fitzgerald, The High Priests of Waste (1972). The discussion of Fitzgerald's employment with the Air Force and his subsequent lawsuits is based primarily on pages 210-275 of Fitzgerald's book.

41 *Supra* note 39, 457 U.S. at 738 n.17.

42 Intimidation of Congressional witnesses is prohibited by 18 U.S.C. §1505 (1988).

On January 6, 1969, an Air Force internal memorandum was prepared outlining three possible ways in which Fitzgerald could be terminated, including a reduction in force. Fitzgerald testified again before the Joint Economic Committee in June 1969, regarding another Air Force procurement program, and again Fitzgerald's superiors attempted to prevent him from testifying. On November 4, 1969, Fitzgerald was notified that his position had been eliminated as part of a reorganization and reduction in force. Sixty Congressmen wrote a letter to then-President Nixon on November 7 protesting Fitzgerald's termination, but to no avail. Fitzgerald's legal battle to regain his position ensued.

Under the federal criminal witness intimidation statute, Fitzgerald's only remedy was to persuade the federal law enforcement officials to begin a criminal prosecution against the officials of the Air Force. Since Fitzgerald was not entitled to sue his superiors in the civil courts, he sought reinstatement in January 1969 through the administrative mechanisms of the U.S. Civil Service Commission. In May 1971 a closed hearing was scheduled on Fitzgerald's allegations. After Fitzgerald sued for an injunction permitting public and media access, open hearings were commenced in early January 1973. At a news conference on January 31, 1973, then-President Nixon stated that he was fully aware of and approved of the decision to dismiss Fitzgerald. In September of that year, the Civil Service Commission recommended that Fitzgerald be reinstated, but also stated that the evidence did not establish that Fitzgerald had been dismissed in retaliation for his Congressional testimony.

Having gained only partial vindication through administrative channels, Fitzgerald then turned to the judicial system for relief. Fitzgerald filed a lawsuit in federal court against various Defense Department and White House officials, including the President. After many procedural twists, the lawsuit eventually was appealed to the United States Supreme Court. On June 15, 1982, nine days before the Supreme Court issued its decision, the Air Force agreed to reassign Fitzgerald to his former position. The Supreme Court dismissed the lawsuit against former President Nixon, ruling that he was entitled to absolute immunity from prosecution, but permitted the lawsuit to continue against other White House aides.[43] Fitzgerald had finally won a Pyrrhic victory to regain his job at the expense of twelve years of litigation. Partially in response to cases such as Fitzgerald's, new legislation was enacted in 1978 to protect whistleblowers in the federal civil service.

As the federal budget continued to increase, taxpayers began to insist that the federal government spend their tax dollars more efficiently by hiring employees on the basis of merit rather than political patronage. Moreover, taxpayers demanded that the federal bureaucracy take steps not only to eliminate unproductive employees, but also to eliminate fraud, waste, or corruption in government spending.

---

[43]*Supra* note 39; *see also* Harlow v. Fitzgerald, 457 U.S. 800 (1982).

One of the principal initiatives of the Carter administration was the overhaul of the federal civil service system. In 1977, President Carter commissioned the Personnel Management Project, which undertook a comprehensive five-month study of the civil service. At several of the public hearings conducted as part of the project, the project staff took testimony from many individuals, including A. Ernest Fitzgerald, Ralph Nader, the director of the National Federation of Federal Employees, and the president of the American Federation of Government Employees. The reforms eventually proposed by the Personnel Management Project included new protections for whistleblowers in the civil service.

The Personnel Management Project culminated in the Civil Service Reform Act of 1978.[44] The CSRA restructured the agencies responsible for administering the federal system of employment, and provided procedures for ensuring that all federal employees are evaluated on the basis of merit, rather than on the basis of political patronage. Another principal purpose of the CSRA was to "provide new protections for employees who disclose illegal or improper Government conduct. . . ."[45] Thus, for the first time the CSRA established that federal whistleblowers may not be discriminated against in the conditions of their employment. The rationale for the whistleblower protection provisions is stated as follows:

> Often, the whistleblower's reward for dedication to the highest moral principles is harassment and abuse. Whistleblowers frequently encounter severe damage to their careers and substantial economic loss. . . . Protecting employees who disclose government illegality, waste, and corruption is a major step toward a more effective civil service. In the vast federal bureaucracy it is not difficult to conceal wrongdoing provided that no one summons the courage to disclose the truth. . . . What is needed is a means to assure [employees] that they will not suffer if they help uncover and correct administrative abuses. . . .[46]

Under the CSRA, an employee may not be retaliated against for complaining about potentially improper conduct to his superiors, to the Special Counsel, or to the Inspector General of the employee's agency.[47]

---

[44]*Supra* note 37.

[45]S. Rep. No. 95-969, 95th Cong., 2d Sess. *reprinted in* 1978 U.S. Code Cong. & Admin. News 2723.

[46]*Id.* at 2730.

[47]The general principle of whistleblower protection is set forth in 5 U.S.C. §2301(b)(9), which states:

> Employees should be protected against reprisal for the lawful disclosure of information which the employees reasonably believe evidences—(a) a violation of any law, rule, or regulation, or (b) mismanagement, a gross waste of funds, and abuse of authority, or a substantial and specific danger to public health or safety.

This general principle is implemented in 5 U.S.C. §2302(b)(8), which provides in relevant part:

> Any employee who has authority to take, direct others to take, recommend, or approve any personnel action, shall not, with respect to such authority. . . (a) take or fail to take a personnel action with respect to any employee or applicant for employment as a reprisal for (A) a disclosure for information by an employee or applicant which the employee or applicant reasonably believes evidences (i) a violation of any law, rule or regulation, or (ii) mis-

The CSRA recognizes that any waste of tax dollars is a matter of public concern which government employees should be encouraged to oppose. Accordingly, the CSRA protects employees who complain not only about "a violation of any law, rule or regulation," but also about "mismanagement, a gross waste of funds, an abuse of authority, or a substantial and specific danger to public health or safety." The CSRA also recognizes that every employee is bound to disagree with his or her supervisor on insignificant issues, and that petty disagreements are not intended to be protected. Thus, the legislative history of the CSRA states that general, nonspecific criticism of an agency is not protected by the CSRA.[48]

The legislative history of the CSRA also states that employees will be protected only if they bring the purportedly improper conduct to the attention of their superiors before making any disclosure outside the agency by which the individual is employed: "It is assumed, however, that before such allegations are brought to the attention of the Special Counsel, an employee will first exhaust whatever internal procedures are available for bringing such allegations to the attention of agency officials."[49]

The drafters of the CSRA recognized the potential for conflict between the principles of merit selection and of whistleblower protection. That is, it is conceivable that incompetent employees might attempt to insulate themselves from termination by becoming whistleblowers. That tension was addressed as follows:

> Finally, it should be noted that this section is a prohibition against reprisals. The section should not be construed as protecting an employee who is otherwise engaged in misconduct, or who is incompetent, from appropriate disciplinary action. If, for example, an employee has had several years of inadequate performance, or unsatisfactory performance ratings, or if an employee has engaged in an action which would constitute grounds for dismissal for cause, the fact that the employee "blows the whistle" on his agency after the agency has begun to initiate disciplinary action against the employee will not protect the employee against such disciplinary action.[50]

While recognizing the importance of protecting responsible whistleblowers, the CSRA also recognizes that irresponsible whistleblowers are not deserving of protection. The legislative history of the CSRA states that "[a]n employee should not be protected, however, for making a disclosure which he knows to be false."[51]

Thus, the CSRA eliminated many of the problems which faced whistleblowers in the federal government such as A. Ernest

---

management, a gross waste of funds, an abuse of authority, or a substantial and specific danger to public health or safety, . . . or (B) a disclosure to the Special Counsel of the Merit Systems Protection Board, or to the Inspector General of an agency or another employee designated by the head of the agency to receive such disclosures. . . .

[48] S. Rep. No. 95-969, p. 35, *reprinted in* 1978 U.S. Code Cong. & Ad. News 2723, 2743.

[49] *Id.* at 2757.

[50] *Id.* at 2744.

[51] *Id.*

Fitzgerald. For the first time, federal law expressly prohibited retaliation against whistleblowers in the federal civil service. Federal employees are protected for complaining about a broad range of conduct, including mismanagement, abuse of authority, gross waste of funds, substantial and specific dangers to the public health and safety, and violations of law.

Petermann v. Teamsters: *The Public Policy Doctrine*

Peter E. Petermann was a member of Local 396 of the International Brotherhood of Teamsters, and was also employed by Local 396 as a business agent. Petermann was promised at the time of hiring that his employment would continue so long as his performance was satisfactory. The Assembly Interim Committee on Governmental Efficiency and Economy of the California Legislature issued a subpoena requiring Petermann to testify before the committee. Petermann alleged that the secretary-treasurer of Local 396 instructed Petermann to make false statements in his testimony before the legislative committee. Contrary to those instructions, Petermann answered truthfully all of the questions asked of him. The day after Petermann's testimony, the secretary-treasurer terminated Petermann's employment as a business agent. Thereafter, Petermann was issued a withdrawal card terminating his membership in Local 396. Petermann sued Local 396 to recover the accrued salary he had lost since his discharge, and challenged the termination of his membership in the union.

In *Petermann v. Teamsters,*[52] the California Court of Appeal noted that Petermann was not promised employment for any specified period of time, and that such employment relationships were generally terminable at the will of the employer. Notwithstanding this general rule, the court noted that an employer's right to terminate at-will employees such as Petermann could be limited by considerations of public policy. The court recognized that "[t]he term 'public policy' is inherently not subject to precise definition." Without attempting to conclusively define public policy, the court held that the public interest in the administration of justice would be undermined if employers could terminate their employees for refusal to commit the crime of perjury. The court reasoned as follows:

> To hold that one's continued employment could be made contingent upon his commission of a felonious act at the instance of his employer would be to encourage criminal conduct on the part of both the employee and employer and serve to contaminate the honest administration of public affairs. This is patently contrary to the public welfare. The law must encourage and not discourage truthful testimony. The public policy of

---

[52] 174 Cal. App.2d 184, 344 P.2d 25 (1959).

> this state requires that every impediment, however remote to the above objective, must be struck down when encountered.[53]

Accordingly, the court allowed Petermann to sue for recovery of his accrued salary.

The union defended both of Petermann's claims for lost salary and restoration of his union membership on the ground that Petermann had failed to take an appeal within the union of both his termination and loss of membership. The court noted that the union's constitution provided a mechanism for members to appeal loss of membership within the union, and required members to do so before resorting to the courts. However, the constitution contained no such mechanism or requirement as to termination of employment as a business agent. Because Petermann had failed to appeal the loss of his membership within the union, the court refused to hear Petermann's claim for restoration of his membership. However, the court agreed to hear Petermann's claim for lost salary arising from termination of his employment as a business agent because he could not appeal his termination from that position under the union's constitution.

The *Petermann* decision was highly significant in two respects. First, the opinion held that the at-will rule of employment was not absolute, and that the at-will rule did not permit termination of employees in violation of public policy. Although the court did not expressly refer to whistleblowing in its opinion, Petermann clearly was a whistleblower in the sense that he disclosed information to a legislative committee against the wishes of his employer. The *Petermann* ruling laid the groundwork for later decisions in the 1970s and 1980s which expressly created causes of action for terminated whistleblowers. In contrast to the *Petermann* decision, which permitted only recovery of damages for breach of contract in the form of lost salary, the rulings of the 1970s and 1980s generally permitted recovery of tort damages including lost salary, amounts for emotional distress, and punitive damages when appropriate. The more recent public policy decisions founded on the *Petermann* decision are discussed in detail in Chapter 5. Further, the *Petermann* decision was significant in that it addressed whether union members should be required to exhaust remedies available to them under union constitutions, or by analogy, under collective bargaining agreements, before bringing suit in the courts. As discussed in detail in Chapter 7, whistleblowers who are union members may be required to exhaust contractual or statutory remedies available to them before pursuing other legal relief.

As *Fitzgerald* and *Petermann* indicate, whistleblowing can take place in many different ways. The following section proposes an overall definition of whistleblowing which includes both the Fitzgerald and Petermann examples, and proposes definitions for several different types of whistleblowing for use in the following chapters.

---

[53] *Id.* at 189

Proposed Definitions of Whistleblowing

The term whistleblower may apply to employees in a wide variety of circumstances. The most common conception of a whistleblower is probably of an employee who reports his or her employer's violation of law to an appropriate law enforcement agency. For instance, in the criminal context an employee might contact the federal or state district attorney, while in the environmental context an employee might contact the U.S. Environmental Protection Agency. In both of these examples, the employee's disclosure is to an enforcement authority outside of the employer's organization. However, an employee's complaints to his or her superiors within his employer's organization may also be protected under some laws.

Most legal protections for employees who are popularly thought of as whistleblowers do not contain any definition of the term, but instead define the circumstances under which employees will be protected from retaliation by employers. For example, the CSRA does not contain any definition of whistleblowing, and the *Petermann* decision actually protected a whistleblower without expressly recognizing that it did so.

To include all employees who have been protected under the statutory and common-law developments discussed in chapters 3 through 6, for the purpose of this book the term whistleblowing will refer not only to employees who make disclosures outside of their organizations, but also to employees who raise questions about improper practices through their employees' internal channels, or who refuse to carry out illegal instructions. Whistleblowing may also be a report, not of an illegal act, but of an act in violation of a code of professional ethics, or of an act which an employee believes might be technically legal, but which might nevertheless be dangerous to the public health and safety. Further, whistleblowing will also refer to employees who choose not to make allegations through internal channels or to the appropriate authorities, but instead make reports directly to the news media, to professional associations, to political groups, or to other organizations not responsible for law enforcement. For present purposes, whistleblowing is defined in the broadest sense to include employees who oppose, either internally or externally, their employers' conduct.

Although whistleblowing will be used in an all-encompassing sense, it may be useful to attempt to categorize the various forms which whistleblowing may take. The first category of whistleblowers, like Fitzgerald and Petermann, may be referred to as "passive" whistleblowers. Neither Fitzgerald nor Petermann actively volunteered their information. Instead, Fitzgerald responded to a request to testify before a Congressional committee, while Petermann obeyed a subpoena issued by a legislative committee. Thus, the term passive whistleblowing will include employees who do nothing more than respond to lawful requests for information from governmental authorities. In addition, passive whistleblowing will be used to refer to employees who refuse to carry out illegal instructions, but who do not publicly disclose such instructions. For example, employees who refuse their employers' instructions to violate the antitrust laws would fall within the category of passive whistleblowers, even though they may take no additional steps to disclose their employers' behavior.

A second category of "active" whistleblowing may be useful to describe employees who voice their concerns regarding their employers' illegal behavior, either internally or externally. Thus, the term active whistleblowing will include employees who take affirmative steps to oppose their employers' conduct within the confines of their employers' organizations, in addition to employees who report illegal practices to persons outside of their employers' organizations.

A third category for "embryonic" whistleblowers may also be useful. That term has been used to describe employees who are terminated before they have the opportunity to oppose their employers' practices, ostensibly because their employers suspected that such employees harbored an intent to actively oppose illegal practices. This category may include either active or passive whistleblowers, because the embryonic whistleblower may be either on the threshold of refusing to perform illegal acts, or of taking the affirmative step of making an internal or external complaint.

The broad definition of whistleblowing suggested above does not imply that all forms of whistleblowing are legally protected, or that the same level of legal protection is given to each category. Indeed, as discussed in chapters 3 through 6, the various legal protections for whistleblowers distinguish between which forms of whistleblowing should or should not be protected.

Common Forms of Whistleblower Protection

The whistleblower protection laws discussed in chapters 3 through 6 prohibit various methods of retaliation against responsible whistleblowers. Because these laws do not differ greatly with respect to which methods of retaliation are prohibited, the common forms of protection will be discussed generally in this section, rather than individually with respect to each statute.

The most obvious method of retaliating against whistleblowers is to terminate their employment. Most whistleblower laws prohibit this method of retaliation. Whistleblowers may also be discriminated against in more subtle ways, such as demotions or transfers to undesirable locations.[54] Most protection laws recognize this, and prohibit any adverse changes in a whistleblower's conditions of employment.

---

[54] M. GLAZER & P. GLAZER, *supra* note 34 at 133-66.

For instance, the CSRA defines discrimination to include failure to promote, demotion, disciplinary action, transfer, adverse performance evaluation, an adverse decision regarding pay, benefits, awards, or training, and any significant change in duties or responsibilities.[55] Many laws also protect whistleblowers who are not dismissed, but who resign because of severe harassment in the workplace. Many courts recognize that such employees were "constructively discharged" by their employer's actions. For example, it is well settled under Title VII that an employee may state a claim if it can be shown that the employer intended to force the employee to resign by creating intolerable working conditions.[56]

Although the precise types of prohibited discrimination vary under each of the particular whistleblower protection laws discussed in chapters 3 through 6, as a general matter most such laws prohibit subtle forms of discrimination as well as prohibiting termination of employment. Before discussing these specific whistleblower protections, the following chapter will discuss many of the general considerations which determine whether or not various forms of whistleblowing are legally protected.

---

[55] 5 U.S.C. §2302(a)(2) (1988).

[56] Comment, *Constructive Discharge Under Title VII and the ADEA,* 53 U. CHI. L. REV. 561 (1986).

2

Balancing Workplace Responsibilities and Conscience

The whistleblower protection laws discussed in chapters 3 through 6 differ regarding the types of whistleblowing that they protect, with some laws containing broad protections, and others containing narrow protections. All of these whistleblower protection laws reflect judgments by legislatures or courts regarding which forms of whistleblowing should be encouraged, and which forms should be discouraged. To place the specific statutes and common-law protections set forth in chapters 3 through 6 in context, this chapter will discuss the various policy considerations which determine whether particular forms of whistleblowing are protected.

The Competing Responsibilities of Employees

Individuals in our society are called upon to fulfill numerous roles in the workplace and in the community. These roles include acting as a subordinate or superior in the workplace, or acting as a member or an officer of community organizations. Each of these roles is accompanied by different rights and responsibilities. The following sections discuss how these responsibilities come to bear upon employees who may wish to disclose improper activities of their employers or their co-workers.

Employment relationships impose duties upon both employers and employees. Employers agree to provide various forms of financial compensation, potential for career advancement, and potential for professional satisfaction, and in return employees agree to carry out their jobs to the best of their abilities. However, employees do not necessarily forfeit rights or duties as citizens by merely accepting employment with an organization. The numerous aspects of employees' duties to their employers, and of employees' rights and duties as citizens, are discussed below.

The Duties of Obedience, Loyalty, and Confidentiality

One of the primary duties implicit in any employment relationship is an employee's duty to obey the reasonable instructions of the employer.[1] This implied duty is qualified, however, in that employees are not required to obey unreasonable instructions which are illegal or contrary to business ethics.[2] While employees may properly refuse to obey illegal or unethical instructions of their employers, it does not necessarily follow that they may also publicly complain about those instructions.

The duty of loyalty to an employer's interests is also implicit in the employment relationship.[3] The duty of loyalty is a flexible concept which varies depending upon the specific circumstances of each employment relationship. Nevertheless, in general, the scope of this duty requires an employee "to act solely for the benefit of the principal in matters entrusted to him, . . . to take no unfair advantage of his position in the use of information or things acquired by him because of his position, . . . [and] not to act or speak disloyally in matters which are connected with his employment except in the protection of his own interests or those of others."[4] In addition to requiring employees not to compete with their employers' businesses, the duty of loyalty prohibits disparagement of the employers' products, and work slowdowns or sabotage.[5] The duty of loyalty is also a qualified duty, in that employees are not prevented from acting outside their employment in a manner which injures their employers' businesses.[6] Thus, the duty of loyalty would not necessarily prevent employees from campaigning for legislation which might require expensive compliance efforts by their employers.

One facet of the duty of loyalty is the obligation not to act for persons whose interests conflict with the employer's interests.[7] This obligation is usually concerned with preventing employees from acting on behalf of their employers' economic competitors. However, this obligation also appears to prevent employees from knowingly gather-

---

[1]RESTATEMENT (SECOND) OF AGENCY §385(1) (1958) [hereinafter "Restatement"]. For an excellent and detailed discussion of the duties of obedience, loyalty, and confidentiality, *see* Blumberg, *Corporate Responsibility and the Employee's Duty of Loyalty and Obedience: A Preliminary Inquiry*, 24 OKLA. L. REV. 279 (1971).

[2]RESTATEMENT §385(1) comment a (1958).

[3]*Id.* at §387, which provides:
Unless otherwise agreed, an agent is subject to a duty to his principal to act solely for the benefit of the principal in all matters connected with his agency.

[4]*Id.* at §387 comment b (1958).

[5]*See generally* Judd, *The Implied Covenant of Good Faith and Fair Dealing: Examining Employees' Good Faith Duties*, 39 HASTINGS L.J. 483 (1988).

[6]RESTATEMENT §387 comment 6 (1958).

[7]*Id.* at §394.

ing information for political organizations with the avowed purpose of putting the employer out of business, even though they are not economic competitors. For example, the obligation to avoid conflicts conceivably would prevent employees of lumber companies from providing sensitive information to environmental groups opposed to all lumbering activities, or employees of nuclear power plants from providing information to antinuclear organizations.

This view of the duty of loyalty is supported by an additional implied duty of confidentiality, which requires an employee "not to use or to communicate information confidentially given him by the principal . . . to the injury of the principal . . . unless the information is a matter of general knowledge."[8] The duty of confidentiality stems from the fact that employers must disclose varying amounts of confidential information to their employees so they may carry out their responsibilities. The duty of confidentiality recognizes that the flow of necessary information between employers and employees would be hampered if employees made unauthorized disclosures of confidential information. This duty applies to unique business methods, trade secrets, customer lists, or other strategic information. Like all of the previous duties, the duty of confidentiality is qualified in that employees may properly disclose information if their employers have committed or are about to commit a crime.[9] This privilege to disclose criminal activities does not necessarily extend to disclosures of unethical behavior, even though employees need not obey instructions to commit unethical acts.

The duties of obedience, loyalty, and confidentiality arise in part from the trust that employers must of necessity repose in employees. It is generally accepted that the greater the degree of trust reposed in employees, the higher the level of duty expected from those employees. Thus, managerial or supervisory employees are generally held to higher standards under these duties than are lower level employees. Moreover, since higher level employees are often required to work on management teams, breaches of the duties of obedience, loyalty, and confidentiality by high level employees may be especially destructive of these close working relationships. For this reason, employers have generally been permitted to require managers to conform to organizational goals and to cooperate with colleagues.[10]

Duties as Citizens to Aid in Law Enforcement

The qualified nature of the duties of obedience, loyalty, and confidentiality, which recognizes that employees may disclose illegal conduct, reflects a longstanding theme of the common law which

---

[8] *Id.* at §395.

[9] *Id.* at §395 comment f.

[10] *See* Bartholet, *Application of Title VII to Jobs in High Places*, 95 HARV. L. REV. 945 (1982).

encourages citizens to report criminal conduct to appropriate authorities. Under the ancient doctrine of misprision of felony, it was a crime for citizens to fail to report felonies they had witnessed.[11] If it were applied to the employment context, the doctrine of misprision arguably would not only permit employees to disclose their employers' illegal conduct, but would require employees to do so or else face criminal liability for failure to disclose illegal conduct.[12]

The doctrine of misprision originated in medieval England which depended largely upon communal action for law enforcement and which lacked the sophisticated federal, state, and local law enforcement agencies common in the United States today. Citizens of medieval England were required to raise a "hue and cry" if they witnessed the commission of a felony, or came across a dead body. All males between the ages of 15 and 60 were required to join the hue and cry, to pursue the criminal, and to follow the instructions of the local constable. However, there were no reported prosecutions for misprision in England until 1960, when the House of Lords ruled that misprision of felony continued to exist as a common-law offense.[13] Under English law, the doctrine of misprision did not require reporting of all offenses, but only of crimes serious enough to be classified as felonies. Moreover, misprision was prosecuted as a misdemeanor instead of a felony offense because it was not viewed as a serious infraction.

The doctrine of misprision is of questionable vitality under the common law of the United States. In an often-quoted decision of the Supreme Court, Chief Justice John Marshall stated:

> It may be the duty of a citizen to accuse every offender, and to proclaim every offense which comes to his knowledge; but the law which would punish him in every case for not performing this duty is too harsh for man.[14]

Most American jurisdictions have declined to recognize misprision in its original form, based on reasons similar to those voiced by the Florida Court of Appeal:

> While it may be desirable, even essential, that we encourage citizens to get involved to help reduce crime, they ought not to be adjudicated criminals themselves if they don't. . . . We cherish the right to mind our own business when our best interests dictate.[15]

---

[11]*See* Glazebrook, *Misprision of Felony—Shadow or Phantom*, 8 AM. J. LEGAL HIST. 189 (1964); Meale, *Misprision of Felony: A Crime Whose Time Has Come, Again*, 28 U. FLA. L. REV. 199 (1975); Comment, *Forcing the Bystander to Get Involved*, 94 YALE L.J. 1787 (1985).

[12]Closely related to the doctrine of misprision is the offense of compounding crimes, which consists of an agreement not to report a crime in return for receipt of consideration. In the employment context, it could be argued that an employee who has witnessed a crime, but failed to report it out of a desire to continue to receive compensation from the employer, has committed the offense of compounding. *See* Note, *Compounding Crimes: Time for Enforcement?*, 27 HASTINGS L.J. 175 (1975).

[13]Sykes v. DPP, 3 W.L.R. 371, 45 Cr. App. R. 230 (1961).

[14]Marbury v. Brooks, 20 U.S. 251, 260 (1822).

[15]Holland v. State, 302 So.2d 806, 810 (Fl. Dist. Ct. App. 1974).

Commentators have criticized the doctrine of misprision on the additional ground that it tends to encourage vigilantism. In the modern era, such self-help by citizens may have the primary effect of disrupting the orderly administration of the criminal justice system.[16] In addition to vigilantism, the doctrine of misprision may present the potential for abuse for political purposes. For example, the two Communist scares of this century, of the 1920s and 1950s, prompted many prosecutions for disloyalty to the United States.[17] Although the doctrine of misprision may serve the salutary purpose of encouraging reports of crime, it also contains the potential for persecution in times of political turmoil when various forms of political conduct are made illegal.

The states which continue to recognize misprision have generally added an additional element to the offense, apart from mere knowledge of a felony and the failure to report it. For example, the Supreme Court of South Carolina imposed the additional requirement that there must be some positive act of concealment of a felony.[18] Other jurisdictions have required the additional element of "an evil motive to prevent or delay the administration of justice."[19] Thus, whatever utility misprision may have served in medieval England, most states have declined to apply misprision under the modern social conditions of the United States.

Although misprision may no longer be a recognized offense under the common law of most states, misprision of felonies in violation of federal law is still a federal offense.[20] The federal misprision statute modifies the original common-law offense in the same way as the state courts have, by expressly requiring the additional element of some affirmative act of concealment. Despite the outmoded nature of the criminal offense of misprision, the underlying principle that citizens should be encouraged to report serious crimes is accepted throughout the United States. As this principle relates to whistleblowing, however, the question is to what extent employees are under an affirmative duty to report felonious criminal behavior of their employers. In most jurisdictions, there appears to be no such affirmative duty imposed by the doctrine of misprision.

The question of whether employees have an affirmative obligation to report their employers' misbehavior invites the related question of whether employees have an affirmative obligation to testify in legal proceedings against their employers. As demonstrated by the cases of A.E. Fitzgerald and P.E. Petermann, employees may also be

---

[16]Comment, *Forcing the Bystander to Get Involved,* 94 Yale L.J. 1787, 1788 (1985).

[17]*See, e.g.*, Lardner v. United States, 216 F.2d 844 (9th Cir. 1954).

[18]State v. Carson, 274 S.C. 316, 262 S.E.2d 918 (1980).

[19]Commonwealth v. Lopes, 318 Mass. 453, 459, 61 N.E.2d 849, 852 (1945).

[20]18 U.S.C. §4 (1988) provides:

Whoever, having knowledge of the actual commission of a felony cognizable by a court of the United States, conceals and does not as soon as possible make known the same to some judge or other person in civil or military authority under the United States, shall be fined not more than $500 or imprisoned not more than three years, or both.

called upon to provide testimony in various legal proceedings, even if that testimony is unfavorable to their employer. While employees have an affirmative duty to obey subpoenas commanding them to testify in legislative or judicial proceedings, there is no legal requirement that employees testify in the absence of a subpoena. As discussed in Chapter 1, some statutes specifically give employees the right to testify against their employers. Title VII, for example, gives employees the right to testify in discrimination lawsuits against their employers. However, it is important to note that Title VII and similar statutes impose no requirement that employees testify in the absence of a subpoena. As a general rule, in the absence of a subpoena or other order compelling employees to give testimony, there appears to be no legal duty imposed upon employees to participate in legal proceedings against their employers.[21]

Ethical Considerations

The previous sections have discussed duties imposed upon employees by the law. However, in the minds of employees considering whether or not to report improper conduct, ethical responsibilities may be equally as compelling as legal responsibilities.

Individual Conscience

Few experiences are as frustrating as witnessing a wrong but feeling unable to correct it. Employees may feel as if they are in such a position when their companies act improperly, and if they fear loss of their jobs if they protest. Similarly, employees who participate in the decisionmaking processes which lead to their organizations' decisions to take improper actions, but who opposed taking such actions, may feel powerless because their voices have gone unheeded. The only reason they do not become whistleblowers may be concern about retaliation. Such self-interest, however, may not seem very weighty in comparison to the public interests threatened by an organization's

---

[21]One commentator has suggested that the legal doctrine of contempt may serve as justification for whistleblowing. S. KOHN & M. KOHN, THE LABOR LAWYER'S GUIDE TO THE RIGHTS AND RESPONSIBILITIES OF EMPLOYEE WHISTLEBLOWERS 5-8 (1988). The authors point out that courts have always had the power to punish interference with their processes, such as intimidation of witnesses. The authors then argue that court protection of witnesses should be extended to protection of whistleblowers, on the basis that whistleblowers may be potential witnesses in legal proceedings. This argument has some flaws. While it is true that courts have always been able to protect witnesses, this protection is premised on the fact that there is an ongoing criminal or civil proceeding before a court which either a prosecutor or a private party has deemed significant enough to commence. The courts may then punish by contempt any person who interferes with witnesses in ongoing proceedings. In contrast, all whistleblower allegations do not necessarily lead to either criminal or civil proceedings, because the allegations may not be borne out, or may not be serious enough to warrant legal proceedings. Thus, under the authors' view, which would protect all whistleblowers regardless of whether any legal proceedings are ever brought based on their allegations, legal protection would be automatic and would not depend on an independent prosecutor's view of whether particular allegations are serious enough to prosecute. Taking this view to its logical conclusion, the contempt power of the courts would protect all employees at all times because they may become potential witnesses. This would extend the contempt power of the courts to an unprecedented and unwarranted extent.

improper activities, and may seem more like cowardice than prudence.[22]

Employees may be subjected to intense peer or social pressure to take ethical positions on volatile issues. For example, hospital employees may feel pressure from their religious beliefs or organizations to oppose abortion practices. Similarly, given the great present concern over drug abuse, employees may feel a strong obligation to report drug usage by co-workers, or lax handling of dangerous drugs in hospitals or pharmaceutical companies. Thus, employees who observe wrongdoing may feel compelled to make disclosures by their own personal sense of ethics.[23]

Professional employees who are sworn to follow ethical codes may experience acute conflicts between their duty to obey those codes, and their duty to their employers. Physicians, nurses, attorneys, architects, engineers, accountants, or other professionals may be required to follow the codes of ethics of their professions, many of which require or strongly encourage disclosure of improper conduct by co-workers or by clients in order to protect the public welfare.

For example, the Principles of Medical Ethics issued by the American Medical Association provide that "[a] physician should expose, without fear or favor, incompetent or corrupt, dishonest or unethical conduct on the part of members of the profession."[24] An absolute requirement of disclosure is contained in the Code of Ethics for Engineers promulgated by the National Society of Professional Engineers, which provides as follows:

> Engineers shall at all times recognize that their primary obligation is to protect the safety, health, property and welfare of the public. If their professional judgment is overruled under circumstances where the safety, health, property or welfare of the public are endangered, they shall notify their employer or client and such other authority as may be appropriate.[25]

Similarly, the Model Rules of Professional Conduct adopted by the American Bar Association absolutely require attorneys to report ethical violations by other attorneys, including co-workers, to the appropriate disclipinary authorities.[26]

Thus, professional employees may often be placed in positions where their responsibilities as employees and their responsibilities under ethical codes are in direct conflict. Such professional employees may feel ethically compelled to become whistleblowers, and may feel

---

[22]For autobiographical accounts of several individuals who became whistleblowers, *see* WHISTLEBLOWING: LOYALTY AND DISSENT IN THE CORPORATION (A. Westin ed. 1971).

[23]*Id.*

[24]*Principles of Medical Ethics and Current Opinions of the Council on Ethical and Judicial Affairs—1989* §9.04, *reprinted in* CODES OF PROFESSIONAL RESPONSIBILITY 219 (R. Gorlin ed. 2d ed. 1990) [hereinafter "Gorlin"].

[25]*Code of Ethics for Engineers* II:1:a (1987), *reprinted in* Gorlin, *supra* note 24 at 69.

[26]*Model Rules of Professional Conduct* Rule 8.3 (1989), *reprinted in* Gorlin, *supra* note 24 at 384.

that they run the risk of professional discipline if they do not make disclosures of misconduct which affects the public safety or welfare.

Consideration for the Rights of Others

Compelling ethical considerations may weigh against whistleblowing. Whistleblowers have ethical responsibilities to the public interest, to their organizations, to their co-workers, and, in the case of professional employees, to their professions. All of these ethical considerations must be weighed in determining whether whistleblowing is the proper course of action.

First, the responsibility to the public interest suggests that potential whistleblowers must consider whether the subject of the potential report is truly a matter of public interest,[27] distinguishing between matters in which the public may be interested, and matters which actually affect the public safety or welfare. For example, it may be of interest to the public that an employer contributes to extreme religious or political organizations, but only in exceptional cases might such information affect the public interest. If it is determined that the subject of the potential report directly affects the public interest, employees must determine whether the public interest is either substantial or insignificant. Since the notion of whistleblowing implies calling attention to an imminent danger that can only be stopped by the act of whistleblowing, potential whistleblowers must consider whether it is possible that whistleblowing will lead to correction of the imminent danger.[28] If the public will not benefit from the act of whistleblowing, then the public interest may be disserved by causing undue waste of public time and resources necessary to investigate the report.[29]

Second, employees' responsibilities to their organizations and co-workers suggest that care be taken to ensure the accuracy of any report of wrongdoing. Whistleblowing by its nature is a form of accusation against an employee's organization, and either directly or indirectly, against another individual in the organization. For instance, a report of corruption within a police precinct not only accuses the police department itself, but implicitly accuses the responsible officer in the precinct of either tolerating, participating in, or negligently failing to uncover corruption. Partly for this reason, the Code of Ethics and Implementation Guidelines issued by the American Society for Public

---

[27]D. Callahan & S. Bok, Ethics Teaching in Higher Education 277-95 (1980); F. Elliston, J. Keenan, P. Lockhart & J. Van Schaick, Whistleblowing: Managing Dissent in the Workplace 126-128 (1985) [hereinafter "Elliston"]. *See also* N. Bowie, Business Ethics 143 (1980). The author states that whistleblowing is ethically permissible if the following conditions are met: (1) the purpose is to prevent harm to others, (2) an internal resolution has been unsuccessfully attempted, (3) there is sufficient evidence that a reasonable person would be persuaded that the alleged violation poses a serious danger, (5) the whistleblower has not participated in the violation, and (6) there is a reasonable chance that the violation can be stopped or corrected.

[28]*Id.*

[29]D. Callahan & S. Bok, *supra* note 27 at 285.

Administration provides that "[a]s a last resort, public employees have a right to make public their criticism but it is the personal and professional responsibility of the critic to advance only well founded criticism."[30] Therefore, employees' responsibilities to their organizations and co-workers suggest that reports of wrongdoing be carefully researched for accuracy before institutional and individual reputations are called into question.

This is especially true in the present legal climate in which corporations and individual managers may be held criminally liable for a wide variety of offenses which were not criminalized until recent years. Many of the health, safety, and environmental statutes enacted in the 1960s and 1970s contain provisions permitting criminal penalties as well as civil penalties for conduct which had not previously been considered criminal.[31] Although most criminal statutes have traditionally required that the defendant act with a guilty mind, or *mens rea*, many of the recent public health and environmental statutes have been construed by the courts to dilute the *mens rea* requirement, and to impose virtually strict liability for violations. In cases involving statutes protecting the public welfare, the Supreme Court has permitted imposition of criminal penalties upon responsible corporate officers who may not have known of, or participated in illegal conduct, but who were in a position to prevent or correct violations.

> [T]he [Food, Drug and Cosmetic] Act imposes not only a positive duty to seek out and remedy violations when they occur but also, and primarily, a duty to implement measures that will insure that violations will not occur. The requirements of foresight and vigilance imposed on responsible corporate agents are beyond question demanding, and perhaps onerous, but they are no more stringent than the public has a right to expect of those who voluntarily assume positions of authority in business enterprises whose services and products affect the health and well-being of the public that supports them. [Citation omitted.][32]

In addition to the relaxed requirements for criminal violations under many recent statutes, stiffer sentences have been advocated for corporate criminal violations. In 1984, Congress passed the Sentencing Reform Act which created the U.S. Sentencing Commission.[33] The Commission issued sentencing guidelines which became effective on November 1, 1987, which stated as follows:

---

[30]*Code of Ethics and Implementation Guidelines* (1985), *reprinted in* Gorlin, *supra* note 24 at 97.

[31]*See, e.g.*, Resource Conservation Recovery Act (RCRA), 42 U.S.C. §6901 *et seq.* (felony penalties up to two years' imprisonment); Toxic Substances Control Act, 15 U.S.C. §2601 *et seq.* (misdemeanor penalties up to one year imprisonment); Federal Water Pollution Control Act Amendments of 1977, 33 U.S.C. §466 *et seq.* (amendments provided for felony penalties up to three years' imprisonment); Comprehensive Environmental Response, Compensation and Liability Act of 1980 (CERCLA), 42 U.S.C. §9601 *et seq.* (felony penalties up to five years' imprisonment).

[32]United States v. Park, 421 U.S. 650, 672 (1975) (upholding conviction under Food, Drug and Cosmetic Act). The courts of appeal have upheld criminal convictions under RCRA in the absence of *mens rea*. *See* United States v. Hayes Int'l Corp., 786 F.2d 1499 (11th Cir. 1986).

[33]Pub. L. No. 98-473, 98 Stat. 1837 (codified throughout Title 18 of the United States Code).

> Under present sentencing practice, courts sentence to probation an inappropriately high percentage of offenders guilty of certain economic crimes, such as theft, tax evasion, antitrust offenses, insider trading, fraud, and embezzlement, that in the Commission's view are serious. If the guidelines were to permit courts to impose probation instead of prison in many or all such cases, the present sentences would continue to be ineffective.
>
> The Commission's solution to this problem has been to write guidelines that classify as "serious" (and therefore subject to mandatory prison sentences) many offenses for which probation is now frequently given.[34]

In addition to the possibility of being held criminally liable for offenses which they did not personally commit or condone, corporate officials also face the prospect of strict sentences under the Sentencing Guidelines.

Similar considerations suggest that employees should explore alternatives short of whistleblowing to correct improper behavior. Unless there is evidence of intentional wrongdoing, employees may be expected to give their employers and co-workers the benefit of the doubt that improprieties were the result of negligence, oversight, mistake, or some other inadvertence rather than an affirmative desire to harm the public. Attempts to informally resolve alleged violations may lead to correction of the problems, and may prevent criminal prosecution of honest but ill-informed officials who would immediately correct problems if they knew about them.

Furthermore, an attempted informal resolution may give employers the opportunity to voluntarily disclose violations without incurring negative publicity. As mentioned in Chapter 1, the Securities and Exchange Commission encouraged voluntary disclosure of questionable corporate payments in the 1970s. The U.S. Department of Defense began a voluntary disclosure program in July 1986, for defense contractors who might have submitted fraudulent claims to the federal government.[35] Although these voluntary disclosure programs do not shield participants from prosecution, participation in the programs would probably be viewed positively by prosecutors who are considering whether to bring criminal charges, or judges who are considering whether a severe sentence should be imposed. Thus, whistleblowers who make reports to outside authorities, without attempting an internal resolution, may prevent their companies from gaining whatever advantages may exist to participating in disclosure programs. Consideration for their organizations and their co-workers strongly suggests that employees should attempt to resolve any alleged violations internally before reporting to outside authorities.[36]

In addition to exploring alternative solutions, employees must take care that their judgments regarding the motives of their co-

---

[34]U.S. Sentencing Commission, Sentencing Guidelines and Policy Statements (1987), pp. 1.8-1.9.

[35]Memorandum, U. S. Dept. of Justice, "Department of Justice Guidelines re: Department of Defense Voluntary Disclosure Program" (July 17, 1987).

[36]D. CALLAHAN & S. BOK, *supra* note 27 at 286.

workers are unbiased. Many whistleblowers desire not only to make a disclosure of wrongdoing, but also to keep their jobs rather than resign in protest. If they succeed in doing so, and if the co-workers accused of improprieties by whistleblowers either lose their jobs or some degree of authority, the disclosures of whistleblowers may significantly alter the power structures of their organizations. This possibility for intentional or subconscious use of whistleblowing for political advantage within an organization requires employees to consider objectively their motives.[37]

Employees' professional responsibilities to their professions may also counsel against whistleblowing. For example, many states leave the matter of professional discipline to professional organizations which police themselves, rather than creating a state agency to oversee professional conduct. For example, the Principles of Medical Ethics state that "[q]uestions of such conduct should be considered, first, before proper medical tribunals in executive sessions or by special or duly appointed committees on ethical relations, provided such a course is possible and provided, also, that the law is not hampered thereby."[38] To the extent that a whistleblower's complaint causes public scrutiny of usually confidential matters, the complaint may undermine the self-policing function of professional associations.

Finally, whistleblowers owe it to themselves and to the public to successfully prevent harm to the public welfare. This requires that their complaints be accurate, fair, and credible. More often than not, anonymous whistleblower complaints lack credibility because the accuracy of the information and motives of the source are unknown, and cannot be objectively assessed. When employees' obligations to their organizations, to their co-workers, and to the public are weighed, anonymous whistleblowing is rarely justified.[39]

Balancing the Tensions

As discussed previously, there is some historical support in the doctrine of misprision for the view that employees have a duty to report serious crimes they have witnessed. However, beyond the narrow category of felony crimes, there is little legal support for the view that employees have an affirmative duty to become whistleblowers. From the legal perspective, except in narrow circumstances, the act of whistleblowing is voluntary rather than required by law.

From an ethical perspective, employees may feel that the act of whistleblowing is required rather than voluntary. However, it should be recognized that the compulsion employees may feel does not neces-

---

[37]*Id.* at 287-88.

[38]*Principles of Medical Ethics and Current Opinions of the Council on Ethical and Judicial Affairs—1989* §9.04, *reprinted in* Gorlin, *supra* note 24 at 219.

[39]D. Callahan & S. Bok, *supra* note 27 at 286-87.

sarily arise from legal sources, but instead from individually held moral or ethical beliefs.[40] In some cases, an employee's decision to blow the whistle is tantamount to a decision that his or her individual ethical views are superior to those of his or her organization. Additionally, whistleblowers who desire to keep their jobs implicitly take the position that their employers may not ethically take adverse employment action against them.

Equally strong ethical arguments can be made against whistleblowing, depending on the circumstances of each case. From the perspective of employers, whistleblowers may be viewed as persons who gain an inside position by accepting a job offer and promotions, who use their inside position to pry into internal affairs, who voluntarily engage in conduct that embarrasses their organizations, who do so on grounds of moral or ethical superiority, and who insist that employers are ethically required to continue treating them as if nothing had happened. The ethical position of whistleblowers is even more tenuous when their disclosures are inaccurate.

Because whistleblowing falls into gray areas of law and of ethics, whether whistleblowing is justified in a particular case depends upon the details of each case, including the size of the employer's organization and the seriousness of the threat to the public safety. Moreover, slight variations in the facts of different cases may lead to dramatically different conclusions regarding the propriety of whistleblowing. The following sections will examine the detailed factual situations that may arise in whistleblowing cases, and will suggest how the principles discussed in the previous sections affect whether a particular instance of whistleblowing is legally or ethically justifiable.

What Whistleblowers May Disclose

Whistleblowers justify their disclosures by placing the public welfare above their organizations' interests. Thus, as suggested above, whistleblowers must first ensure that the subject of their complaint directly affects the health, safety, or welfare of the public.

As suggested by the cases of A.E. Fitzgerald and P.E. Petermann discussed in Chapter 1, whether a particular subject directly affects the public interest varies greatly depending upon whether a whistleblower is employed in the public or private sectors. In the case of Fitzgerald, there is little question that his disclosures regarding massive cost overruns, which allegedly caused unnecessary waste of taxpayers' funds, were directly related to the public interest. Moreover, as discussed in Chapter 1, the CSRA broadly defines the matters about which federal government employees may complain. Similar broad definitions are found in state statutes protecting employees of state

---

[40] M. GLAZER & P. GLAZER, THE WHISTLEBLOWERS: EXPOSING CORRUPTION IN GOVERNMENT AND INDUSTRY 97-132 (1989).

government, as discussed in Chapter 3. Mismanagement and gross waste of funds imply that public funds are being squandered either through inefficiency or waste. An abuse of authority in the public sector might be a political reprisal because a politically appointed superior does not agree with the politics of a subordinate.

The public interest in private sector employment is much less easily defined. For example, it is not immediately obvious whether the public interest would have been implicated if Petermann had made disclosures about cost overruns in a Teamsters apprenticeship or pension program. Although members of the affected union would clearly be interested in such matters, the public interest in the internal finances of particular unions is less direct because no misuse of public funds is involved.

The problem of defining the public interest in relationships between private parties, including private sector employment, has long perplexed judges and scholars.[41] In the American system of government, the legislature has the authority to enact laws in furtherance of the legislature's view of the public interest, because the legislature consists of the elected representatives of the people. Thus, judges and scholars readily agree that legislative enactments, within constitutional limits, are valid expressions of public policy. There is little agreement, however, regarding nonlegislative sources that courts may rely upon as expressions of public policy. As the Maryland Court of Appeals candidly admitted:

> [J]urists to this day have been unable to fashion a truly workable definition of public policy. . . . [J]udges are frequently called upon to discern the dictates of sound public policy and human welfare based upon nothing more than their own personal experience and intellectual capacity.[42]

Furthermore, courts have recognized that each judge's conception of what is in the public interest is likely to vary depending upon each judge's education, habits, talents, and opinions. Because of the subjectivity of defining public policy, and because the judiciary lacks the investigatory and hearing capabilities of legislatures, the American judiciary has been hesitant to intrude upon the legislative function of defining the public interest.

The difficulty of defining the limits of public policy as it applies to private sector employment is illustrated by the opinion of the California Supreme Court in *Foley v. Interactive Data Corp.*[43] David Foley had been employed by Interactive Data Corporation for almost seven

---

[41]*See* Brachtenbach, *Public Policy in Judicial Decisions*, 21 GONZ. L. REV. 1 (1985-86). This article by a Justice of the Washington Supreme Court alludes to the "futility of ascertaining a precise definition of public policy." *See also* Note, *Protecting Employees At Will Against Wrongful Discharge: The Public Policy Exception*, 96 HARV. L. REV. 1931, 1947 (1983), in which the commentator remarks that "[d]eveloping a coherent doctrine of public policy has long been recognized as a source of judicial difficulty and confusion."

[42]Maryland-Nat'l Capital Park & Planning Comm'n v. Washington Nat'l Arena, 282 Md. 588, 605-06, 386 A.2d 1216, 1228 (1978).

[43]47 Cal.3d 654, 254 Cal. Rptr. 211, 765 P.2d 373, 3 IER Cases 1729 (1988).

years, and had risen through a series of promotions to the position of branch manager of the Los Angeles office. Interactive Data Corporation was in the business of marketing computer-based decision-support services, and had customers in the financial community that disclosed confidential information to Interactive Data. When he was hired, Foley was required to sign a "Confidential and Proprietary Information Agreement" in which he acknowledged that he would receive confidential information during his employment, and promised to keep such information confidential.

Foley learned that his immediate supervisor, Vice President Richard Earnest, was to be replaced by Robert Kuhne. Foley also learned that Kuhne was under investigation by the Federal Bureau of Investigation for embezzlement from the Bank of America, Kuhne's prior employer. In January 1983, Foley disclosed this information to Earnest, for the interest and benefit of Interactive Data, because Foley believed that Interactive Data, which did business with the financial community on a confidential basis, had an interest in knowing about a high executive's prior criminal conduct. Earnest allegedly told Foley to forget the rumors he had heard. Shortly thereafter, Earnest and Kuhne allegedly began criticizing Foley's performance, and in March 1983, gave Foley the option of resigning or being terminated. In September 1983, after Foley had been discharged, Kuhne pleaded guilty in federal court to one felony count of embezzlement.

In attempting to determine whether Foley's discharge was contrary to public policy, the court noted that the intermediate California appellate courts had divided upon the issue of whether judges must defer to the legislature in defining public policy. Several intermediate courts had held that public policy was limited to legislative enactments such as statutes or constitutional provisions, and required that a statutory or constitutional basis be identified for public policy claims. Other intermediate courts had suggested that judges were free to define public policy without reference to legislative enactments. Foley attempted to satisfy the requirement of a statutory basis for his claim by relying upon a statute which arguably required Foley to disclose to Interactive Data all information relevant to his employment.

The California Supreme Court declined to decide whether statutes or constitutional provisions were the only sources of public policy. Instead, the court assumed that the statute relied upon by Foley required him to disclose his knowledge to Interactive Data. Nevertheless, the court stated as follows:

> Even where, as here a statutory touchstone has been asserted, we must still inquire whether the discharge is against public policy and affects a duty which inures to the benefit of the public at large rather than to a particular employer or employee. For example, many statutes simply regulate conduct between private individuals, or impose requirements

> whose fulfillment does not implicate fundamental public policy concerns.[44]

Moreover, the court stated that the public policy implicated must be "firmly established" and "substantial."[45] The court then held that the statutory duty to disclose information to Interactive Data relied upon by Foley did not implicate a fundamental concern of public policy, because the duty inured only to the benefit of Interactive Data rather than to the public at large.

The court relied in part on a contractual analysis to justify its result. The court noted the general principle that contracts that are contrary to public policy will not be enforced by the judiciary. Using this analysis, the court pointed out that a contract between Foley and Interactive Data, under which Foley agreed not to make a disclosure such as that regarding Kuhne, would be fully enforceable because it would not be contrary to any compelling mandate of public policy. In contrast, the court noted that its earlier public policy decisions involved public interests that could not be circumvented by an agreement between the parties. For instance, in an earlier decision recognizing a cause of action on behalf of an employee who alleged that he was fired for refusing to violate the antitrust laws, the court stated that a contractual provision that purported to require the employee to violate the antitrust laws would not be enforceable.

This aspect of the *Foley v. Interactive Data Corp.* opinion simply restates a basic point of the law of contracts regarding the unenforceability of illegal bargains. Under this basic contractual doctrine, the courts may refuse to enforce contractual provisions depending upon the following factors:

> (a) the strength of that [public] policy as manifested by legislation or judicial decisions,
> (b) the likelihood that a refusal to enforce the term will further that policy,
> (c) the seriousness of any misconduct involved and the extent to which it was deliberate, and
> (d) the directness of the connection between that misconduct and the term.[46]

By defining public policy as "legislation or judicial decisions," this doctrine provides only general guidance regarding the contours of public policy. Thus, the California Supreme Court's reliance upon the contractual doctrine of unenforceability of illegal bargains does little to clarify how the judiciary should decide whether a fundamental public policy is implicated.

At first glance, because Foley's internal disclosure related to potentially criminal conduct, Foley's disclosure appears to have been directly related to the strong public policies reflected in the criminal

---

[44]*Id.* at 668-669, 254 Cal. Rptr. at 216-17, 765 P. 2d at 378-79, 3 IER Cases at 1733.

[45]*Id.*

[46]RESTATEMENT (SECOND) OF CONTRACTS, at §178.

laws. Moreover, Foley's disclosure superficially appears to have been required by the doctrine of misprision. On closer analysis, however, it is apparent that Foley's disclosure only indirectly affected the public welfare. Foley's disclosure did not bring to light conduct that otherwise would go undetected or unpunished. According to Foley's information, the Federal Bureau of Investigation was already investigating Kuhne's conduct at the Bank of America. Thus, the public interest in detection and punishment of embezzlement was already being served, and Foley's disclosure did nothing to advance that interest. Quite a different case would have been presented if Foley had disclosed first-hand knowledge of potential embezzlement by Kuhne at Interactive Data, and if the criminal activity were not already being investigated by the authorities. In that situation, Foley's disclosure might have served the public interest in detection and punishment of criminal activities in addition to serving Interactive Data's interests. However, under the facts actually presented to the California Supreme Court, Foley's disclosure did nothing to advance the public interest in law enforcement.

The *Foley v. Interactive Data Corp.* decision underscores the reluctance of the judiciary to transform notions of appropriate business practices, or of personal ethics, into legal requirements based on public policy. The California Supreme Court was required to assume that Foley acted solely out of a desire to protect Interactive Data, which many employers might applaud and encourage. Foley may have felt compelled to make the disclosure based on his sense of business or personal ethics. Notwithstanding the ethical concerns Foley may have felt, the court's decision rested upon whether any public interest had been served, rather than whether Foley believed his disclosure to be necessary.

The inherently difficult task of defining the public interest, reflected in the *Foley v. Interactive Data Corp.* decision, suggests that whistleblowers in private sector employment may safely complain about violations of statutes, or rules or regulations authorized by statute, which otherwise might go undetected. However, if their complaints do not concern unreported violations of law, whistleblowers in private sector employment must carefully consider whether their complaints will actually serve the public interest, or will serve only the private interest of their employers or their own personal interests.

When Whistleblowers May Make Disclosures

Individual whistleblowers may discover wrongdoing in many different ways. In the case of P.E. Petermann, the wrongdoing was immediately obvious when he was asked by his employer to commit perjury. A.E. Fitzgerald, however, did not immediately discover evidence of waste, but only learned of the C5-A cost overruns over a considerable period of time while carrying out his duties. These different means of learning of improprieties suggest that the appropriate time for making disclosures will vary from case to case.

In the Petermann example, there might be little purpose served if Petermann had attempted to informally resolve his concerns with his employer. Petermann, according to his allegations, had been requested to commit the serious offense of perjury. Petermann may have been justified in assuming that his employer knowingly requested him to commit perjury, and that Petermann had little chance of changing his employer's mind. Furthermore, Petermann was uniquely qualified to know whether his employer's request was proper, because he himself knew best what he had witnessed. Thus, there was little chance that Petermann might have been mistaken as to whether the illegal request had been made. Given these circumstances, although he chose not to do so, Petermann might have justifiably reported his employer's illegal request to the appropriate authorities shortly after it had been made.

In cases like Fitzgerald's, however, employees may not immediately have sufficient knowledge to determine whether improprieties have taken place. If employees merely suspect wrongdoing, but lack the personal knowledge or expertise to determine with any degree of certainty whether wrongdoing is imminent, the ethical responsibilities and the legal duty of loyalty to the employer would seem to require that employees not immediately assume the worst about their organizations and co-workers. Rather, those duties would impliedly require employees to make reasonable inquiry before blowing the whistle, to ensure that there is an actual danger to the public interest.

Assuming that employees have sufficient information to adequately determine that a real threat exists, the legal and ethical responsibilities of employees would also appear to require that an informal attempt be made within their organizations to resolve the problem. Unless employees have reason to know, like Petermann, that informal efforts would be futile, employees who are loyal to their organizations may legitimately be expected to attempt to resolve the problem without subjecting their organizations or co-workers to unnecessary embarrassment. The requirement of giving an employer a reasonable opportunity to correct improprieties may best serve the public interest. To illustrate, assume an oil refinery worker believes that poor maintenance practices may lead to an oil spill in an ecologically sensitive area. Surely it is to the advantage of the company, as well as to the surrounding community, to encourage the employee to immediately report such concerns within the company so that corrective action can be taken to prevent any toxic spill.

The obligation to attempt an informal resolution would be nullified not only if the attempt would be futile, but also if employees legitimately feared for their own personal safety, or if the emergency nature of the imminent danger did not provide enough time. These situations, however, should be the exception rather than the norm.

The size and complexity of the employer's organization may determine how a whistleblower should attempt an informal resolution. In small organizations, a whistleblower's only recourse may be to an immediate supervisor, or to high-ranking officers. If a whistleblower justifiably believes that the immediate supervisor is powerless to remedy the violation, the whistleblower may be justified in ignoring the chain of command by appealing to management. In larger organizations, however, whistleblowers may be able to appeal to other departments within the organization which are not directly involved in the violation or to a company ombudsman charged with investigating whistleblowers' concerns. In those instances, it may be appropriate to require whistleblowers to pursue those channels before appealing directly to highly placed executives.[47]

Because whistleblowing falls into the gray areas of law and ethics, the decision whether to make a disclosure usually is not clear cut. The difficult nature of deciding whether to make a disclosure suggests that potential whistleblowers should consult with as many trusted advisers as possible before attempting an informal resolution within their organizations. For example, discussions with other members of the whistleblower's trade or profession may help place the whistleblower's technical concerns in perspective. Further, consultation with attorneys or members of the clergy, even though they may not be familiar with technical issues, may help to identify and prioritize the ethical considerations involved that are within their area of expertise.[48] Consultations with attorneys or the clergy may have the added advantage of being legally privileged from disclosure under most circumstances. Thus, neither informal attempts within organizations, nor formal complaints outside of organizations, should be made until the employee has a firm grasp on all of the legal and ethical issues that may come into play.

To Whom Whistleblowers May Make Disclosures

Informal attempts to resolve complaints internally may not succeed. Organizations may decide that a whistleblower's concerns are without merit, or even if well-grounded, that the organization will stand by its original decision. The question then becomes to whom whistleblowers may turn for redress of their concerns. As noted above, the strongest argument for whistleblowing is when employees have personally witnessed the commission of a felony. In those instances, employees have the right, and perhaps even a duty to report such crimes to the appropriate law enforcement agencies. Likewise, employees should be able to report violations of law, apart from fel-

---

[47]ELLISTON, *supra* note 27 at 127.

[48]D. CALLAHAN & S. BOK, *supra* note 27 at 288-289.

onies, to the government agency with authority to enforce the law that was violated.

Beyond these categories of felonies and violations of law, however, it is unclear whether employees in the public or private sectors should be permitted to make disclosures to organizations or persons apart from the appropriate government authorities. Criminal law enforcement agencies and agencies that enforce civil statutes are charged with serving the public interest. The interests of other organizations or personnel to whom disclosures might be made are not necessarily aligned with the public interest. For example, other recipients of whistleblower disclosures might include newspaper, radio, or television reporters, community or political action groups, or professional or religious associations. Whether whistleblowers in the public and private sectors should be permitted to make disclosures to these varied persons depends upon how the public interest is best served in each particular case.

The principles underlying the structure of American government suggest that public sector employees should be given permission to make disclosures to a broad range of persons. Separation of powers, the fundamental principle upon which the federal and state governments of this country are based, is designed to prevent any one branch of government from exercising absolute power. Laws are enacted by the elected legislature, interpreted by the judicial branch, and enforced by the executive branch, which at the highest levels is comprised of an elected president or governor, and his or her appointees.[49] The vast majority of executive branch employees, at middle management and lower levels, are civil service employees who are not subject to removal for political considerations.

In addition to preventing one branch of government from becoming too powerful, another purpose of the separation of powers is to prevent selective enforcement of the laws.[50] Nevertheless, there is potential for selective enforcement within the executive branch arising from the fact that appointed officials may owe political debts to the party or persons that appointed them, and may be reluctant to enforce the law against their supporters. Moreover, due to the political nature of these appointments, officials at high levels in the executive branch may be subject to political pressure to abuse the powers of their offices. For these reasons, the legislative branches of federal and state government have a long tradition of monitoring the activities of the executive branches. Thus, a strong argument can be made that government employees should be able to make disclosures to either the legislative, executive, or judicial branch.

Because the principle of the separation of powers within the government has no application to the private sector, it is less clear whether private sector employees should be permitted to make dis-

---

[49]THE FEDERALIST No. 47 (Rossiter ed. 1961).

[50]*Id.* at No. 48.

closures to the legislative branches of government. For example, the interests of legislators, in contrast to law enforcement officials, include not only enforcement of existing laws, but also gaining favorable publicity for their party or for their reelection. Thus, it is possible that legislators may take up a whistleblower's cause not out of belief in its justice, but out of a desire to use the whistleblower's concerns to advance the legislator's own political purposes. There may be instances when employees may be legitimately concerned that the enforcement agencies in their localities will not act upon their complaints, or when employees know that the identities of other whistleblowers have been disclosed without consent by enforcement agencies. In these instances, employees may be justified in making disclosures to legislators instead of to enforcement agencies.

Most law-abiding citizens, including members of the various forms of the news media, share the objective of enforcing existing laws. However, most newspapers and radio and television stations, due to the pressures in those highly competitive fields, must place a high emphasis on ensuring their economic survival by maintaining circulation or audience. Moreover, the concept of "newsworthiness," or what the public may be interested in, is much broader than the concept of the public health, safety, or welfare discussed earlier in this chapter. Under the landmark Supreme Court decision in *New York Times v. Sullivan*, the media enjoy constitutional protection for printing or broadcasting almost any newsworthy items about public figures, except those which are knowingly false, or are disseminated with reckless disregard for their truth.[51] Thus, there is a significant risk that disclosures by whistleblowers to the news media may be broadcast for their newsworthiness, rather than out of a desire to prevent imminent harm to the public.

These concerns suggest that the duty of loyalty and ethical responsibilities require employees to make disclosures to the news media only as a last resort. Because the fundamental loyalty of government employees is to the public, rather than to organizations or individuals, the government employee's duty of loyalty may allow more frequent resort to the news media than does the private sector employee's duty of loyalty. Perhaps for this reason, the phenomenon of anonymous leaks of information to the news media has been generally tolerated in government employment until recently.[52] Since private sector employees' primary allegiance is to their organizations, leaks of information in private sector employment would appear to be justified only in extraordinary circumstances.

For similar reasons, disclosures to political or community action groups may be justified only in extreme circumstances. It is difficult to imagine a situation in which a whistleblower with a legitimate concern would be unable to obtain a response from either government

---

[51]New York Times Co. v. Sullivan, 376 U.S. 254 (1964).

[52]S. Bok, Lying: Moral Choice in Public and Private Life 183 (1979).

agencies, legislators, the judiciary, or the news media. Thus, the instances in which the public interest would be advanced by disclosures to political or community action organizations would appear to be rare.

How Whistleblowers May Make Disclosures

Whistleblowing by its nature is disruptive of the status quo. By calling into question an organization's decisions or practices, whistleblowers necessarily cause disharmony in their organizations.[53] Moreover, a harmful side-effect of a whistleblowing may be a reduction in the dissemination of information within an organization necessary to conduct the organization's affairs, due to fear that information might be misinterpreted or abused. Nevertheless, as in the case of misprision of felony, some degree of disruption may be required by law in order to achieve broader social goals. Duties of loyalty and professional ethics require that employees make their disclosures in a manner that minimizes the damage to their organizations.

As noted earlier in this chapter, employees owe a duty of confidentiality as to their employers' trade secrets, customer lists, or other proprietary information. Since it is not uncommon for whistleblower complaints to arise out of confidential aspects of their employers' affairs, whistleblowers often find themselves in a dilemma. In order for their concerns to be objectively evaluated by appropriate authorities outside of their organizations, employees may feel the need to disclose confidential information that is sufficiently detailed so that an outside expert can make an independent assessment of their concerns. However, disclosure of detailed confidential information may violate the duty of confidentiality, and may subject employees to legal liability to their employers.[54] In these situations, whistleblowers may wish to protect themselves against legitimate adverse actions by their employers by disclosing confidential information only to the extent absolutely necessary, and only if the authority to which the information is disclosed expressly agrees to keep such information confidential.

In addition to minimizing potential harmful effects of disclosures of confidential information, considerations of loyalty and ethics also suggest that whistleblowers must attempt to minimize the disruption caused by their disclosures. The legitimate self-interest of whistleblowers also favors minimizing the disruptive effects of their disclosures. Because most whistleblowers desire to keep their positions and to maintain previous working relationships, whistleblowers can maintain a measure of credibility with their co-workers by minimizing disruption.

---

[53]D. Callahan & S. Bok, *supra* note 27 at 281.

[54]*See* Uniform Trade Secrets Act, 14 U.L.A. 541 (1980).

Moreover, whistleblowers who conduct themselves in a way which maximizes disruption run the risk of forfeiting legal protection which may otherwise exist for their disclosures. No right is absolute, including the right to disclose or oppose illegal conduct. As discussed in Chapter 8, numerous authorities have recognized that employees may forfeit qualified rights to engage in conduct otherwise protected by law, by doing so in an extreme manner. For these reasons, prudent whistleblowers would be well-advised to attempt to minimize the animosity and disruption which their disclosures may generate.

For What Reasons Whistleblowers May Make Disclosures

The ethical justification for whistleblowing, which is placing the public interest before all others, logically requires that employees' disclosures be motivated by a good-faith desire to protect the public. From either a legal or ethical perspective, unfounded complaints motivated by personal desires for political advantage or economic gain do not deserve legal protection.[55] It is equally clear that truthful disclosures based on purely altruistic motives should be protected. However, whistleblower disclosures may have varying degrees of accuracy, and whistleblowers may act out of mixed public and personal motives. Whether disclosures of questionable accuracy or of questionable motivation should be legally protected may vary in different cases.

As discussed earlier in this section, whistleblowers owe it to themselves, to their organizations, and to the public to make careful inquiries to ensure that their disclosures are accurate. From the standpoint of employers, who have much to lose by inaccurate disclosures, only disclosures which are truthful and accurate should be protected. From the public's point of view, depending upon the gravity of the threat to the public safety, it would be better to encourage disclosures made in good faith, which after investigation prove to be unfounded, than to discourage all disclosures which cannot be absolutely verified. Thus, in cases where the danger to the public is serious, the public has an interest in encouraging well-researched disclosures made in good faith, even if the ultimate conclusion of the investigation into the disclosure reveals that the perceived danger did not actually exist. In cases where the subject of the disclosure is less serious, however, the public has an interest in encouraging only accurate disclosures, regardless of the whistleblower's good faith, so that public resources are not unnecessarily wasted in investigating the disclosures. As a matter of policy, therefore, well-researched whistleblower disclosures regarding serious threats to the public safety, made in good faith, should be legally protected. In situations where the threat to the public safety is not serious, the better policy may be to

[55]D. CALLAHAN & S. BOK, *supra* note 27 at 286-288; N. BOWIE, *supra* note 27 at 143.

protect only disclosures regarding actual legal violations or improprieties.

Disclosures of questionable motivation pose more of an analytical problem than those of questionable accuracy. Employees may be partially motivated by various reasons apart from concern for the public interest. For instance, bureaucratic battles over the jurisdiction of competing government agencies are commonplace. Although less publicized, internecine squabbles between departments or divisions undoubtedly occur in the private sector as well. Whistleblower disclosures may be partially motivated by a desire to gain some advantage in such internal political disputes. It is also possible that whistleblower disclosures may be motivated by personal desires for publicity, for financial gain if whistleblowers are promised compensation for their disclosures, or for revenge based on years of repressed frustration with the way an individual has been treated by his or her employer. Finally, false or unscrupulous disclosures may be made "in the periods of hysteria and witch-hunting we are as a nation sometimes guilty of."[56]

In most instances, disclosures that are based solely upon motives apart from protecting the public do not merit legal protection, because the law should not encourage disruption of employment relationships for personal gain or revenge. However, disclosures based upon mixed public and personal motives may deserve protection depending upon the seriousness of the threat to the public. As discussed in Chapter 8, legal tests have been developed to evaluate the mixed motives of employers who terminate the employment of whistleblowers. Under those standards, an employer is liable for retaliation against a whistleblower if the employer would not have taken adverse action in the absence of the disclosure. However, an employer is not liable if it would have taken adverse action even if the whistleblower had not made the disclosure. A similar standard may be appropriate for evaluating employees' motives. That is, if a whistleblower would not have made a disclosure, except for personal motivations, then the employee should not be protected because abuse of whistleblower protection may be encouraged. However, if a disclosure would have been made in the absence of personal motivations, then the employee should be protected because the potential for abuse is minimized. Because of the overriding public interest in disclosure of such threats, an exception to this framework may be justified in circumstances in which the subject of the disclosure presents a serious, imminent danger to the public.

The tensions discussed in this chapter have been resolved in different ways by Congress, the state legislatures, and the American judiciary in creating the various whistleblower protections which are discussed in the following chapters.

[56]Swaaley v. United States, 376 F.2d 857, 863 (Ct. Cl. 1967).

3

Protections for Government Employees

More than three million people were employed by the federal government in 1987, excluding military employees.[1] Almost 14,000,000 persons are employed by state, county, municipal, and other local governments throughout the country.[2] Most of these public employees enjoy whistleblower protections arising from either constitutional or statutory sources, which are the subject of this chapter.

Constitutional Protections for Government Employees

The First Amendment to the United States Constitution provides in part that "Congress shall make no law . . . abridging the freedom of speech, or of the press; or the right of the people peaceably to assemble, and to petition the government for a redress of grievances." Although by its terms the First Amendment places limits only upon Congress, the Supreme Court has applied those limits to state governments as well through the Fourteenth Amendment.[3] By virtue of this judicial interpretation, the First Amendment now limits the restrictions that either federal or state governments may place upon freedom of speech.

Until the 1950s, however, the Supreme Court drew a distinction between the free speech rights of citizens and those of public employees, on the ground that government employment was a privilege upon which governments could place whatever restrictions were necessary to ensure the efficient functioning of government agencies, including restrictions on free speech. One of the most famous expressions of this

---

[1]United States Department of Commerce, *Statistical Abstract of the United States 1989*, No. 512, at 318.

[2]*Id.* No. 479, at 293.

[3]Murdock v. Pennsylvania, 319 U.S. 105 (1942).

view was Justice Holmes' dictum in a case in which a policeman had been dismissed for violating a city regulation requiring political neutrality:

> [T]here is nothing in the Constitution . . . to prevent the city from attaching obedience to this rule as a condition to the office of policeman. . . . The petitioner may have a constitutional right to talk politics, but he has no constitutional right to be a policeman. . . . The servant cannot complain, as he takes the employment on terms which are offered to him.[4]

The privilege doctrine was greatly eroded during the 1950s in a series of cases invalidating laws which required public employees to take oaths of loyalty as a condition of employment.[5]

In the landmark case of *Pickering v. Board of Education*,[6] the Supreme Court held that the First Amendment provided limited protection for public employees who publicly criticized the policies of their employers. Pickering, a public school teacher, had been dismissed because he wrote a letter criticizing the fiscal policies of the local school board to the editor of a newspaper. The Court held that Pickering's statements were protected by the First Amendment because they were directed at issues of legitimate public concern, and therefore could not provide a ground for his dismissal. Nevertheless, the Court took care to indicate that the free speech rights of public employees were not unlimited. The Court stated that "the State has interests as an employer in regulating the speech of its employees that differ significantly from those it possesses in connection with the regulation of the speech of the citizenry in general."[7] Although it refrained from setting down general rules regarding such governmental interests, the Court suggested that Pickering's statements might not have been protected if he had had a close working relationship with the school board, such that his statements might have jeopardized discipline or harmony in the workplace. In addition, the Court indicated that Pickering's statements might not have been protected if the statements "in any way either impeded . . . proper performance of his daily duties . . . or . . . interfered with the regular operation of the schools. . . ."[8]

The *Pickering* ruling, which protected public statements, was interpreted to protect "the public employee who arranges to communicate privately with his employer rather than to spread his views before the public."[9] The combination of these rulings establishes a qualified

---

[4]McAuliffe v. Mayor of New Bedford, 155 Mass. 216, 220, 9 N.E. 517 (1892).

[5]*See* Weyman v. Updegraff, 344 U.S. 183 (1952); Slochower v. Board of Educ., 350 U.S. 551 (1956); Shelton v. Tucker, 346 U.S. 479 (1960). For a discussion of the erosion of the privilege doctrine, see Note, *Government Employee Disclosures of Agency Wrongdoing*, 42 U. CHI. L. REV. 530 (1975), and Heffron, *Protection of the Constitutional Rights of Federal Employees*, 3 COOLEY L.REV. 297 (1985).

[6]391 U.S. 563, 1 IER Cases 8 (1968).

[7]*Id.* at 568, 1 IER Cases at 10.

[8]*Id.* at 572-73, 1 IER Cases at 12.

[9]Givhan v. Western Line Consol. School Dist., 439 U.S. 410, 415-16 (1979).

constitutional protection for both internal and external whistleblowers, but only for those who complain about matters of public concern in a manner that does not disrupt public employment. Indeed, the Supreme Court recently indicated that some categories of speech may be protected by the First Amendment only if the speech occurred within the employer's organization, and would not be protected if publicly expressed.

In *Rankin v. McPherson*,[10] Ardith McPherson was a clerical employee in the county constable's office who overheard a radio report about the attempted assassination of then-President Reagan. McPherson said to a co-worker, within the confines of the constable's office, "[I]f they go for him again, I hope they get him."[11] After another co-worker reported the comment to the constable, who asked McPherson whether she made the statement, McPherson replied, "Yes, but I didn't mean anything by it."[12] The constable then terminated McPherson's employment based primarily on his concern for the image of his law enforcement office.

The Court held that McPherson's comment was protected by the First Amendment because it related to a matter of serious public concern, and because it did not amount to a threat to kill the President.[13] Taking into account the time, place, and manner of McPherson's comment, the Court stated as follows:

> [There was not] any danger that McPherson had discredited the office by making her statement in public. McPherson's speech took place in an area to which there was ordinarily no public access; her remark was evidently made in a private conversation with another employee.[14]

Finally, the Court also stated that McPherson's level of responsibility should be considered in determining whether the functioning of the constable's office had been impaired:

> Where, as here, an employee serves no confidential, policy-making, or public contact role, the danger to the agency's successful function from that employee's private speech is minimal.[15]

Unlike Pickering's speech, which was a public disclosure of sensitive information, McPherson's comment was more in the nature of a personal opinion. Thus, while McPherson technically was not a whistleblower, the *Rankin v. McPherson* decision indicates that internal complaints of whistleblowers, which do not publicly discredit an agency and thereby undermine its functions, may be protected to a greater extent than external, public complaints.

---

[10]483 U.S. 378, 2 IER Cases 257 (1987).

[11]*Id.* at 381, 2 IER Cases at 257.

[12]*Id.* at 382, 2 IER Cases at 258.

[13]*Id.* at 386-87, 2 IER Cases at 260.

[14]*Id.* at 389, 2 IER Cases at 261.

[15]*Id.* at 390-91, 2 IER Cases at 261.

Other decisions have underscored the limited extent of the protection established by *Pickering* and its progeny. In *Connick v. Myers*,[16] a whistleblower's criticism was held to be unprotected because the criticism was not directly related to matters of public concern, and was made in a manner that disrupted the activities of the employer. Myers was an assistant district attorney in Orleans Parish who had competently performed her duties for over five years. When told that she would be assigned to different duties, she objected to Connick, the District Attorney, and several other supervisors. In response to one of her supervisors' suggestion that her concerns were not shared by others in the office, Myers circulated a questionnaire to 15 co-workers concerning the office transfer policy, office morale, the level of confidence in supervisors, the need for a grievance committee, and whether employees felt pressured to work in political campaigns. Connick terminated Myers on the day the questionnaire was circulated, on the grounds that she had refused the transfer, and that he considered the questionnaire to be an act of insubordination. Connick was particularly upset by a question asking whether employees "had confidence in and would rely on the word" of supervisors in the office.

The Court held that most of Myers' questionnaire did not address matters of public concern, but instead reflected Myers' dissatisfaction with her transfer to other duties. The Court stated that Myers did not "seek to bring to light actual or potential wrongdoing or breach of public trust on the part of Connick," but instead only attempted "to gather ammunition for another round of controversy with her superiors."[17] The Court held that Myers' question regarding pressure to work on political campaigns was protected because it related to a matter of public concern, yet ultimately the Court held that the disruptive potential of the questionnaire in a small office requiring close working relationships justified Myers' dismissal. Moreover, the time, place, and manner of Myers' questionnaire was viewed as disruptive, in that "the manner of distribution required not only Myers to leave her work but for others to do the same in order that the questionnaire be completed."[18] Thus, *Connick v. Myers* indicates that whistleblower complaints that are directly related to whistleblowers' personal grievances may not be constitutionally protected.

Despite the indications in *Pickering v. Board of Education* and *Connick v. Myers* that disruptive speech may justify dismissal, several courts have recognized that whistleblowing by its nature often causes disruption and demoralization, and that the mere potential for disruption alone does not necessarily forfeit First Amendment protection. This concept was articulated by one court as follows:

> An employee who accurately exposes rampant corruption in her office no doubt may disrupt and demoralize much of the office. But it would be

[16]461 U.S. 138, 1 IER Cases 178 (1983).

[17]*Id.* at 148, IER Cases at 182-83.

[18]*Id.* at 153, 1 IER Cases at 184.

> absurd to hold that the First Amendment generally authorizes corrupt officials to punish subordinates who blow the whistle simply because the speech somewhat disrupted the office.[19]

The distinction between whistleblowing that is so disruptive it loses legal protection, and whistleblowing that is not seriously disruptive, is highly dependent on the facts of each case, as discussed in Chapter 8.

Assuming that a public employee has engaged in whistleblowing in a legally protected fashion, the remedy for violation of a whistleblower's First Amendment rights varies depending upon whether the whistleblower is employed by the federal, state, or local government. Federal employees who have a remedy under the Civil Service Reform Act may also have an implied right of action under the First Amendment, patterned after a *Bivens* cause of action arising under the Fourth Amendment.[20] Employees of state governments may have no affirmative right of action at all, but only a constitutional defense against adverse personnel actions.[21] County and local employees may bring civil actions under 42 U.S.C. §1983, which are discussed in detail in Chapter 6.

Statutory Protections for Federal Employees

As discussed in Chapter 1, the Civil Service Reform Act of 1978 (CSRA) comprehensively reformed the civil service laws of the federal government.[22] The principal purpose of the Act was to codify the merit system principles by restructuring the agencies responsible for administering the federal system of employment, and by providing procedures for ensuring that all federal employees are evaluated on

---

[19]Porter v. Califano, 592 F.2d 770 (5th Cir. 1979); Wulf v. Wichita, 644 F. Supp. 1211, 1224, 1 IER Cases 895, 905 (D. Kan. 1986) (quoting Porter v. Califano).

[20]Although the United States Constitution prohibits many governmental abuses, the Constitution itself does not create remedies for violations of its provisions. In Bivens v. Six Unknown Named Agents of Fed. Bureau of Narcotics, 403 U.S. 388 (1971), the Supreme Court created an implied right of action under the Fourth Amendment which prohibits unreasonable searches and seizures. However, in Bush v. Lucas, 462 U.S. 367 (1983), the Court refused to create an implied right of action under the First Amendment for federal employees who had remedies under the CSRA. The key factor distinguishing *Bivens* was that the plaintiff in that case had no remedy available, apart from an implied constitutional action. *Bush v. Lucas* has been differently interpreted by the various circuit courts of appeal. Two circuit courts held that the CSRA preempts all other judicial remedies for whistleblowers. Hallock v. Moses, 731 F.2d 754, 116 LRRM 2407 (11th Cir. 1984); Braun v. United States, 707 F.2d 922 (6th Cir. 1983). The District of Columbia Circuit has held that the CSRA precludes a *Bivens* action for damages, but not for equitable relief. Hubbard v. United States Env't. Protection Agency, 809 F.2d 1 (D.C. Cir. 1986). The Ninth Circuit has held that a *Bivens* action is available for less drastic types of adverse employment actions. Kotarski v. Cooper, 799 F.2d 1342 (9th Cir. 1986); *but see* Daly-Murphy v. Winston, 820 F.2d 1470 (9th Cir. 1987).

[21]The United States Supreme Court recently held that states are not "persons" within the meaning of 42 U.S.C. §1983 (1988). Will v. Michigan Dep't of State Police, __U.S.__, 57 USLW 4677 (1989). Thus, §1983 does not apply to state government actions, but only to county and other local government actions.

[22]Pub. L. No. 95-454, 92 Stat. 1111 (1978) (the Civil Service Reform Act is codified at various sections throughout 5 U.S.C.).

the basis of merit. Another fundamental purpose of the Act was to provide new protections for employees who disclose illegal or improper government conduct.

The Act replaced the former Civil Service Commission with two organizations: (1) the Office of Personnel Management, charged with personnel management and agency advisory functions, and (2) the Merit Systems Protection Board (MSPB or Board), charged with ensuring adherence to merit system principles and laws. The Act empowers the Special Counsel of the Board to protect whistleblowers from improper reprisals by petitioning the Board to stay retaliatory actions against whistleblowers, and to commence disciplinary proceedings against individuals who improperly discipline whistleblowers. Thus, the Special Counsel is given broad investigative and prosecutorial powers under the Act in order to protect federal employees from reprisals. The substantive provisions of the Act provide that employees may not lawfully be subjected to retaliation for having disclosed information regarding potentially improper conduct either to their superiors, to the Special Counsel, or to the Inspector General of the employees' agencies.

In addition to prosecutions by the Special Counsel, known as "corrective action" proceedings, the Act also provides that employees may seek relief on their own behalf by appealing directly to the Board, in what is known as a "Chapter 77" appeal. The Board may then hold a hearing on employees' appeals of purportedly retaliatory action. Thus, the Act contemplates that aggrieved employees may either petition directly to the Board on their own behalf, or may request the Special Counsel to institute corrective action against supervisors allegedly retaliating against them. Employees may appeal decisions of the Board in Chapter 77 cases directly to the U.S. court of appeals, which has exclusive jurisdiction to review final orders of the Board. The Act has also been construed to permit employees to appeal decisions of the Board in a corrective action case brought by the Special Counsel directly to the U.S. court of appeals.[23]

After the Special Counsel makes an investigation and recommends certain action to the Board, the Board may conduct an evidentiary hearing into the facts underlying the conclusions of the Special Counsel. In such a hearing before the Board, the Special Counsel bears the burden of proving by the preponderance of the evidence the existence of prohibited personnel practices. In order to make out a *prima facie* case, the Special Counsel must prove that the official accused of taking the retaliatory action against the whistleblower had actual or constructive knowledge that the whistleblower had made a protected disclosure. If the employee prevails in a corrective action proceeding brought by the Special Counsel, the Board may award attorneys' fees to the employee for any independent counsel.[24]

---

[23]Frazier v. Merit Sys. Protection Bd., 672 F.2d 150, 109 LRRM 2959 (D.C. Cir. 1982).

[24]*Id.*

The remedy provided by the Act is essentially a "make-whole" remedy supplemented by disciplinary sanctions against officials found to have improperly retaliated against whistleblowers. The Board is empowered to reinstate an employee to the same position he or she would have held in the absence of the improper reprisals, and is also empowered to award attorneys' fees if the employee is represented by separate counsel. The disciplinary actions which may be taken against violators of the Act range from reprimands to the severe sanction of dismissal and disbarment from the federal civil service for up to five years.[25]

Whistleblower Protection Act of 1989

Although the CSRA was intended to protect federal employees who reported improprieties, many employees complained during the 1980s that the Special Counsel was not investigating their complaints in a timely fashion, and was not prosecuting meritorious cases. Moreover, several employees complained that their identities had been disclosed by the Special Counsel, permitting the agencies to engage in retaliation. In response to these criticisms, Congress enacted the Whistleblower Protection Act of 1989 in order to strengthen protections for whistleblowers.[26]

To speed up the response time of the Special Counsel, the Act provides deadlines by which whistleblower complaints must be prosecuted, and requires that whistleblowers be informed of the progress of investigations. To improve the effectiveness of MSPB proceedings and Special Counsel investigations, the Act clarifies the subpoena powers of the MSPB and the Special Counsel. The Act also requires the Special Counsel to submit an annual report to Congress regarding the number of complaints filed and their disposition.

To help prevent retaliation against whistleblowers while their cases are pending, the Special Counsel is specifically prohibited from disclosing the identity of whistleblowers, except when necessary to prevent imminent danger to the public or to prevent criminal activity. Moreover, the Act allows the MSPB, the Special Counsel, and individual whistleblowers to seek orders protecting employees while investigations or enforcement proceedings are pending. To prevent delay tactics by agencies which seek court review of MSPB rulings, the Act requires that prevailing whistleblowers be granted all relief awarded to them during the pendency of any review in the appellate courts. Further, the Act specifies that losing agencies must pay the attorneys' fees and costs of the prevailing whistleblowers. Apart from these procedural modifications, the only new substantive protection contained in the Act is a provision allowing preferential transfers of

---

[25]5 U.S.C. §7701(g) (1988).

[26]Pub. L. No. 101-12, 103 Stat. 16, *codified at* 5 U.S.C.A. §1201 (West Supp. 1990).

whistleblowers who request transfers to other agencies because of fear of retaliation.

The CSRA is the primary source of protection for civil service employees of the federal government. Other narrower sources of protection include two statutes protecting the rights of federal employees to communicate with Congress. The first statute, mentioned in the discussion regarding A.E. Fitzgerald in Chapter 1, makes intimidation of witnesses in Congressional investigations punishable by significant fines and imprisonment. The second statute expressly guarantees federal employees the right to furnish information to any member or committee of Congress.[27] However, neither of these statutes creates a right of action against employers who violate their provisions.

The CSRA does not reach non-civil service employees of the federal government, including approximately 185,000 employees of the Department of Defense who manage and operate military clubs, exchanges, and recreation programs for members of the military service. In 1984 Congress enacted protections for such employees which are substantially similar to those provided by the CSRA.[28]

Personnel in the armed forces have long had the right to communicate with members of Congress.[29] However, until recently there were no specific procedures for handling complaints of military personnel who alleged that they were subjected to reprisals because they communicated with members of Congress. In 1988 Congress strengthened this right of communication by prohibiting reprisals against military personnel who communicate either with members of Congress or with an Inspector General of a military department.[30] Moreover, Congress required that complaints of military whistleblowers be quickly resolved by the Inspector General of the Department of Defense, who is authorized to correct any adverse action and to discipline individuals engaging in reprisals.[31]

Protections for State and Local Government Employees

State Laws Protecting Government Whistleblowers

Twenty-four states have enacted whistleblower statutes that protect state or local government employees. Those states are Alaska (enacted in 1989), Arizona (1985), California (1979), Colorado (1988), Delaware (1983), Florida (1986), Illinois (1981), Indiana (1981), Iowa (1985), Kansas (1984), Kentucky (1986), Maryland (1982), Missouri

[27]5 U.S.C. §7211 (1988).

[28]Department of Defense Authorization Act of 1984, 10 U.S.C. §1587 (1988).

[29]10 U.S.C.A. §1034 (West Supp. 1990).

[30]Department of Defense Authorization Act of 1988, 10 U.S.C.A. §1034 (West Supp. 1990).

[31]10 U.S.C.A. §1034(d)(5)(6) (West Supp. 1990).

(1987), North Carolina (1989), Oklahoma (1982), Oregon (1983), Pennsylvania (1987), South Carolina (1988), Tennessee (1989), Texas (1983), Utah (1985), Washington (1982), West Virginia (1988), and Wisconsin (1984). A description of these statutes is set forth in Appendix A. Further, as discussed in Chapter 4, eleven other jurisdictions have enacted laws which provide substantially similar protections for both public sector and private sector employees. Thus, a total of thirty-five states have passed statutes which protect whistleblowers employed by state or local governments. Some statutes apply only to employees of the state government and not to employees of the political subdivisions of the state, while other statutes apply to employees at all levels of government.

There is little controversy regarding the topics about which government sector whistleblowers may complain, in contrast to the topics which are protected in the private sector. Most state laws protecting whistleblowers employed by state or local governments are patterned after the CSRA, which protects complaints about violations of law, or about gross waste and abuse of authority. The topics of complaints protected in each jurisdiction are also set forth in detail in Appendix A.

Although there is wide agreement concerning the topics of protected complaints, there is less agreement concerning to whom such complaints may be made. In this regard, the statutes protecting employees in state and local governments fall into three general categories. The primary concern underlying the first category of statutes is to protect the legislative oversight of the executive branch of government. These statutes limit the number of persons to whom complaints may be made regarding the topics of mismanagement and political abuses. The second category of statutes is more broad, and does not limit the persons to whom complaints about mismanagement and political abuses may be made. A third category of statutes is noteworthy in that these laws not only protect whistleblowers, but also create incentives encouraging employees to report improper activities. The following sections discuss these three categories, and several common elements found throughout.

Legislative Oversight

The statutes enacted by California, Colorado, Connecticut, Delaware, Florida, Iowa, Kansas, Kentucky, Maine, Missouri, Oklahoma, Washington, and Wisconsin share the intent to protect government employees who communicate with legislators or other government agencies with oversight responsibilities. These statutes provide different protections depending on whether a complaint is about a legal violation, or about mismanagement or political abuse. Under most of these statutes, legal violations may be reported to any appropriate enforcement authority, while complaints about mismanagement or political abuses must be reported to legislative or executive bodies with oversight responsibilities. For example, the Iowa statute prohibits reprisals "for disclosure of information . . . to a member of the General Assembly, the legislative service bureau, the legislative fiscal bureau, or the respective caucus staffs of the General Assembly. . . ."[32] The laws of Colorado, Kansas, Kentucky, Maine, Missouri, Oklahoma, and Wisconsin contain similar protections for communications with the legislative branch, some of which are more narrow than others. For example, the Maine statute protects employees of the state who testify before legislative committees, and protects employees of the public utilities who testify before the Public Utilities Commission. The shared element in all of these statutes is protected communication with some segment of the legislative branch.

More limited mechanisms for oversight are provided by the laws of California, Connecticut, Delaware, Florida, and Washington. Rather than protecting communications with the legislative branch, these statutes protect employees who make reports of abuses to a designated government official. For example, the laws of Connecticut and Florida protect employees who make reports to the attorneys general of those states. The California, Delaware, and Washington statutes protect employees who make reports to the auditors of those states. Although the types of communications protected by these statutes are more limited than in the statutes protecting communications with the legislative branch, the narrower statutes also are aimed at ensuring that the executive branch is effectively monitored.

The significance of which branches of government may be contacted in a protected manner is illustrated by the Colorado case, *Lanes v. O'Brien*.[33] George Lanes was initially employed by the Department of Revenue. He reported to the Legislative Audit Committee regarding practices he believed to be fraudulent. He was dissatisfied with the response to his report, and wrote a letter to every member of the Colorado General Assembly regarding his views. The next day Lanes' employment was terminated. If Lanes had been employed in a jurisdiction protecting only reports to designated officials, his letter to the General Assembly would not have been protected. However, because the Colorado statute protected disclosures of information to any "person," which the court construed to include members of the legislature, the court held that Lanes' conduct was protected and overturned his termination.[34]

General Protection for Reports

The majority of jurisdictions that protect state government employees do not draw any distinction between persons to whom reports of illegal conduct may be made, and those to whom reports of

---

[32] IOWA CODE §19.A.19 (1989).

[33] 746 P.2d 1366 (Colo. App. 1987).

[34] *Id.* at 1371-73.

mismanagement and political abuses may be made. Eleven states protect all kinds of reports made to appropriate state or federal agencies. For example, Florida and five other jurisdictions protect reports to "a public body." These statutes either do not define the term "public body" any further, or define the term very broadly. Similarly, Pennsylvania and four other jurisdictions protect reports made to an "appropriate authority," without defining that term.

Twelve jurisdictions protect complaints made to any persons, not simply to governmental agencies. For example, the Oregon statute protects "disclosures" regarding protected subjects, and does not require that a disclosure be made to a government authority. Similarly, South Carolina protects "reports" without specifying to whom such reports may be made. The Colorado law protects reports made to "any person," as well as those made to legislative committees. These statutes apparently would protect employees who make disclosures to the press. In *Lanes v. O'Brien*, for instance, the court rejected the employer's argument that the fact that Lanes wrote a letter to a newspaper regarding his concerns, in violation of a departmental regulation, constituted sufficient grounds for termination. The court rejected his argument, and held that the departmental regulation was invalid to the extent it conflicted with the whistleblower protection statute.[35] Only two states, Kentucky and Utah, specifically protect communications with the media.

Incentives to Make Reports

South Carolina and Texas are the only states that provide incentives to make reports. Both states create a rebuttable presumption that employees, against whom adverse employment action is taken within a specified period after making a protected report, have been wrongfully retaliated against in violation of the whistleblower protection law. This time period is one year under the South Carolina statute, and 90 days under the Texas statute.

South Carolina and Texas also provide unusual financial incentives to report wrongdoing. Much like the federal False Claims Reform Act discussed in Chapter 6, the South Carolina statute provides that 25 percent of the estimated net savings resulting from the first year of implementation of an employee's report, up to $2,000, must be awarded to an employee whose report results in savings of public funds.

The Texas, California, and Alaska statutes are the only state laws to allow prevailing employees to recover punitive damages as a potential incentive for whistleblowing. The North Carolina statute allows treble damages for willful retaliation against whistleblowers. Every other state statute provides a make-whole remedy providing for reinstatement, backpay, and in most instances, reasonable attorneys'

---

[35] *Id.* at 1371.

fees. Under the Texas, California, Alaska, and North Carolina statutes, prevailing employees may recover additional amounts in order to punish the defendant.

Reasonable Opportunity to Correct Violations

The subjects about which government employees may complain encompass not only legal violations, but also matters such as corruption, gross waste of funds, or abuses of authority. In the case of suspected legal violations, since it would be presumptuous for employees to immediately conclude that their superiors intentionally violated the law, the duty of loyalty might require employees to give their employers a reasonable opportunity to correct the violations. In the case of inefficiency or gross waste of funds, the employer may not have intentionally violated any law, but only acted in an inappropriate manner. In the case of abuses of authority, however, it may be more appropriate and less disloyal for an employee to presume that the abuses were intentional. Because of the broad categories of irregularities about which public employees may complain, and because the primary loyalty of government employees is to the public welfare rather than to particular agencies or supervisors, there appears to be less reason to require public employees to allow their employers a reasonable opportunity to correct suspected improprieties. In addition, due to the political tensions that may exist between political appointees and civil service employees, the likelihood of retaliation may be greater if government employees are required to give notice of their intention to report questionable activities.

For these reasons, most statutes protecting government employees do not require that employees give their employers a reasonable opportunity to correct improper activities. Indeed, both Kentucky and Missouri specifically provide that employers may not require their employees to give notice that they intend to make reports about improper conduct. Only Alaska, Indiana, Maine, Utah, and Wisconsin allow government agencies to impose a requirement that employees give their superiors, or some other agency within the government, an opportunity to correct suspected improprieties.

Protecting the identity of whistleblowers is also a concern of several statutes. The majority of jurisdictions protects not only employees who actually make reports, but, as exemplified in the Pennsylvania law, also protects employees who are "about to report" improprieties. These provisions are aimed at removing any incentive employers may have to attempt to identify embryonic whistleblowers before they make formal reports. Furthermore, the laws of California, Connecticut, Illinois, and Oregon require the state agencies that receive reports from whistleblowers to keep their identity confidential. The Tennessee statute allows whistleblowers to request that their identity be kept confidential, and requires the authorities to honor such requests. As further protection for the identity of whistleblowers, most statutes protect persons making reports on behalf of other employees.

Common Protections and Remedies

To ensure that employees are aware of the protections available to them, many jurisdictions require employers to post notices informing employees about the whistleblower protection laws. Furthermore, to indicate the serious nature of violations of the whistleblower protection laws, many statutes impose some form of penalty upon supervisors who retaliate against whistleblowers. The mildest penalty is imposed by the Colorado statute, which requires that an entry be made in the offending supervisor's personnel records. Some of the most severe penalties are imposed by Oklahoma, which provides that supervisors may forfeit their positions and be ineligible for state employment for up to five years, and California which subjects violators to fines of up to $10,000, and imprisonment for up to one year.

As a further indication of the serious nature of retaliation against whistleblowers, most jurisdictions permit employees to bring civil actions in addition to whatever relief may be available under civil service rules. The majority of jurisdictions also provides that these civil actions do not preempt, but are supplemental to, any other available remedies. For example, the California statute permits employees to sue the official who retaliated against them for damages, including punitive damages and reasonable attorneys' fees, if the appropriate administrative agency does not issue timely decisions on the employees' administrative complaints.

Common Safeguards Against Abuses

The potential for abuse of whistleblower protections is recognized by most jurisdictions. The almost universal method of protection against abuse is the requirement that an employee's complaint be made in good faith. One variant of this requirement is contained in the Pennsylvania statute, which provides that complaints about merely technical or minimal violations are not protected. Several states, such as Wisconsin, expressly require that an employee's report be made without regard to "receipt of anything of value for the employee or the employee's immediate family."[36]

Many statutes recognize the possibility that employees may attempt to avoid unpleasant work assignments by leaving their work areas, or by refusing assignments, ostensibly based on concerns about improper activities. For example, the Kansas and Kentucky statutes provide that they shall not be construed to permit employees to leave their assigned work areas without following the rules applying to leaves of absence, unless they are requested to appear before a legislative committee. Many jurisdictions attempt to remove any incentive to

---

[36]WIS. STAT. ANN. §230.83(2) (1989).

avoid work by specifying that employers are not required to compensate employees for their time spent testifying in legislative or judicial proceedings. Furthermore, very few states specifically protect employees who refuse to work based upon concerns about the propriety of their assignments. This limited protection for refusal to work appears to be the result of the difficulty of determining what constitutes gross waste, inefficiency, or abuse of authority, categories which are more ambiguous than the category of legal violations.

Several states recognize that some government employees are privy to records not available to the public, and that the confidentiality of such records must be respected. These jurisdictions provide that whistleblowers who publicly disclose confidential information are not protected. The Maine statute, for instance, does not protect employees of public utilities who disclose trade secrets or corporate strategy. The Kansas law does not protect employees who disclose information that "is confidential under any provision of law."[37] Finally, the Arizona statute provides that persons who make disclosures in a manner prohibited by law are not protected.

Unique Aspects of Various Statutes

The state laws protecting whistleblowers in government employment vary regarding whether state, county, or local government employees are protected. Some statutes protect only employees at one level of government, while others protect employees at all levels of government. However, most statutes provide the same type of protection for all covered employees. Two exceptions to this general pattern are Connecticut and Tennessee. The Connecticut statute provides different degrees of protection for employees at different levels of government. The Connecticut law protects employees of the state government who report either legal violations or mismanagement. The protection for employees of lower levels of government, however, is limited to reports of legal violations, and does not protect complaints regarding corruption, unethical conduct, gross waste of funds, or abuse of authority. This distinction may reflect the Connecticut legislature's reluctance to interfere in the affairs of local government. The Tennessee statute protects only public education employees who make reports of waste or mismanagement of public education funds.

Another almost universal aspect of the state whistleblower protection laws is that these statutes apply only to government employers. The Florida statute is the exception to this rule, extending its protections to employees of companies contracting with government agencies.

---

[37]KANSAS STAT. ANN. §75-2973 (1988).

Civil Service Rules

Notwithstanding the thirty-five state whistleblower protection statutes referred to in the previous section, there are some categories of government employees in those states that are not covered by the statutes. For example, almost one-half of the statutes protect only employees of the state government, and not employees of the various political subdivisions of the state. Furthermore, in the fifteen jurisdictions that have not enacted whistleblower protection laws, employees at all levels of government may have no specific protection for whistleblowing.

Despite the lack of specific protection for many whistleblowers in government employment, some protection may be available under state civil service regulations which generally require "cause" for termination of government employment. Under these regulations, whistleblowers may argue that the termination of their employment is unrelated to any legitimate reason designed to further the efficiency of the civil service, but instead is a reprisal for responsible whistleblowing activities. For example, Massachusetts has not enacted a whistleblower statute protecting government employees. However, the Massachusetts civil service regulations require "just cause" for removal of government employees.[38] Under the Massachusetts regulations, employees may contend that mere reprisal for whistleblowing does not constitute sufficient cause to justify dismissal from employment. Similar protection under civil service regulations may be available to employees at lower levels of government, in jurisdictions that protect whistleblowers employed by the state, but not by political subdivisions of the state.

From the perspective of employees, the civil service protections are much less satisfactory than those afforded by specific whistleblower protection laws. Unlike the whistleblower statutes, the civil service regulations may not provide an affirmative right of action, including a damages remedy, against the government or the superior. Instead, the civil service regulations may only provide a defense for employees in actions taken against them by the government or their superior. Further, unlike the whistleblower protection laws, which provide specific definitions of what activities will or will not be protected, the just cause standard also gives civil service commissions wide latitude to decide whether particular whistleblowers should or should not be protected. Thus, although government whistleblowers in jurisdictions which do not specifically protect them may find shelter under civil service regulations, they should not presume that such regulations will protect any and all forms of whistleblowing.

---

[38] MASS. GEN. LAWS ANN. ch. 31, §43 (West 1990).

As discussed in this chapter, the majority of states have concluded that whistleblowers in the public sector deserve broad protection for disclosures regarding a wide variety of topics. As will be discussed in the following chapter, there is less of a consensus regarding the circumstances under which whistleblowers in the private sector should be protected.

4

Statutory Protections in the Private Sector

In the 1980s, fourteen states enacted statutes protecting private sector whistleblowers. In addition, Congress enacted more than a dozen statutes protecting private sector whistleblowers who work in safety-sensitive industries, or who disclose violations of federal workplace safety or environmental protection regulations. Further, over a dozen other states created protections for private sector whistleblowers by judicial recognition of a common-law remedy for wrongful discharge in violation of public policy, as is discussed in Chapter 5. These state and federal protections reflect a growing consensus in favor of protecting responsible whistleblowers whose disclosures are made to prevent serious harm to the public welfare and safety. Apart from this general agreement regarding serious danger to the public, however, there is little agreement among the state and federal protections regarding the various issues that arise in whistleblower cases, such as the scope of protected complaints, the strength of remedies available, and overlap with other sources of whistleblower protection. The following sections of this chapter discuss the protections for private sector whistleblowers provided by state and federal statutes.

State Statutory Protections

Eleven states have enacted laws that provide similar protections for both private sector and public sector employees: Connecticut (enacted in 1983), Hawaii (1987), Louisiana (1981), Maine (1985), Michigan (1981), Minnesota (1987), New Hampshire (1988), New Jersey (1986), New York (1986), Ohio (1988), and Rhode Island (1984).

Only private sector employees are protected by laws enacted by California (1985), Tennessee (1990), and Wisconsin (1990). As is true with respect to the statutes protecting public sector employees, these statutes vary widely regarding the nature of protected conduct, the remedies available, and other provisions. A description of these statutes is set forth in Appendix B. To illustrate how the various state legislatures have resolved many of these issues, the following whistleblower laws will be discussed in detail: Louisiana, Rhode Island, and Ohio, which protect relatively narrow ranges of conduct; Michigan, which was one of the first statutes to protect a relatively broad spectrum of activity; New York and New Jersey, which have several important aspects not contained in other laws; and California and Wisconsin, which both have features deserving comment.

Louisiana, Rhode Island, and Ohio

The most controversial question concerning private sector whistleblowers is how to define complaints that are made in the public interest. As discussed in Chapter 2, unlike in the public sector, not all waste or mismanagement in the private sector has a direct impact on the public treasury. Therefore, private sector whistleblower statutes tend to define more narrowly the subjects about which whistleblowers may complain than do statutes applying to the public sector, as exemplified by the legislation of Louisiana, Rhode Island, and Ohio.

The Louisiana statute specifically protects public and private sector employees who disclose violations of environmental laws.[1] The Rhode Island whistleblower protection statute contains fairly broad provisions protecting all public sector employees who complain about violations of virtually any law, but protects only private sector

[1]LA. REV. STAT. ANN. §30:2027 (West 1989), IERM 559:2. The relevant text follows:

A. No firm, business, private or public corporation, partnership, individual employer, or federal, state, or local governmental agency shall act in a retaliatory manner against an employee, acting in good faith, who reports or complains about possible environmental violations.

B. Any employee against whom an action is taken as a result of reporting or complaining of a violation of any state, federal, or local environmental statute, ordinance, or regulation may commence a civil action in a district court of the employee's parish of domicile, and shall recover from his employer triple damages resulting from the action taken against him and all costs of preparing, filing, prosecuting, appealing, or otherwise conducting a law suit, including attorney's fees, if the court finds that Subsection A of this Section has been violated. In addition, the employee shall be entitled to all other civil and criminal remedies available under any other state, federal, or local law. . . . "Damages" for the purposes of this section shall include, but not be limited to, lost wages, lost anticipated wages due to wage increase, or loss of anticipated wages which would have resulted from a lost promotion, any property lost as a result of lost wages, lost benefits, and any physical or emotional damages resulting therefrom. This section shall not have any application to any employee who, acting without direction from his employer or his agent, deliberately violates any provision of this Subtitle or of the regulations, or permit or license terms and conditions in pursuance thereof.

employees when violations of toxic waste laws are involved.[2] Ohio's whistleblower statute protects only reports about felonies or other criminal offenses that are likely to cause an imminent risk of physical harm, or to present a hazard to public health or safety.[3] Thus, the

---

[2]R.I. GEN. LAWS §36-15-1 *et seq.* (1989), IERM 581:2, provides in relevant part as follows:

* * *

Public body means all of the following:
(i) A state officer . . . in the executive branch of state government.
(ii) An agency . . . of the legislative branch of state government.
(iii) A county, city, town, or regional governing body. . . .
(iv) Any other body which is created by state or local authority. . . .
(v) A law enforcement agency. . . .
(vi) The judiciary and any member or employee of the judiciary.

* * *

An employer shall not discharge, threaten or otherwise discriminate against an employee regarding the employee's compensation, terms, conditions, location, or privileges of employment 1) because the employee . . . reports or is about to report to a public body, verbally or in writing, a violation, the employee knows or reasonably believes has occurred or is about to occur, of a law or regulation or rule promulgated under the law of this state, a political subdivision of this state, or the United States, unless the employee knows or has reason to know that the report is false, or 2) because an employee is requested by a public body to participate in an investigation hearing or inquiry held by that public body, or a court action.

* * *

An employee shall show by clear and convincing evidence that he or she or a person acting on his or her behalf was about to report to a public body, verbally or in writing, a violation, the employee knew or reasonably believed had occurred or was about to occur, of a law of this state, a political subdivision of this state, or the United States.

* * *

A court . . . shall order, as the court considers appropriate, reinstatement of the employee, the payment of back wages, full reinstatement of fringe benefits and seniority rights, actual damages, or any combination of these remedies. A court may also award the complainant all or a portion of the costs of litigation, if the court determines that the award is appropriate.

* * *

The provisions of this chapter shall also apply to any [private sector] employee or employer . . . who disposes of toxic waste in violation of said chapter.

[3]OHIO REV. CODE ANN. §4113.52 (Anderson 1989), IERM 576:3, provides in relevant part as follows:

* * *

If an employee becomes aware in the course of his employment of a violation of any state or federal statute or any ordinance or regulation of a political subdivision that his employer has authority to correct, and the employee reasonably believes that the violation is a criminal offense that is likely to cause an imminent risk of physical harm to persons or a hazard to public health or safety or is a felony, the employee orally shall notify his supervisor or other responsible officer of his employer of the violation and subsequently shall file with that supervisor or officer a written report that provides sufficient detail to identify and describe the violation. If the employer does not correct the violation or make reasonable and good faith effort to correct the violation within 24 hours after the oral notification or the receipt of the report, whichever is earlier, the employee may file a written report that provides sufficient detail to identify and describe the violation with the prosecuting authority of the county or municipal corporation where the violation occurred, a peace officer, or any other appropriate public official or agency that has regulatory authority over the employer and the industry, trade, or business in which he is engaged.

If an employee makes a report . . . the employer, within 24 hours after the oral notification was made or the report was received or by the close of business on the next regular business day following the day on which the oral notification was made or the report was

Louisiana, Rhode Island, and Ohio legislatures appear to have been concerned only about infractions of federal, state, or local laws which have a bearing on the public health or safety.

Although these statutes narrowly define the topics about which whistleblowers may complain, they strongly protect employees who make disclosures about those topics. All three statutes protect employees who complain about violations of any federal, state, or local statutes, ordinances, or regulations. Moreover, because complaints about possible environmental violations do not have to be made to any particular persons or agencies, the Louisiana statute appears to protect employees who make internal complaints to their employers. The Ohio statute expressly protects such internal whistleblowers by requiring employees to make an oral report to their supervisor, which may be followed by a written report to the appropriate authorities if the employer does not reasonably attempt to correct the violation within 24 hours. The Ohio statute protects employees even before they report internally, by prohibiting retaliation against employees who make internal inquiries to ensure that their reports of violations are accurate.

These statutes are also favorable to employees in the sense that they impose relatively strict penalties upon employers. All three

---

received, whichever is later, shall notify the employee, in writing, of any effort of the employer to correct the alleged violation or hazard or of the absence of the alleged violation or hazard.

If an employee becomes aware in the course of his employment of a violation of Ch. 3704 [Air Pollution Control], 3734, [Solid and Hazardous Wastes], 6109 [Safe Drinking Water], or 6111 [Water Pollution Control], of the revised code, that is a criminal offense, the employee may directly notify, either orally or in writing, any appropriate public official or agency that has regulatory authority over the employer and the industry, trade, or business in which he is engaged.

If an employee becomes aware in the course of his employment of a violation by a fellow employee of any state or federal statute, any ordinance or regulation of a political subdivision, or any work rule or company policy of his employer and the employee reasonably believes that the violation either is a criminal offense that is likely to cause an imminent risk of physical harm to persons or hazard to public health or safety or is a felony, the employee orally shall notify his supervisor or other responsible officer of his employer of the violation and subsequently shall file with that supervisor or officer a written report that provides sufficient detail to identify and describe the violation.

[N]o employer shall take any disciplinary or retaliatory action against an employee for making any report . . . , or as a result of the employee's having made any inquiry or taken any other action to ensure the accuracy of any information reported under either such division. No employer shall take any disciplinary or retaliatory action against any employee for making any report . . . if the employee made a reasonable and good faith effort to determine the accuracy of any information so reported, or as a result of the employee's having made any inquiry or taken any other action to ensure the accuracy of any information reported under that division.

An employee shall make a reasonable and good faith effort to determine the accuracy of any information reported. . . . If the employee who makes a report under either division fails to make such an effort, he may be subject to disciplinary action by his employer, including suspension or removal, for reporting information without a reasonable basis to do so. . . .

If an employer takes any disciplinary or retaliatory action against an employee as a result of the employee's having filed a report . . . , the employee may bring a civil action for appropriate injunctive relief or for the remedies set forth in this section, or both, within 180 days after the date the disciplinary or retaliatory action was taken, in a court of common pleas in accordance with the rules of civil procedure.

[This act] does not diminish or impair the rights of a person under a collective bargaining agreement, or permit disclosures that would diminish or impair the rights of any person to the continued protection of confidentiality of communications if a statute or common law provides such protection.

statutes recognize the seriousness of retaliation against responsible whistleblowers by allowing employees to sue in the courts without exhausting any administrative relief. The remedy provided by the Louisiana statute is one of the most severe provided by any whistleblower protection statute. Employees may recover treble damages, costs, attorneys' fees, backpay, benefits, and compensation for any physical or emotional damages resulting from the discrimination. Damages under the Rhode Island and Ohio statutes are limited to the more usual categories of reinstatement, backpay, actual damages, and costs of litigation. The Ohio statute also allows awards of attorneys' fees and interest on the amount of backpay. The Ohio statute also imposes a duty upon employers to respond in writing to whistleblower complaints within 24 hours of receipt regarding the efforts being taken to correct the alleged violation or the absence of the alleged violation.

The Ohio statute is unique because it is the only statute that directly addresses the potential problem of complaints stemming from a desire to retaliate against a co-worker. Most whistleblower protection statutes guard against this possibility by protecting only complaints made in good faith, like the Louisiana statute, or complaints that an employee does not have reason to know are false, like the Rhode Island statute. Nevertheless, because neither statute specifically requires employees to exhaust internal channels, irresponsible whistleblowers who complain directly to outside authorities for the purpose of harming a co-worker could be protected, if they could make a plausible argument that they acted in good faith. The Ohio statute prevents such a possibility by requiring that reports about alleged criminal activity by fellow employees be reported only within the company rather than directly to an outside authority. This approach has the advantage of permitting employers to screen personnel disputes before they escalate to the level of formal complaints to outside authorities. Conversely, the Ohio approach may have the disadvantage of discouraging complaints by employees who believe that their supervisors will not correct illegal activities of their co-workers.

The Louisiana, Rhode Island, and Ohio legislatures have limited the kinds of whistleblower complaints that deserve protection. At the same time, however, those legislatures have indicated their serious intent to discourage retaliation against protected whistleblowers by affording strong protections and liberal remedies. This inverse relationship between the scope of complaints and the strength of protections occurs in most whistleblower statutes. In general, the more broadly the statutes define protected whistleblower complaints, the more diluted is the strength of the remedies provided, and the statutes such as those in Louisiana, Rhode Island, and Ohio, which narrowly define protected conduct tend to contain stronger protections. This inverse relationship is also reflected in the statutes discussed in the following sections.

Michigan

In contrast to the previous three statutes which provide strong protections for a narrow range of complaints, the Michigan whistleblower statute contains less generous protections for a broader range of complaints. The Michigan statute is useful for purposes of illustration because the whistleblower protection statutes of Connecticut, Hawaii, Maine, Minnesota, and New Hampshire contain substantially similar provisions.

The Michigan Whistleblowers' Protection Act[4] was passed in 1981 in response to a specific industrial accident which caused widespread public damage. In the mid-1970s, the Michigan Chemical Company mistakenly shipped a toxic fire retardant (PBB) to feed grain cooperatives in place of a nutritional supplement for farm animals. Cattle, pigs, and other livestock began dying in large numbers. While investigations were underway, employees of Michigan Chemical were allegedly warned by their supervisors not to volunteer information about the mistaken shipments of PBB. Due in part to the delays caused by the suppression of the employees' information, the cause of death of the livestock was not discovered for approximately six months. By the time that the PBB mistakenly shipped by Michigan Chemical was identified as the cause, foods contaminated by PBB probably had been consumed by humans. Although the accident itself may have been unavoidable, the damage to livestock and to people who consumed contaminated foods might have been lessened if employees had not been intimidated.[5]

In response to this accident, the Michigan legislature enacted broad protections for both private and public sector employees who report suspected violations of any federal, state, or local law. The protected subjects are obviously much broader than the narrow subjects protected by the previous three statutes. However, the statute provides only a make-whole remedy rather than a punitive remedy, such as provided by the Louisiana statute. The statute authorizes employees to sue in the courts, which may award reinstatement, backpay, and any actual damages, including reasonable attorneys' fees, and may impose a civil fine of up to $500. Because the Michigan Chemical Company employees appeared to believe that they had no protection if they spoke to investigators, the statute specifically requires employers to post notices advising employees of their rights under the statute. Many whistleblower statutes likewise contain a posting requirement.

---

[4]MICH. COMP. LAWS ANN. §15.361 *et seq.* (West 1981), IERM 563:7.

[5]Barcia, *Update on Michigan's Whistleblowers' Protection Act*, 1 DET. C. L. REV. 1 (1988). In this article, the author of the Michigan statute, State Senator James A. Barcia, discusses the events leading to passage of the act.

Despite its broad substantive coverage, the Michigan statute is less protective of embryonic whistleblowers than is the narrower Ohio statute. Although the Act protects employees who are "about to report" legal violations, it requires employees to prove by clear and convincing evidence that they were about to report a violation. This evidentiary standard requires more weighty proof than the preponderance of the evidence standard, but is not as strict as the requirement in criminal cases of proof beyond a reasonable doubt. Under Michigan's approach, loyal whistleblowers who oppose their companies' practices within their organizations have a heavier burden of proving that they were about to report to outside authorities than in other jurisdictions. Moreover, the Michigan law does not require employers to respond to internal whistleblower complaints.

Finally, the Michigan statute was the first to address whether its protections superseded any protections provided by other sources, such as collective bargaining agreements. The Act specifically states that it shall not diminish any person's rights under any collective bargaining agreement. Thus, a terminated whistleblower could seek relief under both the Act and the collective bargaining agreement. Approximately one-half of the private sector whistleblower statutes contain a similar provision. However, the Michigan courts have held that the Act precludes any common law claim for wrongful discharge in violation of public policy, apart from contractual relief under a collective bargaining agreement, on the ground that the legislature impliedly intended the Act to be the exclusive remedy for whistleblowers.[6]

New York and New Jersey

Like the Michigan statute, both the New York and New Jersey whistleblower protection statutes protect employees who report violations of any federal, state, or local statute. However, the New York statute qualifies the type of violation that may be reported by stating that the violation must create and present "a substantial and specific danger to the public health or safety."[7] The scope of protection pro-

---

[6]Covell v. Spengler, 141 Mich. App. 76, 366 N.W.2d 76 (1985). Several evidentiary problems under the Act were addressed in Melchi v. Burns Int'l Sec. Servs., Inc., 597 F. Supp. 575 (E.D. Mich. 1984). First, the court stated that it would evaluate evidence using the burdens of proof developed in Title VII cases, which are discussed in Chapter 8. The court also stated that, although the act required an employee to act in good faith in order to be protected, an employee would be protected even if he or she acted partially in bad faith. 597 F. Supp. at 585-86. However, because of the presence of a bad-faith motive, the court limited the damages recovered by the plaintiff to back pay, and denied the plaintiff's requests for other benefits and attorneys' fees.

[7]N.Y. LAB. LAW §740 (McKinney 1989), IERM 573:6. The relevant text of the statute is as follows:

* * *

An employer shall not take any retaliatory personnel action against an employee because such employee does any of the following:

(a) discloses, or threatens to disclose to a supervisor or to a public body an activity, policy or practice of the employer that is in violation of law, rule or regulation which violation creates and presents a substantial and specific danger to the public health or safety;

vided by the New Jersey statute, entitled the "Conscientious Employee Protection Act,"[8] depends upon whether an employee's conduct falls into the categories of "participation" or "opposition" referred to in Chapter 1, and discussed in detail in Chapter 6. The New Jersey law protects active whistleblowers, or those who actually complain about violation of any federal, state, or local laws. However, passive whistleblowers who object to or refuse to participate in allegedly improper practices, without actually making a complaint, have broader protection. They may object not only to legal violations, but also to criminal or fraudulent activities, or to practices which are "incompatible with a clear mandate of public policy concerning the public health, safety or welfare." New York similarly protects passive whistleblowers who oppose improper practices, but only in the narrow category of violations which create a substantial specific danger to the public health or safety.

Both New York and New Jersey require employees to attempt to resolve their complaints internally by giving their employers a reasonable opportunity to correct the alleged violations. In return, both statutes protect embryonic whistleblowers who disclose or threaten to disclose alleged violations to their supervisors. A unique aspect of the New Jersey statute is that employers are required to designate an

---

(b) provides information to, or testifies before, any public body conducting an investigation, hearing or inquiry into any such violation of a law, rule or regulation by such employer; or

(c) objects to, or refuses to participate in any such activity, policy or practice in violation of a law, rule or regulation.

The protection against retaliatory personnel action provided by paragraph (a) of subdivision two of this section pertaining to disclosure to a public body shall not apply to an employee who makes such disclosure to a public body unless the employee has brought the activity, policy or practice in violation of law, rule or regulation to the attention of a supervisor of the employer and has afforded such employer a reasonable opportunity to correct such activity, policy or practice.

An employee who has been the subject of a retaliatory personnel action in violation of this section may institute a civil action in a court of competent jurisdiction for relief as set forth in subdivision five of this section within one year after the alleged retaliatory personnel action was taken.

In any action brought pursuant to . . . this section, the court may order relief as follows: [an injunction to restrain continued violation of this section; the reinstatement of the employee; the reinstatement of full fringe benefits and seniority rights; lost wages, benefits and other remuneration; and reasonable costs, disbursements, and attorney's fees.]

A court, in its discretion, may also order that reasonable attorney's fees and court costs and disbursements be awarded to an employer if the court determines that an action brought by an employee under this section is without basis in law or in fact.

Nothing in this section shall be deemed to diminish the rights, privileges, or remedies of any employee under any other law or regulation or under any collective bargaining agreement or employment contract; except that the institution of an action in accordance with this section shall be deemed a waiver of the rights and remedies available under any other contract, collective bargaining agreement, law, rule or regulation or under the common law.

[8]N.J. Rev. Stat. §34:19-1 (1988 & West Supp. 1990), IERM 571:3. The relevant text of the New Jersey statute is as follows:

"Supervisor" means any individual with an employer's organization who has the authority to direct and control the work performance of the affected employee, who has authority to take corrective action regarding the violation of the law, rule or regulation of which the employee complains, or who has been designated by the employer. . . .

"Retaliatory action" means the discharge, suspension or demotion of an employee, or other adverse employment action taken against an employee in the terms and conditions of employment.

ombudsman within their organizations to receive whistleblower complaints. Employees who complain to either their own supervisors or to the ombudsman are protected. By providing an alternative means of complaining, this feature may encourage employees who fear retaliation from their own supervisors to complain about violations which might otherwise go unreported.

The problem of duplication of remedies is resolved identically by the New York and New Jersey statutes, which both provide make-whole remedies. Both laws specify that they do not impair any rights employees may have from any other source, including other laws or collective bargaining agreements. However, both provide that an employee's election to file a lawsuit in the courts under the whistleblower protection statutes constitutes a waiver of any other remedies available under other statutes, collective bargaining agreements, or the common law. The New York and New Jersey statutes are the only whistleblower protection laws that contain such an exclusivity provision.

One other provision of the New York statute is worthy of note. The New York law does not protect independent contractors, who are only temporarily employed. The New Hampshire statute is similarly limited. The rationale of this provision is not set forth in the statute itself, but appears to be based on the recognition that independent contractors may not have as much loyalty to their employers as full-time employees. Thus, the New York and New Hampshire legislatures

---

An employer shall not take any retaliatory action against an employee because the employee does any of the following:

a. Discloses, or threatens to disclose to a supervisor or to a public body an activity, policy or practice of employer that the employee reasonably believes is in violation of a law, or a rule or regulation promulgated pursuant to law;

b. Provides information to, or testifies before, any public body conducting an investigation, hearing or inquiry into any violation of law, or a rule or regulation promulgated pursuant to law by the employer; or

c. Objects to, or refuses to participate in any activity, policy or practice which the employee reasonably believes:

(1) is in violation of a law, or a rule or regulation promulgated pursuant to law;

(2) is fraudulent or criminal; or

(3) is incompatible with a clear mandate of public policy concerning the public health, safety or welfare.

The protection against retaliatory action provided by this act pertaining to disclosure to a public body shall not apply to an employee who makes a disclosure to a public body unless the employee has brought the activity, policy or practice in violation of a law, or a rule or regulation promulgated pursuant to law to the attention of a supervisor of the employee by written notice and has afforded the employer a reasonable opportunity to correct the activity, policy or practice. Disclosure shall not be required where the employee is reasonably certain that the activity, policy or practice is known to one or more supervisors of the employer or where the employee reasonably fears physical harm as a result of the disclosure provided, however, that the situation is emergency in nature.

An employer shall conspicuously display notices of its employees' protections and obligations under this act, and use other appropriate means to keep its employees so informed. Each notice posted pursuant to this section shall include the name of the person or persons the employer has designated to receive written notifications. . . .

Nothing in this act shall be deemed to diminish the rights, privileges, or remedies of any employee under any other federal or state law or regulation or under any collective bargaining agreement or employment contract; except that the institution of an action in accordance with this act shall be deemed a waiver of the rights and remedies available under any other contract, collective bargaining agreement, state law, rule or regulation or under the common law.

appear to have been concerned that there was an increased probability that independent contractors might make improperly motivated complaints, and that this factor weighed against protection of such persons.

Two significant cases have been decided under the New Jersey statute. In *Littman v. Firestone Tire & Rubber Co.,*[9] the court emphasized that the fraud complained of under the New Jersey statute must directly affect the public. The plaintiff alleged that he was terminated because he objected to an alleged fraud upon the company committed by a co-worker. The court dismissed the case because the fraud was allegedly perpetrated on the company, not on the public. This case suggests that the New York and New Jersey statutes may be construed to protect only complaints about conduct which poses a direct danger to the public health, safety, or welfare.

Second, in *Parker v. M & T Chemicals*[10] the court rejected an attempt to exempt attorneys employed directly by corporations from coverage. The defendant argued that the ethical rules applying to attorneys allow a client, including a corporation, to terminate an attorney's employment for any reason, and that the New Jersey law improperly limited a client's discretion. The court disagreed with this argument, stating that its holding would encourage employers not to coerce their attorneys to engage in illegal conduct.

California and Wisconsin

The private sector whistleblower protection statutes of California and Wisconsin deserve mention because of their limited nature. The California statute is notable for its brevity. Unlike the laws discussed earlier in this chapter, which all specify the procedures and remedies available to whistleblowers who have suffered retaliation, the California statute contains only a prohibition of retaliation against private sector employees who report violations of law to the appropriate authorities.[11] The statute does not protect internal whistleblowers. Moreover, the statute contains no procedural or remedial provisions. Instead, the statute leaves it to the California courts to resolve the

---

[9]715 F. Supp. 90, 4 IER Cases 1023 (S.D.N.Y. 1989).

[10]236 N.J. Super. 451, 566 A.2d 215, 4 IER Cases 1766 (1989).

[11]The California private sector whistleblower statute is codified at CAL. LABOR CODE §1102.5 (West Supp. 1990), IERM 545:15, and provides in its entirety as follows:

(a) No employer shall make, adopt, or enforce any rule, regulation, or policy preventing an employee from disclosing information to a government or law enforcement agency, where the employee has reasonable cause to believe that the information discloses a violation of state or federal statute, or violation or noncompliance with a state or federal regulation.

(b) No employer shall retaliate against an employee for disclosing information to a government or law enforcement agency, where the employee has reasonable cause to believe

numerous questions regarding available remedies, overlap with other protections available under collective bargaining agreements, and so forth, which are presently unresolved.

The Wisconsin private sector statute is one of the narrowest in terms of coverage. The Wisconsin statute protects only private sector employees who complain regarding violations of Wisconsin employment laws regulating wages, hours, child labor, workplace safety, and discrimination. The statute provides an administrative remedy for whistleblowers who are terminated or subjected to discriminatory treatment.

Summary

The fourteen state legislatures which have enacted private sector whistleblower protection statutes have been highly conscious of the competing duties owed by whistleblowers to their employers and to their communities. Most of these jurisdictions recognize the duty of loyalty by requiring that employees report their concerns internally, and that employers be given a reasonable opportunity to correct alleged improprieties. In return, most statutes protect not only whistleblowers who complain outside their organizations, but also embryonic whistleblowers who complain only inside their organizations. Moreover, most jurisdictions recognize that employers must be afforded discretion to maintain performance standards by taking adverse action against non-performing employees. To that end, almost every statute contains a requirement that complaints be made in good faith, rather than for ulterior motives such as preventing employers from enforcing performance standards.

Most jurisdictions also recognize the responsibilities owed by employees to the public welfare by protecting complaints of alleged violations of almost any law, rule, or regulation promulgated by the legislative or executive arms of most levels of government. However, because the public interest in private sector employment is less pervasive than in government employment, no jurisdiction protects employees who complain about waste or mismanagement. Moreover, no statute has gone so far as to protect whistleblowers who complain about alleged violations of ethical codes. Even the New Jersey statute, the title of which suggests that any complaints made by conscientious employees about any topic are protected, recognizes that there are limits on the topics about which whistleblowers in the private sector may make disclosures.

---

that the information discloses a violation of state or federal statute, or violation or noncompliance with a state or federal regulation.

(c) This section shall not apply to rules, regulations, or policies which implement, or to actions by employers against employees who violate, the confidentiality of the lawyer-client privilege of Article 3 (commencing with Section 950), the physician-patient privilege of Article 6 (commencing with Section 990) of Chapter 4 of Division 8 of the Evidence Code, or trade secret information.

Federal Environmental, Workplace Safety, and Public Health Statutes

A broad range of federal statutes regulate the conduct of businesses with respect to the environment, workplace safety, and public health. To enhance their enforcement, many of these statutes protect employees who complain about violations under varying circumstances. These statutes are described in detail in Appendix C. Several statutes focus on particular safety-sensitive industries, such as the Federal Mine Safety and Health Act (MSHA) which regulates the mining industry, and the Energy Reorganization Act (ERA) which regulates the nuclear power industry.[12] Other federal statutes focus on particular wage, hour, and pension practices, on workplace safety, or on environmental issues, and may apply across industry boundaries. The statute of this kind most frequently invoked by whistleblowers is the Occupational Safety and Health Act (OSHA).[13] These federal statutes vary widely with respect to the substantive protection provided, the agencies responsible for their enforcement, and the procedures and remedies provided by the responsible agencies. To show how the characteristics of these statutes vary, the provisions of MSHA, OSHA, and several other federal laws will be discussed below.[14]

Mine Safety and Health Act (MSHA)

Close to one-half million mine workers in the United States are subjected daily to the physical hazards of working underground with powerful machinery and explosives. Dust may cloud their vision or

---

[12]The employee protection provision of the Federal Mine Safety and Health Act is codified at 30 U.S.C. §815 (1988), and of the Energy Reorganization Act is codified at 42 U.S.C. §5851 (1988). Other industry-specific statutes which contain employee protection provisions include the following: Department of Defense Authorization Act of 1987, 10 U.S.C. §2409 (1988); Longshoremen's and Harbor Worker's Compensation Act, 33 U.S.C. §948(a) (1988); Migrant Seasonal and Agricultural Worker Protection Act, 42 U.S.C. §300j-9 (1988); Railroad Safety Authorization Act, 45 U.S.C. §441 (1988); Safe Containers for International Cargo Act, 46 U.S.C. §1506 (1988); and the Surface Mining Control and Reclamation Act of 1977, 30 U.S.C. §1293 (1988). *See* Appendix C for more detailed descriptions of these statutes.

[13]The employee protection provision of the Occupational Safety and Health Act is codified at 29 U.S.C. §660 (1988). Other statutes focusing on specific concerns across industry lines, which contain employee protection provisions, are as follows: *Wage, Hour and Pension Practices*: Employee Retirement Income Security Act (ERISA), 29 U.S.C. §1140 (1988); Fair Labor Standards Act, 29 U.S.C. §215(a)(3) (1988); and the Protection of Jurors' Employment Act, 28 U.S.C. §1875 (1988); *Workplace Safety*: Federal Employers' Liability Act (FELA), 45 U.S.C. §60 (1988); *Environmental Protection*: Asbestos Hazard Emergency Response Act, 15 U.S.C. §2641 (1988); Asbestos School Hazard Detection and Control Act, 20 U.S.C. §3608 (1988); Comprehensive Environmental Response, Compensation and Liability Act of 1980 (CERCLA), 42 U.S.C. §9601 (1988); and the Hazardous Substances Releases Act, 42 U.S.C. §9610 (1988). *See* Appendix C for more detailed descriptions of these statutes.

[14]Many states have enacted environmental, workplace safety, and public health statutes analogous to the federal laws discussed in this chapter. Moreover, many of these state statutes contain antiretaliation provisions akin to the federal laws. These statutes are beyond the scope of this work.

impair their breathing, and noise may impair their communication with each other. Safety concerns are not limited to immediate hazards such as explosions, dangerous machinery, and slides, but also include health problems that manifest themselves gradually, such as black lung disease and hearing impairment. MSHA was tailored by Congress and has been interpreted by the agency charged with its enforcement to fit the hazards unique to the mining industry.

Many mine safety concerns must be immediately addressed. To encourage immediate reports of safety problems, MSHA contains what may be the most liberal protections for employees who make safety complaints. Miners are permitted to orally request immediate inspections of safety hazards by a representative of the Federal Mine Safety and Health Administration (FMSHA).[15] Such requests are protected if they are made to a supervisor, or even to a union representative. In addition to protecting informal verbal safety complaints, MSHA has been interpreted to allow miners to refuse to work in hazardous conditions. Such conditions include not only circumstances immediately dangerous to life and limb, but also conditions such as excessive coal dust or noise which may in the long term lead to black lung disease or hearing loss. Unlike many of the state whistleblower protection statutes which limit the right to refuse to work to conditions involving an imminent and substantial danger of serious injury, MSHA protects a much broader range of refusals to work because of the unique hazards in mines.

MSHA's procedures and remedies are among the most favorable for employees. FMSHA immediately investigates complaints of retaliation and is required to order reinstatement of miners within 15 days of their complaints, if the complaints are not frivolously brought.[16] Meritorious cases are prosecuted by the FMSHA, and are heard by administrative law judges (ALJ) from the Federal Mine Safety and Health Review Commission (FMSHRC), a body independent of the FMSHA. Miners may be reinstated with backpay and interest and, if they prevail, are entitled to an award of attorneys' fees. Review of the decisions of ALJs may be sought before the FMSHRC itself, which will uphold the decisions if there is substantial evidence to support them. Judicial review of the FMSHRC's decision may be sought in the United States Circuit Court of Appeals in which the alleged retaliation occurred. Thus, MSHA effectively protects employees who complain about mine safety by broadly defining the types of complaints protected, by quickly reinstating responsible miners who make legitimate complaints, and by requiring that the attorneys' fees of successful miners be reimbursed by their employers. Although there is no private right of action created by MSHA, one court has held

---

[15]Munsey v. Federal Mine Safety & Health Review Comm'n, 595 F.2d 735 (D.C. Cir. 1978); Simpson v. Federal Mine Safety & Health Review Comm'n, 842 F.2d 453 (D.C. Cir. 1988).

[16]30 U.S.C. §815(c)(2) (1988).

that MSHA does not preempt state law claims for wrongful discharge in violation of public policy.[17]

Occupational Safety and Health Act (OSHA)

The focus of OSHA is much broader than that of MSHA. OSHA regulates workplace safety in many varied industries across the nation. As a consequence, the employee protection provisions of OSHA are not tailored to any specific circumstances, but are drafted in general terms to apply to a wide variety of circumstances. From the employees' perspective, the administrative protections of OSHA are far less generous than those of MSHA.

The conduct protected by OSHA includes requests for inspection, which may be made if an employee believes that a safety violation threatens physical harm or presents an imminent danger.[18] If a violation presents a threat of death or serious physical harm, and cannot be remedied, the OSHA inspector must recommend that the Secretary of Labor seek injunctive relief. Employees are authorized to sue to compel the secretary to seek injunctive relief if the secretary arbitrarily refuses to do so. In addition, employees are allowed to accompany OSHA inspectors on walkaround inspections of an employer's premises. Like MSHA, employees have the right under OSHA to refuse to work in conditions that present an imminent danger of death or serious injury, and that cannot be corrected through a request for inspection, or in conditions that the employer refuses or is unable to correct.[19] This right is narrower than that provided under MSHA, which does not necessarily require that conditions pose an immediate threat to life or limb.

Employers may not retaliate against employees for exercising any of these rights. The procedures and remedies of OSHA, compared with those of MSHA, are limited. Victims of retaliation may file a complaint with the Secretary of Labor, who has discretion, but is not required to institute an action on behalf of the employee in an appropriate United States District Court for reinstatement and backpay. Nor is there any provision for expedited reinstatement of discharged employees. Moreover, employees whose claims are not prosecuted by the Secretary of Labor may not commence civil actions on their own behalf.[20]

MSHA and OSHA provide an instructive contrast. The whistleblower protections of MSHA are specifically designed to take into account the special circumstances of the mining industry, with

---

[17]Echard v. Devine, 726 F. Supp. 1045 (N.D.W.Va. 1989).

[18]29 U.S.C. §657(f)(1) (1988).

[19]The right to refuse work is set forth in 29 C.F.R. §1977.12(b), and was upheld by the Supreme Court in Whirlpool Corp. v. Marshall, 445 U.S. 1 (1980).

[20]Taylor v. Brighton Corp., 616 F.2d 256 (6th Cir. 1980).

stronger protections as a result. OSHA addresses whistleblowers in a much broader range of industries, some of which are less hazardous than others, with weaker protections as a result. This contrast between MSHA and OSHA is similar to the inverse relationship between the breadth of whistleblower protections and the strength of whistleblower remedies present in the state statutes protecting private sector whistleblowers. Due to the political compromises that are necessary to enact sweeping whistleblower protections, such as OSHA and the state statutes, it appears that broad substantive protections have been achieved only by sacrificing strong remedies. The example of MSHA, however, suggests that both liberal protections and strong remedies can be combined in whistleblower protection statutes that are narrowly framed to address the specific problems of particular industries.

Other Federal Sources of Protection

Not all of the federal whistleblower protection statutes discussed in Appendix C contain elaborate enforcement mechanisms like those contained in MSHA and OSHA. For instance, the Public Health Service Act states that employees may not be discriminated against if they refuse to participate in abortions, but provides no procedural framework for resolving complaints of discrimination.[21] The International Safe Containers for Cargo Act allows the Secretary of Labor to commence a civil action on behalf of employees who report the existence of unsafe containers, but does not require the secretary to take any action at all.[22] In contrast, the Protection of Juror's Employment Act is not enforced by an administrative agency, but permits employees to apply to the United States District Court for appointment of counsel. However, such relief is solely within the court's discretion.[23]

The federal whistleblower protection statutes have been criticized because of the variance in substantive protection, statutes of limitations, investigative agencies, and remedies.[24] Partially in response to such criticism, Congress is presently considering legislation to create uniform protections for whistleblowers who expose health and safety violations in all industries.[25] The proposed legisla-

---

[21]42 U.S.C. §300a-7 (1988).

[22]46 U.S.C. §1506 (1988).

[23]28 U.S.C. §1875 (1988).

[24]Fidell, *Federal Protection of Private Sector Health and Safety Whistleblowers*, 2 ADMIN. L.J. 84 (1988).

[25]The proposed legislation is entitled the Uniform Health and Safety Whistleblowers Protection Act, and was introduced in the 100th Congress, Second Session as Senate Bill 2095. The proposed legislation would centralize enforcement and adjudication of all whistleblower complaints under the Secretary of Labor, and would supersede pre-existing laws such as MSHA. The penalties under the legislation include punitive damages, a remedy which is extremely rare under existing whistleblower protection statutes. If the secretary did not follow the enforcement

tion may suffer from the defect of overbreadth. OSHA's broad coverage resulted in lesser degrees of protection for whistleblowers. In contrast, the overbreadth of the proposed omnibus whistleblower protection statute, which contains broad substantive coverage and imposes heavy penalties, would probably have the opposite result by imposing overly severe restrictions upon smaller and less hazardous businesses. As the model of MSHA demonstrates, the risk of crafting inappropriate remedies clearly is less significant if statutes are tailored to specific industries.

While most of the federal statutes discussed in this chapter are aimed at health, safety, or environmentally sensitive industries, one whistleblower statute addresses the defense contracting industry due to perceptions of fraudulent conduct in that industry. In 1987, Congress passed legislation prohibiting retaliation against employees of defense contractors who disclose substantial violations of defense contracting laws to either members of Congress, or to authorized representatives of the Departments of Defense or Justice.[26] Employees may seek protection under this law by filing an administrative complaint with the Inspector General of the Department of Defense. However, in *Mayo v. Questech*,[27] the court ruled that this law does not give whistleblowers the right to sue for damages if they have been subjected to retaliation, but are limited to the administrative remedy. To some extent, this legislation may provide protections which overlap with those provided by the False Claims Reform Act discussed in Chapter 6.

Department of Labor Jurisdiction

The exception to the general lack of uniformity among federal protections is the whistleblower jurisdiction of the Department of Labor (DOL). The DOL enforces the whistleblower protection provisions contained in the Safe Drinking Water Act, the Federal Water Pollution Control Act, the Toxic Substances Control Act, the Solid Waste Disposal Act, the Clean Air Act, the Energy Reorganization Act of 1974, and the Surface Transportation Assistance Act of 1978.[28]

---

requirements of the proposed legislation, employees would be permitted to sue on their own behalf in the United States district courts. Because the proposed legislation would apply to any and all industries, and would expose employers to punitive damages, the proposed legislation would dramatically alter the employment law of the nation.

[26]Department of Defense Authorization Act of 1987, Pub. L. No. 100-26, §3(5), 10 U.S.C. §2409 (1988).

[27]727 F. Supp. 1007, 4 IER Cases 1850, 51 FEP Cases 1246 (E.D.Va. 1989).

[28]The whistleblower protection provisions of these statutes are found as follows: Safe Drinking Water Act, 42 U.S.C. §300j-9(i) (1988); Federal Water Pollution Control Act, 33 U.S.C. §1367 (1988); Toxic Substances Control Act, 15 U.S.C.A. §2622 (1988 & West Supp. 1990); Solid Waste Disposal Act, 42 U.S.C. §6971 (1988); Clean Air Act, 42 U.S.C. §7622 (1988); Energy Reorganization Act of 1974, 42 U.S.C. §5851 (1988); and Surface Transportation Assistance Act of 1978, 49 U.S.C. §2305 (1988). *See* Appendix C for more detailed descriptions of these statutes.

All of these statutes contain provisions which prohibit reprisal against employees who complain of purported violations of the respective statutes. The DOL has issued extensive regulations that set forth uniform substantive coverage, uniform procedures requiring prompt resolution of complaints, and uniform remedies.[29] The DOL enforcement mechanism handles the third largest number of whistleblower complaints after OSHA and MSHA, respectively.[30] Moreover, the DOL's enforcement process is significant because Congress' proposed whistleblower legislation would centralize enforcement of all health and safety whistleblower complaints within the DOL, and would pattern enforcement of whistleblower complaints, in several respects, after the present DOL model. For these reasons, the DOL's whistleblower jurisdiction is discussed in detail.

The substantive coverage of the statutes enforced by the DOL is not settled. The statutes themselves are written to protect only complaints made to government agencies. Thus, the statutes themselves appear to provide the narrower form of protection for "participation" in activities to enforce the statutes, rather than for "opposition" to unlawful practices. Nevertheless, several United States courts of appeals have interpreted the DOL statutes to protect whistleblower complaints through employers' internal channels, as well as complaints to the appropriate agency. The Secretary of Labor accepts these interpretations in carrying out his or her enforcement responsibilities.[31]

Internal or external whistleblowers who believe that they have suffered retaliation must file a complaint with the Office of the Administrator of the Wage and Hour Division of the DOL within 30 days after the alleged discrimination. The Wage and Hour Administrator is required to conduct a priority investigation and, within 30 days of receipt of the complaint, render a notice of determination which states whether the complaint is meritorious. If either party disagrees with the determination of the Wage and Hour Administrator, a request for a hearing may be filed within five days with the Chief Administrative Law Judge of the DOL. The ALJ to whom the case is assigned must notify the parties of a hearing date within seven days after receipt of the request for hearing. The hearing must be on the record, and both parties have the right to be represented by counsel and to present all forms of evidence. The parties are also permitted to file pre-hearing

---

[29]The DOL regulations are set forth at 29 C.F.R. pt. 24.

[30]Fidell, *Federal Protection of Private Sector Health and Safety Whistleblowers*, 2 ADMIN. L.J. 1, 11 (1988).

[31]The Ninth and Tenth Circuit Courts of Appeals have held that internal whistleblower complaints are protected under §210 of the Energy Reorganization Act, 42 U.S.C. §5851 (1988). Mackowiak v. University Nuclear Sys., Inc., 735 F.2d 1159 (9th Cir. 1984); Kansas Gas & Elec. Co. v. Brock, 780 F.2d 1505, 1 IER Cases 1767, 121 LRRM 3133 (10th Cir. 1985), *cert. denied*, 478 U.S. 1011 (1986). However, the Fifth Circuit has held that only complaints to the appropriate enforcement agency are protected. Brown & Root, Inc. v. Donovan, 747 F.2d 1029, 1 IER Cases 413, 118 LRRM 2301 (5th Cir. 1984).

briefs. The ALJ is required to issue a recommended decision within 20 days after the hearing has terminated. The recommended decision is then forwarded to the Secretary of Labor, who is required to issue a final order within 90 days after the complaint of discrimination was filed.

The typical discovery tools of depositions, interrogatories, requests for production of documents, and requests for admissions are generally available in proceedings before ALJs from the DOL.[32] However, if these time limits were strictly followed, they would appear to drastically limit the discovery available to parties. Because these time limits have not been strictly followed, with the result that several months may be available to the parties before the date the hearing is actually held, the ALJs have considered requests by parties for formal discovery on a case-by-case basis.[33]

In addition to the typical relief of reinstatement with backpay, compensatory damages may also be available in DOL whistleblower cases. In a case under the Energy Reorganization Act, the Sixth Circuit Court of Appeals ruled that a prevailing employee is entitled to recover compensatory damages for medical expenses and injury to reputation, as well as attorneys' fees and other litigation expenses. After this ruling, the Secretary of Labor awarded the employee $10,000 for mental pain and suffering and injury to reputation, and over $11,000 in attorneys' fees and expenses.[34] Furthermore, one of the statutes that the secretary enforces, the Surface Transportation Assistance Act, permits the secretary to order pre-hearing reinstatement of a terminated whistleblower. This portion of the Act was challenged on constitutional grounds, on the theory that requiring employers to reinstate employees prior to a hearing on the merits deprives employers of property without due process. The Supreme Court upheld the statute as written, but also ruled that the secretary was required to disclose to employers the evidence provided in support of employees' complaints.[35]

Judicial review of the secretary's decision may be obtained by filing a petition for review in the United States Circuit Court of Appeals in which the alleged violation occurred, within 60 days after the issuance of the secretary's decision. If an employer has been found to have violated any of the statutes enforced by the secretary, and the employer fails to comply with an order of the secretary, either the

---

[32]The generic rules governing procedures before ALJs from the DOL are set forth in 29 C.F.R. pt. 18, and permit use of standard discovery methods, as well as allowing motions for summary judgment.

[33]*See, e.g.*, Drew v. Jersey Central Power & Light Co., No. 81-ERA-3 (March 5, 1981) (ALJ permitted to issue *subpoena duces tecum* requiring company to produce employee's personnel file).

[34]Deford v. Secretary of Labor, 700 F.2d 281 (6th Cir. 1983).

[35]Brock v. Roadway Express, Inc., 481 U.S. 252, 2 IER Cases 1, 125 LRRM 2001 (1987).

employee or the secretary may file an action in the United States District Court to enforce the order of the secretary. In such an enforcement action, the district courts are empowered to grant injunctive relief, compensatory damages, exemplary damages, and costs of litigation including reasonable attorneys' fees. The courts are split on the issue of whether the statutory remedy under these DOL statutes preempts any public policy cause of action under state common law.[36] In sum, the DOL procedures are designed to provide speedy relief to whistleblowers who are victims of retaliation, and to provide a remedy which provides not only reinstatement with backpay, but also allows for awards of compensatory damages and attorneys' fees.

Other Options for Protection

In addition to the three major federal areas of whistleblower protection activity discussed above (MSHA, OSHA, and the DOL), there are 17 other federal statutes protecting whistleblowers which contain their own substantive coverages, procedures, and remedies, as set forth in Appendix C. Additional federal sources of whistleblower protection probably will continue to be enacted. Moreover, imaginative lawyers probably will continue to pursue whistleblower claims under many laws which originally may not have been intended to protect whistleblowers. For example, some of the most creative whistleblower claims have been pursued under the Racketeer Influenced and Corrupt Organizations Act (RICO). As discussed in Chapter 1, RICO was enacted because Congress perceived that organized crime was infiltrating and corrupting legitimate businesses and labor unions. One of the most attractive aspects of RICO is a provision for treble damages for injury to the business or property of a person

---

[36]Several courts of appeals have ruled that Section 210 of the Energy Reorganization Act preempts any common-law relief. Norman v. Niagara Mohawk Power Corp., 873 F.2d 634 (2d Cir. 1989); Willy v. Coastal Corp., 855 F.2d 1160, 4 IER Cases 819 (5th Cir. 1988); Kansas Gas & Elec. Co. v. Brock, 780 F.2d 1505, 1 IER Cases 1767, 121 LRRM 3133 (10th Cir. 1985); *but see* Norris v. Lumbermen's Mut. Gas Co., 4 IER Cases 1030 (1st Cir. 1989). The federal district courts have split on this issue. *Compare* Snow v. Bechtel Constr., Inc., 647 F. Supp. 1514, 1 IER Cases 1264, 123 LRRM 3245 (C.D.Cal. 1986) (federal remedy preempts common-law claims) *with* Stokes v. Bechtel N.AM. Power Corp., 614 F. Supp. 732 (N.D.Cal. 1985) (no preemption) and Gaballah v. PG&E, 711 F. Supp. 988, 4 IER Cases 1039 (N.D.Cal. 1989) (same). The state courts also are divided on this question. *Compare* Chrisman v. Philips Indus., Inc., 242 Kan. 772, 751 P.2d 140, 3 IER Cases 181 (1988) (common-law claims preempted) *with* Wheeler v. Caterpillar Tractor Co., 108 Ill. 2d 502, 485 N.E.2d 372, 121 LRRM 3186 (1985) (no preemption).

However, in English v. General Elec. Co., 493 U.S. ___, 58 USLW 4679 (1990), the Supreme Court ruled that a whistleblower's common-law claim for intentional infliction of emotional distress was not preempted by §210. The Court did not directly decide whether a claim for wrongful discharge in violation of public policy was preempted, because the plaintiff had abandoned that cause of action. Although it did not overrule any of the decisions discussed above, the reasoning of the Court suggests that the decisions of the courts of appeals which held that §210 preempted any common-law relief may no longer be valid.

Moreover, the courts have split on the question whether the Surface Transportation Assistance Act, *supra* note 28, preempts state law claims for wrongful termination in retaliation for complaints about unsafe trucking conditions. Watson v. Cleveland Chair Co., 789 S.W.2d 538, 4 IER Cases 1779 (Tenn. 1989) (STAA preempts state law claims); *but see* Todd v. Frank's Tong Serv., Inc. 784 P.2d 47, 4 IER Cases 1535 (Okla. 1989) (contra).

harmed by RICO violations. The attempted use of RICO by whistleblowers, which has had mixed success, indicates that counsel may continue to seek innovative protections for private sector whistleblowers under federal laws wherever possible.[37]

---

[37]The Racketeer Influenced and Corrupt Organizations Act of 1970 is codified at 18 U.S.C. §§1961-1968 (1988), and the Congressional Statement of Findings and Purpose is set forth in Pub. L. No. 91-452, Section 1. The federal courts have sharply debated whether the civil remedies of RICO should be permitted to be used against legitimate business rather than criminal enterprises, and whether the class of persons entitled to pursue civil RICO claims should be broadly or narrowly construed. In Sedima, S.P.R.L. v. Imrex Co., 473 U.S. 479, 500 (1985), the Supreme Court resolved many of these questions in favor of a broad interpretation of civil RICO, and expressly recognized that "in its private civil version, RICO is evolving into something quite different from the original conception of its enactors." *See also* H.J. Inc. v. Northwestern Bell Tel. Co., 57 USLW 4951 (1989). Perhaps one of the farthest reaching uses of RICO has been as the basis for wrongful discharge claims by whistleblowers who contend that they were dismissed for having refused to participate in RICO violations, or for having protested conduct of their employers which arguably violated RICO.

Several cases have permitted RICO claims by whistleblowers where the employee has alleged that he or she refused to participate in RICO violations, refused to participate in a cover-up of the violations, and was dismissed for his or her failure to do so. In those cases, the courts have stated that the injury to the employee was related directly enough to the employer's alleged violation of RICO to satisfy the causation requirements of the statute. However, because RICO by its terms allows recovery only for injuries to a plaintiff's "business and property," the courts have only permitted recovery of lost wages or other economic losses, and have not permitted recovery for emotional distress, damage to reputation, or other elements of damage falling into the category of personal injuries. *See, e.g.,* Shearin v. E.F. Hutton, 885 F.2d 1162 (3d Cir. 1989); Williams v. Hall, 683 F. Supp. 639 (E.D. Ky. 1988); Komm v. McFliker, 662 F. Supp. 924, 2 IER Cases 467 (W.D. Mo. 1987); Callan v. State Chem. Mfg. Co., 584 F. Supp. 619 (E.D. Pa. 1984) (no recovery allowed for mental anguish or harm to business reputation). *But see* Hecht v. Commerce Clearing House, Inc., 897 F.2d 21 (2d Cir. 1990) (RICO cause of action does not exist for whistleblowers). Whistleblowers who merely protested RICO violations have fared less well. Several cases have held in these situations that the employees' injuries were not directly caused by the employers' violation of RICO. According to one court, "[f]iring [the plaintiff] under these circumstances was wrong, but it did not violate the RICO Act." Nodine v. Textron, Inc., 819 F.2d 347, 349 (1st Cir. 1987); *see also* Burdick v. American Express Co., 865 F.2d 527 (2d Cir. 1989); Cullom v. Hibernia Nat'l Bank, 859 F.2d 1211 (5th Cir. 1988); Morast v. Lance, 807 F.2d 926, 2 IER Cases 1230 (11th Cir. 1987). In view of the general reluctance of the federal judiciary to expansively construe the civil RICO statute, notwithstanding the Supreme Court's decision in *Sedima*, no safe generalizations can be made regarding whether whistleblowers may rely upon protection under RICO. Nevertheless, individuals, employers and their counsel should be aware of the possibility of relief under RICO, and especially of the availability of treble damages under this law.

5

Common-Law Protection: The Public Policy Doctrine

At the same time that the state legislatures and Congress have been enacting whistleblower protection statutes of varying scope, the judiciary in a majority of jurisdictions has created common-law protections for employees who allege that they were wrongfully discharged in retaliation for their conduct in furtherance of public policy. In many jurisdictions, the public policy doctrine has been construed to protect whistleblowers under various circumstances. An analysis of the jurisdictions that have created public policy causes of action, and that have specifically protected whistleblowers, is set forth in Appendix D.

The public policy cases prohibit discharge of employees in three general circumstances: (1) where an employee was discharged for refusing to commit an illegal act; (2) where an employee is discharged for exercising a statutory right; and (3) where an employee is discharged for carrying out an important civic duty. The public policy doctrine has been extended in several jurisdictions to protect whistleblowers under either the rubric of one of these three general categories, or as an extension of these general categories.

The public policy doctrine is significant not only because it creates new protections for employees, but also because it may permit imposition of tort remedies against employers, including amounts for emotional distress and punitive damages. The tort measure of damages generally permits more extensive recoveries than the majority of the state whistleblower protection statutes. The following overview of the development of the public policy doctrine will help to place the common-law protections for whistleblowers in context.

Refusal to Commit an Illegal Act

Federal and state laws prohibit many different forms of misconduct, providing criminal sanctions for the more serious acts, and civil penalties for other violations of law. Moreover, the severity of punishment varies within the categories of criminal and civil violations. Public policy cases arise under a wide variety of criminal or civil laws. As might be expected, the judiciary has been more willing to create public policy claims in cases involving the more serious violations in either category.

Refusal to Commit a Crime

The most compelling case for protection of at-will employees is when employers instruct their employees to commit a crime. Whether the crime is a felony or a misdemeanor, the employees are forced to choose between disobeying the instruction or disobeying the criminal law. Depending on the nature of the crime, the employees may be subject to fines or imprisonment. Moreover, even if they are not explicitly told as much, employees may believe that they will be fired for insubordination if they refuse to commit the crime.

Employees who refuse to commit crimes are passive whistleblowers in the sense that they are opposing illegal conduct. They differ from other whistleblowers because they may not actively campaign within their employer's organization against the allegedly illegal practices, or may not voice their objections outside of their employer's organization. They may be the most reliable of all whistleblowers because they have direct personal knowledge of their employer's instruction. Thus, they are not required to speculate about whether the activities of other individuals in the organization may be violating the law. This category of whistleblowers is the least controversial because their behavior is the least disruptive or threatening to their employers' organizations. Thus, most courts have readily responded to the dilemma facing employees who have been forced to choose between their jobs and committing crimes by creating a cause of action for them.

One of the first cases to recognize the public policy doctrine was the 1959 case of *Petermann v. Teamsters*,[1] which was discussed in detail in Chapter 1. In brief, the plaintiff contended that the reason for his discharge was that he failed to commit perjury in an administrative hearing at the request of his employer. The court noted that perjury is a criminal offense, as is solicitation of the commission of perjury, and stated:

> The presence of false testimony in any proceeding tends to interfere with the proper administration of public affairs and the administration of justice. It would be obnoxious to the interests of the state and contrary to public policy and sound morality to allow an employer to discharge any employee, whether the employment be for a designated or unspecified duration, on the ground that the employee declined to commit perjury, an act specifically enjoined by statute. The threat of criminal prosecu-

---

[1]174 Cal. App. 2d 184, 344 P.2d 25, 1 IER Cases 5, 44 LRRM 2968 (1959).

> tion would, in many cases, be a sufficient deterrent upon both the employer and employee, the former from soliciting and the latter from committing perjury. However, in order to more fully effectuate the state's declared policy against perjury, the civil law, too, must deny the employer his generally unlimited right to discharge an employee whose employment is for an unspecified duration, when the reason for the dismissal is the employee's refusal to commit perjury. To hold otherwise would be without reason and contrary to the spirit of the law. The public policy of this state as reflected in the Penal Code sections referred to above would be seriously impaired if it were to be held that one could be discharged by reason of his refusal to commit perjury.[2]

Accordingly, the plaintiff was allowed to sue for breach of his employment contract, and to recover any lost compensation owed under the contract. Several other jurisdictions have recognized public policy claims based on the strong public interest in discouraging perjury.[3]

The *Petermann* doctrine was largely dormant throughout the 1960s. However, during the 1970s and 1980s, numerous other jurisdictions applied the *Petermann* rationale to employees who alleged that they were discharged for refusing to commit crimes apart from perjury. For example, the Arizona Supreme Court held that an employee's refusal to participate in his employer's theft scheme was protected in *Vermillion v. AAA Pro Moving & Storage*.[4] Similarly, the plaintiff's refusal to violate food labeling laws was protected by the Connecticut Supreme Court in *Sheets v. Teddy's Frosted Foods*.[5] In that case, Emard Sheets was employed by a food processing company as its quality control director. In the course of his employment, Sheets began to notice deviations from the specifications contained in the company's labels because some vegetables were substandard and some meats were underweight. These deviations meant that the company's products violated the representations in defendant's labels, which therefore violated the Connecticut Uniform Food, Drug & Cosmetic Act. Sheets alleged that he was terminated because of his attempts to ensure that the company's products complied with the applicable labeling laws. The Connecticut Supreme Court noted that the applicable labeling laws imposed criminal penalties on anyone who violates such laws, and that it is not necessary to prove intent to defraud or mislead in order to impose criminal sanctions. The court stated that "[t]he plaintiff's position as quality control director might have exposed him to the possibility of criminal prosecution under [these labeling laws], . . . [which were] intended to 'safeguard the public health and promote the public welfare by protecting the consuming

---

[2]*Id.* at 188-89, 344 P.2d at 27, 1 IER Cases at 6, 7, 44 LRRM at 2969-70.

[3]Wiskotoni v. Michigan Nat'l Bank-West, 716 F.2d 378, 1 IER Cases 250, 114 LRRM 2596 (6th Cir. 1983) (employee who testified before grand jury protected); Sides v. Duke Hosp., 74 N.C. App. 331, 238 S.E.2d 818, 1 IER Cases 512, 120 LRRM 2091 (1985) (nurse who testified in medical malpractice action protected); DeRose v. Putnam Mgmt. Co., 398 Mass. 205, 496 N.E.2d 428, 1 IER Cases 1672 (1986) (employee who refused to implicate co-worker in criminal trial protected).

[4]146 Ariz. 215, 704 P.2d 1360, 119 LRRM 2337 (1985).

[5]179 Conn. 471, 427 A.2d 385, 115 LRRM 4626 (1980).

public from injury by product use and the purchasing public from injury by merchandising deceit.'"[6] The court created a public policy cause of action for the plaintiff, stating that "an employee should not be put to an election whether to risk criminal sanction or to jeopardize his continued employment."[7]

The significance of the public policy cases decided in the last two decades, in addition to reinforcing and extending the rationale of *Petermann*, is that they created a tort cause of action allowing recovery of compensatory and punitive damages. The plaintiff in *Petermann* sought only a contract measure of damages, consisting chiefly of lost wages owed under the contract of employment. Most of the cases of the 1970s and 1980s, however, also allowed the plaintiffs to recover amounts for emotional distress arising from the termination of their employment, and for punitive damages if the employer's conduct was sufficiently reprehensible. Thus, in most jurisdictions, the public policy doctrine not only protects employees who refuse to perform illegal acts, but also provides a powerful deterrent in the form of tort damages.

Refusal to Violate the Civil Law

Employees who are instructed to perform acts in violation of civil statutes that would not result in criminal fines or imprisonment are not faced with the choice between losing their jobs and the risk of criminal sanctions. Rather, if employees know that the requested act would violate a law or regulation, employees would be forced to choose between possibly losing their jobs and their civic obligation to obey the law. Most jurisdictions have not drawn a distinction between violations of criminal or civil statutes, but have protected employees who allege that they were discharged for refusing to violate virtually any legal requirement. Because the courts have expanded the public policy doctrine to include protection for refusal to commit many illegal acts, public policy cases have arisen under a wide variety of statutes not susceptible to easy generalization. This section discusses public policy cases in the areas of environmental regulation, unfair business practices, medical care, and unlawful sexual behavior, for the purpose of illustrating the broad range of conduct which may give rise to a public policy claim.

Just as Michigan was one of the first jurisdictions to enact a whistleblower protection statute, the Michigan courts were also among the first to create public policy causes of action to protect employees who refused to perform illegal acts in violation of environmental laws. In *Trombetta v. Detroit, Toledo & Ironton Railroad Co.*,[8]

---

[6] *Id.* at 478, 480, 427 A.2d at 389, 115 LRRM at 4629.

[7] *Id.*

[8] 81 Mich. App. 489, 265 N.W.2d 385, 115 LRRM 4361 (1978).

Frank Trombetta alleged that he was discharged because he refused to manipulate sampling results included in pollution control reports that were required to be filed with the state. Such manipulation of pollution control reports was prohibited by Michigan law. The court allowed him to sue without discussing whether he might have been personally subjected to criminal or civil sanctions. Environmental concerns were also present in *Hauck v. Sabine Pilots, Inc.*,[9] where the employee alleged that he was discharged because he refused to pump the bilges of his employer's ship at a place where such pumping was prohibited by federal law. The Texas appellate court recognized a public policy claim limited to the facts of the case.

Several public policy cases have arisen under the antitrust laws. In *Tameny v. Atlantic Richfield Co.*[10] Gordon Tameny alleged that he had been discharged for refusing to participate in a price fixing conspiracy, which supposedly violated California's unfair business practice laws. The California Supreme Court stated that "fundamental principles of public policy and adherence to the objectives underlying the state's penal statutes require the recognition of the rule barring an employer from discharging an employee who has simply complied with his legal duty and has refused to commit an illegal act."[11] Similarly, several federal courts have protected employees who alleged that they were terminated because they refused to engage in practices violating the federal antitrust laws.[12]

The public interest in safe medical care has also been the basis for numerous public policy cases. In *O'Sullivan v. Mallon*,[13] a case before the New Jersey courts, Frances O'Sullivan alleged that she was employed by the defendants as an x-ray technician until she was discharged for refusing to perform catheterizations. O'Sullivan contended that she refused to perform such procedures on the grounds that she was not properly trained to perform them, and that it was legally permissible for such procedures to be performed only by a licensed nurse or physician. After O'Sullivan's discharge, the State Board of Medical Examiners concluded that any such procedure performed by her would be in violation of the State Medical Practice Act. The court protected O'Sullivan's conduct based on the following reasoning:

> [A]n employment at will may not be terminated by an employer in retaliation for an employee's refusal to perform an illegal act. This rule

---

[9]687 S.W.2d 733, 119 LRRM 2187 (Tex. 1985).

[10]27 Cal. 3d 167, 164 Cal. Rptr. 839, 610 P.2d 1330, 1 IER Cases 102, 115 LRRM 3119 (1980).

[11]*Id.* at 174, 164 Cal. Rptr. at 843, 610 P.2d at 1333-34, 1 IER Cases at 104, 115 LRRM at 3122.

[12]*See, e.g.*, McNulty v. Borden, Inc., 474 F. Supp. 1111, 115 LRRM 4563 (E.D. Pa. 1979). *See also* Perry v. Hartz Mountain Corp., 537 F. Supp. 1387, 115 LRRM 4934 (S.D. Ind. 1982) ("[Plaintiff] is under a statutory duty to refrain from engaging in conspiracies in restraint of trade. [Citation omitted.] By alleging that Hartz discharged him for refusing to continue his participation in an anti-competitive conspiracy, [plaintiff] has stated a claim. . . .").

[13]160 N.J. Super. 416, 390 A.2d 149, 115 LRRM 5064 (1978). *See also* Hobson v. McLean Hosp. Corp., 402 Mass. 413, 522 N.E.2d 975, 3 IER Cases 1217 (1988) (hospital employee who alleged that she was discharged for attempting to enforce fire code regulations against patients attempting to cook their own meals protected).

is especially cogent where the subject matter is the administration of medical treatment, an area in which the public has a foremost interest and which is extensively regulated by various state agencies.[14]

The public policy doctrine was probably extended to its furthest limits in cases alleging violations of laws regulating sexual behavior. For example, in *Lucas v. Brown & Root, Inc.*,[15] an employee alleged that she was discharged for refusing to sleep with her supervisor. The court relied upon an Arkansas statute prohibiting prostitution to create a public policy cause of action on behalf of the employee. The court reasoned:

> A woman invited to trade herself for a job is in effect being asked to become a prostitute. If this were a criminal prosecution, it might be argued that a job is not a "fee" within the meaning of this statute, and a court, applying the maxim that criminal statutes are to be strictly construed, might agree, holding that "fee" means only money, and not other things of value. But in this civil action no such narrow interpretation is required or appropriate. A wage paying job is logically and morally indistinguishable from the payment of cash. Indeed, it necessarily involves the payment of cash.
>
> Plaintiff should not be penalized for refusing to do what the law forbids. And if she can prove that this is in fact what happened, and that her employer is responsible for it, she can recover damages for breach of contract. For it is an implied term of every contract of employment that neither party be required to do what the law forbids.[16]

The Arizona Supreme Court also upheld a public policy claim in *Wagenseller v. Scottsdale Memorial Hospital*,[17] in which an employee was allegedly discharged because he refused to "moon" fellow employees during a skit on a company retreat. The court reasoned that such conduct would have violated Arizona's laws against indecent exposure.

Refusal to Commit a Tort

The creation of public policy claims in the foregoing cases involving criminal or civil violations is understandable in view of the public policy expressed by the legislatures against such activity. However, there are other types of wrongful conduct that are not prohibited by criminal or civil statutes, but are punished solely by the law of tort. Thus, the courts have traditionally drawn a distinction between "public wrongs," which are punished by criminal or civil statutes, and "private wrongs" which are sanctioned solely by tort law.[18]

---

[14]*Id.* at 418, 390 A.2d at 150, 115 LRRM at 5065.

[15]736 F.2d 1202, 1 IER Cases 388, 116 LRRM 2744 (8th Cir. 1984).

[16]*Id.* at 1205, 1 IER Cases at 390-391, 116 LRRM at 2746-47.

[17]147 Ariz. 370, 710 P.2d 1025, 1 IER Cases 526 (1985).

[18]The distinction between criminal and civil wrongs is well-developed in Hitchler, *Crimes and Civil Injuries*, 39 DICK. L. REV. 23 (1934).

Despite the less serious character of tort violations, the public policy doctrine was extended by the Oregon courts to protect an employee who refused to commit a tort in *Delaney v. Taco Time International*.[19] Reginald Delaney alleged that he had been discharged for failing to sign a false and potentially defamatory statement about an employee under his supervision. The court noted that two provisions of the Oregon Constitution prohibited defamatory statements, and stated that "[t]hese two sections indicate that a member of society has an obligation not to defame others. . . . [P]laintiff here was discharged for fulfilling a societal obligation. We hold that defendant is liable for wrongfully discharging plaintiff because plaintiff refused to sign the potentially defamatory statement."[20]

An apartment manager who refused to commit the civil offense of trespass, by entering apartments without permission of the tenants, was protected by the Maryland Court of Special Appeals in *Kessler v. Equity Management, Inc.*[21] The apartment manager also refused to go through the tenants' private papers. The court protected this conduct as well, stating that the manager would have subjected herself to civil liability for violation of the tenants' rights of privacy. The *Delaney* and *Kessler* decisions indicate that the courts may extend the public policy doctrine to protect employees who are terminated because they refuse to expose themselves to civil liability.

Refusal to Violate Ethical Codes

As is apparent from the foregoing cases, the most compelling source of public policy is a state's criminal laws. Thus, the courts have had little difficulty in defining the elusive term "public policy" to include violations of the criminal law and, by extension, violations of a state's legislative enactments prohibiting various types of conduct through civil penalties. In cases involving professional employees, however, employees often do not contend that the public policy that would be offended by their discharge is contained in a legislative enactment. Rather, professional employees often contend that they were discharged because they refused to engage in unethical activities in violation of a professional code of conduct. Because many professional codes of conduct are promulgated by private professional associations rather than by state legislatures, the courts have had difficulty deciding whether to include professional codes within the definition of public policy.

The New Jersey Supreme Court discussed this issue in detail in *Pierce v. Ortho Pharmaceutical Corp.*[22] Dr.Grace Pierce was a physician who was employed as director of medical research by a manufac-

---

[19]297 Or. 10, 681 P.2d 114, 1 IER Cases 367, 116 LRRM 2168 (1984).

[20]*Id.* at 17, 681 P.2d at 118, 1 IER Cases at 370, 116 LRRM at 2171.

[21]82 Md. App. 577, 572 A.2d 1144, 5 IER Cases 545 (1989).

[22]84 N.J. 58, 417 A.2d 505, 1 IER Cases 109, 115 LRRM 3044 (1980).

turer of therapeutic and reproductive drugs. Her responsibilities were to oversee development of therapeutic drugs, and to establish procedures for testing such drugs for safety, effectiveness, and marketability. Pierce alleged that she had been discharged because she opposed development of a drug for treatment of diarrhea in infants, children, and elderly persons. She felt that one of the components of the drug might be harmful, and therefore that the drug should not be tested on children or elderly persons. Pierce opposed development of the drug because she felt that working on the development of the drug would violate the Hippocratic oath. She did not contend that development and testing of the drug would violate any state or federal statutory regulation, or any principle of ethics of the American Medical Association, or that participation in the research would expose her to a claim for malpractice. The court began its analysis by adopting a broad definition of public policy:

> [A]n employee has a cause of action for wrongful discharge when a discharge is contrary to a clear mandate of public policy. The sources of public policy include legislation; administrative rules, regulations or decisions; and judicial decisions. In certain instances, a professional code of ethics may contain an expression of public policy. However, not all such sources express a clear mandate of public policy. For example, a code of ethics designed to serve only the interests of a profession or an administrative regulation concerned with technical matters probably would not be sufficient. Absent legislation, the judiciary must define the cause of action in case-by-case determinations. . . . Employees who are professionals owe a special duty to abide not only by federal and state law, but also by the recognized code of ethics of their profession. That duty may oblige them to decline to perform acts required by their employers. However, an employee should not have the right to prevent his or her employer from pursuing its business because the employee perceives that a particular business decision violates the employee's personal morals, as distinguished from the recognized code of ethics of the employee's profession.[23]

The court found that Pierce could not prevail because she did not allege that continued development of the drug would violate any ethical prohibition. Rather, Pierce contended only that development of the drug would create unnecessary controversy for the employer's business.

Pharmacy regulations concerning potentially dangerous drugs were the subject of *Kalman v. Grand Union Co.*[24] In this instance, the employee was a pharmacist-in-charge at a pharmacy located in the defendant's grocery store. Kalman contended that he was discharged because he protested the closing of the pharmacy on a holiday in violation of state regulations requiring that the pharmacy be kept open. Kalman was concerned that he might be subject to professional discipline as a pharmacist if the state regulations were not followed. The New Jersey appellate court stated:

> Plaintiff argues persuasively that the requirement that the pharmacy area be open and tended by a pharmacist whenever the premises are

[23]*Id.* at 71-72, 417 A.2d at 512, 1 IER Cases at 115, 115 LRRM at 3049-50.

[24]183 N.J. Super. 153, 443 A.2d 728, 115 LRRM 4803 (1982).

open is, indeed, an expression of public policy. An unsecured, unsupervised drug counter creates a risk that potentially dangerous substances will be dispensed by unqualified persons or stolen by patrons. The purpose of requiring that pharmacists be registered is to protect the public from the dangers attendant upon the sale of drugs by unqualified persons. [Citations omitted.] Thus plaintiff is correct that he was vindicating a clear mandate of public policy when he reported defendant's plan to the Board of Pharmacy. We note that a Board of Pharmacy regulation imposed upon him the duty of so reporting: the pharmacist-in-charge is responsible for ensuring compliance with the provisions of the Pharmacy Act, Rules of the Board of Pharmacy and the Controlled Dangerous Substances Act.[25]

The public interest in controlling access to potentially dangerous drugs is readily apparent. However, the public interest in proper accounting practices is less obvious. In *Suchodolski v. Michigan Consolidated Gas Co.*,[26] the Michigan Supreme Court refused to create a public policy claim for the plaintiff, who worked as a senior auditor. Arthur Suchodolski contended that he was discharged for complaining about the gas company's internal accounting practices, and argued that the Code of Ethics of the Institute of Internal Auditors recommended against the defendant's practices. The court stated "that this case only involves a corporate management dispute and lacks the kind of violation of a clearly mandated public policy that would support an action for retaliatory discharge. The code of ethics of a private association does not establish public policy."[27]

A distinction between professional ethical responsibilities, that may embody public policy, and personal ethical preferences, that may not, was drawn by the New Jersey intermediate court in *Warthen v. Toms River Community Memorial Hospital.*[28] Corrine Warthen, a

---

[25]*Id.* at 158, 443 A.2d at 730, 115 LRRM at 4805.

[26]412 Mich. 692, 316 N.W.2d 710, 115 LRRM 4449 (1982).

[27]*Id.*

[28]199 N.J. Super. 18, 488 A.2d 229, 118 LRRM 3179 (1985). *See also* Lampe v. Presbyterian Medical Center, 41 Colo. App. 465, 590 P.2d 513, 115 LRRM 4313 (1978). The plaintiff was a licensed professional nurse employed as head nurse of the intensive care unit. The plaintiff contended that she was discharged because she refused to comply with the hospital's request that she reduce the amount of overtime work by nurses in the intensive care unit, because she could not do so without jeopardizing the care of the patients. The plaintiff contended that her discharge violated state statutes that declared that the public health and safety required licensing of professional nurses, and that gave a state board of nursing the power to revoke the license of any professional nurse who acted in a negligent manner. The court refused to recognize a cause of action on behalf of the plaintiff, stating as follows:

> [T]he plaintiff in this case relies on a broad, general statement of policy contained in a statute which created the State Board of Nursing and which gives that Board the authority to discipline a nurse who negligently or wilfully acts in a manner inconsistent with the health or safety of persons under her care. Given the general language used in the statute relied on in this case, we cannot impute to the General Assembly an intent to modify the contractual relations between hospitals and their employees in such situations. Neither can we impute an intent to create a claim for relief based upon a mere possibility of disciplinary action. . . .

Id. at 489, 590 P.2d at 515-16, 115 LRRM at 4315.

Another case involving a difference of professional opinion, rather than any ethical violation, was presented in Rozier v. St. Mary's Hosp., 88 Ill. App. 3d 994, 411 N.E.2d 50, 115 LRRM 4391 (1980). The plaintiff contended that she was fired from the hospital in retaliation for reporting abusive conduct by other hospital employees toward patients for whom the plaintiff had responsibility. Plaintiff contended that her discharge violated public policy because she was fired for showing concern for her patients, and for exercising her First Amendment right of free

registered nurse, was dismissed for having refused to perform a kidney dialysis procedure upon a terminally ill patient because of her moral, medical, and philosophical objections to the procedure. Although the family of the patient wanted the treatment performed to keep the patient alive, Warthen declined to do so based upon a nursing code that stated that a nurse might decline to perform procedures in certain circumstances. The court rejected Warthen's claim partially on the ground that the nursing code was not a sufficiently clear expression of public policy, and partially on the ground that the "plaintiff was motivated by her own personal morals. . . . She makes no assertion that she ever referred to her obligations and entitlements pursuant to her code of ethics."[29]

The circumstances of professional employment are even more complicated than nonprofessional employment. Not only do professionals owe a duty of loyalty to their employer, and a duty to their communities, but professionals also owe extremely strong duties to their clients or patients. When whistleblowers who are professional employees have compromised their duties to clients or patients, the courts have generally refused to protect them.

In *Harman v. LaCrosse Tribune*,[30] the plaintiff was a shareholder in a law firm which had a newspaper as one of its clients. Harman was also a member of the county board of supervisors. The newspaper published a series of articles that criticized members of the county highway department for alleged misuse of county property for private purposes. Harman investigated the information contained in the newspaper articles and concluded that such information was insufficient to determine if the newspaper's allegations were true. Accordingly, he issued a press release stating that the newspaper's editor and two reporters had deliberately furnished false information to a newspaper for publication, and urged prosecution of the editor and reporters. The other shareholders of Harman's law firm voted to discharge him from the firm for breaching his duty of loyalty to one of the firm's clients. Harman contended that his discharge violated his free speech rights established by the First Amendment to the United States Constitution. The Wisconsin appellate court noted that the applicable Code of Professional Responsibility restricts an attorney's right of free speech when the speech would adversely affect a client, and that the duty of loyalty runs from each attorney employed by a law firm to every client of the firm. The court held as follows:

---

speech. The court declined to create a cause of action based on plaintiff's free speech rights because there was no state action on the part of the privately owned hospital.

However, an employee who questioned the professional qualifications of a fellow emergency medical technician was found to be protected in Gould v. Campbell's Ambulance Serv., Inc., 130 Ill. App. 3d 598, 474 N.E.2d 740 (1984).

[29] 199 N.J. Super. at 26, 488 A.2d at 234.

[30] 117 Wis. 2d 448, 344 N.W.2d 536, 115 LRRM 3252 (1984). *See also* Klages v. Sperry Corp., 118 LRRM 2463 (E.D. Pa. 1984). In *Klages*, the general counsel of the employer contended that he had been discharged for investigating potential securities law violations by the employer's executives. The court recognized a claim for the plaintiff because of the public policy in favor of disclosing securities law violations.

> [The plaintiff] breached his duty of loyalty to the [newspaper] when he publicly accused its editor and two reporters of criminal behavior in a manner on which the firm had advised the [newspaper], and called for their prosecution. His discharge under this circumstance does not "clearly contravene the public welfare" or "gravely violate paramount requirements of public interest."[31]

Further, one court rejected the claim of an attorney whose complaints regarding allegedly unethical conduct were viewed by the court as being too vague. In *McGonagle v. Union Fidelity Corp.*,[32] an attorney employed by an insurance company refused to approve a mail advertising campaign based on his belief that the campaign would violate the regulations of several states. The court noted that the attorney failed to specifically allege which regulations would be violated, and dismissed his claim because "[w]e are left with only his opinion as to such conduct being ("qualitatively") violative of a state's unspecified insurance laws."[33] Although not articulated in this manner, the court may have required the attorney to specifically allege how the company's conduct was improper because of the attorney's presumably intimate knowledge of the company's practices.

The foregoing cases indicate that no easy generalizations can be made regarding whether the courts will protect employees discharged because of refusal to commit ethical violations. Because the public interest may be implicated by some ethical violations but not by others, the precise character of the alleged violation may determine whether legal protection exists. However, it appears that the judiciary is reluctant to protect employees regarding mere differences in professional opinion, or employees who violate ethical obligations to their clients or patients.

Discharge for Exercise of Statutory Rights

The second major branch of the public policy doctrine has been recognized in cases where a law expresses a public policy by conferring rights upon employees, but does not directly provide any protection for those rights. These cases most often arise when employees allege that they were discharged in retaliation for filing claims for workers' compensation, and where the state workers' compensation law does not provide an express remedy for employees filing for such benefits. In these instances, the courts have implied a remedy from the workers' compensation statutes in order to protect the exercise of the right to seek workers' compensation.

---

[31] *Id.* at 454, 344 N.W.2d at 540.

[32] 383 Pa. Super. 223, 556 A.2d 878 (1989).

[33] *Id.*, 556 A.2d at 885.

Workers' Compensation Benefits

The Indiana Supreme Court was one of the first to recognize a cause of action in these circumstances. In *Frampton v. Central Indiana Gas Co.*,[34] the court noted as follows:

> Workmen's compensation acts are designed to afford injured workers "an expeditious remedy both adequate and certain, and independent of any negligence on their part or on the part of the employer." Prior to workmen's compensation, workers were faced with the harshness of the common law. The employee's only remedy was an action at law against the employer—actions which were rarely successful.[35]

The court stated that the social purpose behind the workmen's compensation legislation is to shift the economic burden for employment-connected injuries from the employee to the employer, and that workers' compensation legislation should be liberally construed in favor of the employee so as to not negate the Act's humane purposes. Moreover, the court reasoned:

> The Act creates a *duty* in the employer to compensate employees for work-related injuries (through insurance) and a *right* in the employee to receive such compensation. But in order for the goals of the Act to be realized and for public policy to be effectuated, the employee must be able to exercise his right in an unfettered fashion without being subject to reprisal.[36]

---

[34]260 Ind. 249, 297 N.E.2d 425 (1973). *See also* Hansen v. Harrah's, 100 Nev. 60, 675 P.2d 394, 115 LRRM 3024 (1984); Clanton v. Cain-Sloan Co., 677 S.W.2d 441, 117 LRRM 2789 (Tenn. 1984); Firestone Textile Co.v. Meadows, 666 S.W.2d 730, 114 LRRM 3559, 1 IER Cases 1800 (Ky. 1983); Murphy v. City of Topeka, 6 Kan. App. 2d 488, 630 P.2d 186, 115 LRRM 4433 (1981); Lally v. Compugraphics, 85 N.J. 668, 428 A.2d 1317, 115 LRRM 4634 (1981); Shanholtz v. Monongahela Power Co., 165 W. Va. 305, 270 S.E.2d 178, 115 LRRM 4387 (1980); Kelsay v. Motorola, Inc., 74 Ill. 2d 172, 384 N.E.2d 353 (1979); Brown v. Transcon Lines, 284 Or. 597, 588 P.2d 1087, 115 LRRM 5072 (1978); Sventko v. Kroger Co., 69 Mich. App. 644, 245 N.W.2d 151, 115 LRRM 4613 (1976). In addition to these common-law protections, many states have created statutory rights of action for employees who have been retaliated against for filing workers' compensation claims. *See* Love, *Retaliatory Discharge for Filing a Workers' Compensation Claim: The Development of a Modern Tort Action*, 37 Hastings L.J. 551, 555 nn.30-33 (1986).

The rationale of these cases was carried one step further, to protect an employee who had been discharged because he refused to fire his workers' compensation lawyer, in A.J. Foyt Chevrolet, Inc. v. Jacobs, 578 S.W.2d 445 (Tex. Civ. App. 1979). *See also* Pytlik v. Professional Resources Ltd., 887 F.2d 1371 (10th Cir. 1989) (employee who allegedly was terminated for contacting a workers' compensation attorney was protected).

The outer limits of protection were probably reached in Darnell v. Impact Indus., 119 Ill. App. 3d 763, 457 N.E.2d 125, 115 LRRM 5012 (1983). The plaintiff alleged that she was discharged, after working one day, for having filed a workers' compensation claim against her previous employer. The defendant argued that plaintiff had been discharged for having falsely answered, in the negative, the questions "Have you had a serious illness or injury in the past five years," and "Have you ever received compensation for injuries," contained in her job application. The court held that there was sufficient evidence for a jury to find that plaintiff had been discharged for filing a workers' compensation claim with her previous employer, rather than for the defendant's proffered reason of falsifying her employment application. However, the dissent argued that the plaintiff should not have been allowed to state a cause of action because of her admitted falsification of the employment application, and stated, "[t]his case illustrates the extent to which an employer can be compelled to defend a suit under facts which, I believe, fully justify the employer's prerogative to discharge an employee." *Id.* at 770, 457 N.E.2d at 129, 115 LRRM at 5015. *See also* Goins v. Ford Motor Co., 131 Mich. App. 185, 347 N.W.2d 184, 116 LRRM 3231 (1983) (claim recognized for employee who alleged that he was discharged for filing a workers' compensation claim against his previous employer).

[35]260 at 250, 297 N.E.2d at 427.

[36]*Id.* at 251, 297 N.E.2d at 427.

The court then noted that the state statutes in question provided that "'[n]o contract or agreement, written or implied, no rule, regulation, or *other device* shall, in any manner operate to relieve any employer in whole or in part of any obligation created by this act.' We believe the threat of discharge to be a 'device' [within the meaning of the statute], and hence, in clear contravention of public policy."[37] The court analogized an action for retaliatory discharge for filing a workers' compensation claim to actions for "retaliatory eviction" for a tenant's reporting health or safety code violations to an appropriate administrative body. The court noted that actions for retaliatory eviction are permitted in order to further the important public policy of improving the quality of housing. The court then held that a retaliatory discharge, if proved, would entitle the employee to tort damages. At least ten other jurisdictions have created public policy claims in these circumstances.[38]

The foregoing cases attempt to protect employees' rights to receive workers' compensation benefits. An effort to protect employees' pension benefits was rejected in *Ingersoll-Rand Co. v. McClendon,*[39] in which the Supreme Court held that the federal Employee Retirement Income Security Act (ERISA) preempted an employee's claim that he had been terminated four months before the vesting of his pension benefits. The Court reversed the decision of the Texas Supreme Court that had created a public policy cause of action for the employee.

Refusal to Take a Polygraph

Twenty-one jurisdictions prohibit private sector employers from requiring employees to submit to polygraph examinations, popularly known as "lie-detectors," as a condition of employment.[40] Nine of these jurisdictions prohibit employers from even asking applicants or employees to take a polygraph examination.[41] However, many of

---

[37]*Id.* at 252, 297 N.E.2d at 428.

[38]*See* Love, *Retaliatory Discharge for Filing a Workers' Compensation Claim*, 37 HASTINGS L.J. 551 (1986).

[39]59 USLW 4033 (1990), *rev'g* 779 S.W.2d 69, 4 IER Cases 1515 (1989).

[40]Those 21 jurisdictions are as follows: ALASKA STAT. §23.10.037 (1984); CAL. LABOR CODE §432.2 (West 1989); CONN. GEN. STAT. §31-51g (West 1987); DEL. CODE ANN. tit. 19, §704 (1979 & Supp. 1988); D.C. CODE ANN. §36-801 (1988); HAWAII REV. STAT. §§378-26 *et seq.* (1985); IDAHO CODE §§44-903 (1977); IOWA CODE ANN. §79.29 (West 1990); ME. REV. STAT. ANN. tit. 32, §7166 (West 1988); MD. ANN. CODE ART. 100, §95 (1990); MASS. ANN. LAWS ch. 149, §19B (West 1990); MICH. COMP. LAWS ANN. §§37.201-.208 (West 1985); MINN. STAT. ANN. §§181.75-.76 (West 1990); MONT. CODE ANN. §39-2-304 (1989); NEB. REV. STAT. §81-1932 (1987); N.J. STAT. ANN. §2C:40A-1 (1982 & West Supp. 1990); OR. REV. STAT. §§659.225-.227 (1989); 18 PA. CONS. STAT. ANN. §7321 (Purdon 1983 & Supp 1990); R.I. GEN. LAWS §28-6.1-1 (1989); WASH. REV. CODE ANN. §§49.44.120-.130 (West 1990); and W. VA. CODE §21-5-5b (1989). These statutes are also contained throughout the BNA Labor Relations Reporter, State Laws, Vols. 4 and 4A.

[41]These jurisdictions are: ALASKA STAT. §23.10.037 (1984); CONN. GEN. STAT. §31-51g(b)(1) (West 1987); DEL. CODE ANN. tit. 19, §704(b) (1979); D.C. CODE ANN. §36-802(a) (1988); MASS. ANN. LAWS ch. 149, §19B (West 1990); MICH. COMP. LAWS ANN. §37.203 (West 1985); MINN. STAT. ANN. §181.75 (West 1990); N.J. STAT. ANN. §2C:40A-1 (1982 & West Supp. 1990); and W. VA. CODE §21-5-5b (1989). These statutes are also contained throughout the BNA Labor Relations Reporter, State Laws, Vols. 4 and 4A.

these statutes do not provide a remedy for employees who are discharged for refusing to submit to a polygraph examination. The courts of the states that prohibit polygraphs have generally recognized public policy causes of action for such employees. For example, in *Ambroz v. Cornhusker Square, Ltd.*,[42] the Supreme Court of Nebraska held that an employee who refused to take a polygraph examination could sue for wrongful discharge on the basis of a Nebraska statute which limited the use of polygraphs to public law enforcement employment.

This protection from dismissal does not necessarily extend to employees who are discharged for having failed a polygraph examination. In *Townsend v. L.W.M. Management, Inc.*,[43] the Maryland Court of Special Appeals stated that it would be contrary to public policy to discharge an employee who refused to submit to a polygraph exam, in view of Maryland's statute prohibiting employers from requiring a polygraph examination as a condition of employment. The court found that the employee was required to take the examination, and that this requirement violated the Maryland statute. Nevertheless, the court found that the employee was discharged because of the polygraph results, not because of the refusal to take the examination. The Maryland statute only prohibited the submission to a polygraph exam as a condition of employment. Because the statute did not expressly preclude using polygraph results as the basis for terminating employees, the court ruled in favor of the employer.

This issue may be mooted to some extent by the Employee Polygraph Protection Act, passed by Congress in 1988.[44] For instance, the New York Court of Appeals refused to create a new tort remedy for negligent administration of a polygraph examination based in part on the "detailed, far-reaching" provisions of the Act.[45] The Act prohibits private sector employers from using polygraphs, except under specified conditions as part of ongoing investigations of economic loss or injury. Even in these narrow circumstances, employers may not take adverse action against employees based solely on the results of a polygraph. Instead, the Act requires additional supporting evidence beyond polygraph results. The Act allows employees to sue, in either state or federal court, for reinstatement, lost compensation and attorneys' fees. This comprehensive federal remedy may decrease the number of claims asserted under state law.

---

[42]226 Neb. 899, 416 N.W.2d 510, 2 IER Cases 1185 (1987). However, in Zaccardi v. Zale Corp., 856 F.2d 1473, 3 IER Cases 1249 (10th Cir. 1988), the court held that no public policy claim existed, under New Mexico law, for an employee who was dismissed for refusing to take a polygraph examination, because New Mexico had no statute restricting the use of polygraphs.

[43]64 Md. App. 55, 494 A.2d 239 (1985). *See also* Johnson v. United Parcel Serv., 722 F. Supp. 1282, 4 IER Cases 1513 (1989) (no remedy for violation of Maryland polygraph statute if discharge not based on refusal to submit to polygraph).

[44]The Employee Polygraph Protection Act is codified at 29 U.S.C. §§2001-2009 (1988).

[45]Hall v. United Parcel Serv., 76 N.Y.2d 27, 556 N.Y.S.2d 21, 555 N.E. 2d 273, 5 IER Cases 616 (1990). *But see* Ellis v. Buckley, 720 P.2d 875, 4 IER Cases 1668 (Colo. 1989) (allegations of harsh administration of polygraph examination were sufficient to state claim for intentional infliction of emotional distress).

Exercise of Free Speech

The most far-reaching extension of the public policy doctrine occurred in a case that held that employees may not be discharged for exercise of their First Amendment right of free speech. This theory is a dramatic break with precedent because prior cases had unanimously required that governmental action be present in order for a constitutional violation to exist.

In *Novosel v. Nationwide Insurance Co.*,[46] decided by the United States Court of Appeals for the Third Circuit, the plaintiff alleged that his employer circulated a memorandum soliciting the participation of all employees in an effort to lobby the state legislature to support a no-fault insurance reform act. The plaintiff contended that he was discharged because he refused to participate in the lobbying effort and privately opposed the company's political stand. Following Pennsylvania precedents, the court stated that Pennsylvania law permitted a cause of action for wrongful discharge where the employment termination abridges a significant and recognized public policy. The court then reviewed the significant body of case law protecting the First Amendment rights of state and local government employees. Although those cases relied upon the presence of governmental action in order to find a constitutional violation, the court stated that "[t]he protection of important political freedoms, however, goes well beyond the question whether the threat comes from state or private bodies. The inquiry before us is whether the concern for the rights of political expression and association which animated the public employee cases is sufficient to state a public policy under Pennsylvania law."[47] The court suggested that the distinction between corporations and the government was no longer useful given the relationship between economic power and the political process:

> The special status of corporations has placed them in a position to control vast amounts of economic power which may, if not regulated, dominate not only the economy but also the very heart of our democracy, [and] the

[46] 721 F.2d 894, 1 IER Cases 286, 114 LRRM 3105 (3d Cir. 1983). The only case which hints at a similar result is Jones v. Memorial Hosp. Sys., 677 S.W.2d 221, 117 LRRM 2915 (Tex. App. 1984). The plaintiff in that case was employed as a registered nurse in the intensive care unit of the defendant hospital. During the course of her employment, plaintiff wrote an article published in a local publication which described the conflict between the wishes of terminally ill patients and their families and the orders of the attending physicians at the hospital. Plaintiff contended that her discharge violated the Texas Constitution, which provided that "every person shall be at liberty to speak, write or publish his opinions on any subject, being responsible for the abuse of that privilege; and no law shall ever be passed curtailing the liberty of speech or of the press." TEX. CONST. art. I, §8. *Id.* at 224, 117 LRRM at 2916. The court determined that the plaintiff's conduct was constitutionally protected because her article related to matters of public concern, in that the article dealt with "the ethical and social questions concerning a patient's right to die." Id. at 224, 117 LRRM at 2917 (quoting TEX. CONST. art. IV, §8). Given the early procedural posture of the case, the court declined to decide whether or not the plaintiff had to prove that the hospital was an entity of the state government in order to satisfy the state action requirement. Accordingly, *Jones* does not necessarily go as far as *Novosel* to do away with the state action requirement traditionally imposed in order to find a constitutional violation.

[47] 721 F.2d at 899.

> electoral process. . . . [The desired end] is not one of equalizing the resources of opposing candidates for opposing positions, but rather of preventing institutions which have been permitted to amass wealth as a result of special advantages extended by the State for certain economic purposes from using that wealth to acquire an unfair advantage in the political process. . . .[48]

It is questionable whether *Novosel* is an authoritative statement of Pennsylvania law. No Pennsylvania court has adopted the *Novosel* reasoning, nor have the courts of any other jurisdiction. Rather, several jurisdictions have recognized that transposing the constitutional right of free speech from the context of government employment to the context of private sector employment would revolutionize private sector employment relations, and have refused to do so.[49]

Discharge for Engaging in Important Civic Duties

The two branches of the public policy doctrine previously discussed created causes of action for employees who were asked to violate express statutes prohibiting certain conduct, or for employees who were discouraged from exercising rights expressly granted by statute. The third branch of the public policy exception does not necessarily rely on any express statutory prohibitions or rights. Rather, in these cases the courts determine that the employees were discharged for having engaged in activities which the courts deem to be important civic obligations. Thus, although the employees in these cases may not have been under a statutory compulsion to act in the manner that they did, the courts viewed their participation in such activities as being socially useful, and ruled that employers should not be permitted to discourage such activities.

The leading case establishing this branch of the public policy doctrine is the decision of the Oregon Supreme Court in *Nees v. Hocks*.[50] In that case, the plaintiff was summoned for jury duty, and was given a letter by her employer that stated that the employer could do without the plaintiff's services for a short period of time but not for a month, and asked that she be excused from service. The plaintiff presented the letter to the court clerk, but told the clerk that she would like to serve on jury duty. The plaintiff was discharged because, according to the defendant, she had requested to be placed on jury duty. The court noted that the state constitution provided for a jury

---

[48]*Id.* at 900, 1 IER Cases at 291, 114 LRRM at 3110.

[49]Rozier v. St. Mary's Hosp., 88 Ill. App. 3d 994, 411 N.E.2d 150, 115 LRRM 4391 (1980); Schultz v. Indus. Coils, Inc., 125 Wis. 2d 520, 373 N.W.2d 74 (1985).

[50]272 Or. 210, 536 P.2d 512, 115 LRRM 4571 (1975). A similar result was reached in Reuther v. Fowler & Williams, Inc., 255 Pa. Super. 28, 32, 386 A.2d 119, 120, 115 LRRM 4690, 4691 (1978), where the plaintiff alleged that he had been discharged in retaliation for having served on a jury for a week. The court reasoned that "[t]he jury system and jury service are of the highest importance to our legal process," and held that the plaintiff should be protected for performing his civic duty.

trial in all civil cases, and noted that several state statutes restricted exemptions from jury duty to exceptional cases. Although it did not rely on this provision for its decision, the court also noted that a state statute provided that a juror who refuses to serve on a jury without reasonable cause may be fined $20 for each day the juror does not serve. The court then reasoned:

> These actions by the people, the legislature and the courts clearly indicate that the jury system and jury duty are regarded as high on the scale of American institutions and citizen obligations. If an employer were permitted with impunity to discharge an employee for fulfilling her obligation of jury duty, the jury system would be adversely affected. The will of the community would be thwarted.[51]

Service as an election officer was viewed as an important public obligation by the California courts in *Kouff v. Bethlehem-Alameda Shipyard.*[52] The plaintiff alleged that he had been discharged because he took a day off in order to serve as an election officer. A California statute provided that election officers shall not "be liable to any penalty, nor shall any deduction be made from his usual salary or wages, nor shall he be suspended or discharged from his service or employment. . . ." The court stated that "[g]ranting that under the general law an employee at will may be discharged without any cause, this particular statute interposes an exception to that rule, the basis of which is the necessity of drawing on industry for such temporary public servants as election officers."[53]

Candidacy for public office has also been held to fall in this category. In *Davis v. Louisiana Computing Corp.*,[54] the plaintiff was employed by a corporation which derived about 60 percent of its business from local government agencies. Davis became a candidate for the local city council, and opposed a candidate supported by numerous local politicians. Davis contended that his discharge violated a state statute which provided that an employer that discharges an employee who becomes a candidate for public office may be subjected to a fine of less than $1,000, and imprisonment for not more than six months. The Louisiana Intermediate Court of Appeal stated:

> We note the "business" justification for firing plaintiff in this case is a real one: plaintiff's candidacy would antagonize persons who could withdraw business from plaintiff's employer. In that sense, plaintiff by his candidacy made himself a detriment to his employer and was "disloyal" to his employer. But the policy of the statute is unmistakable: the employer may not control political candidacy of his employees. We see no exemption from the legislative purpose because of the nature of the employer's business.[55]

---

[51]272 Or. at 219, 536 P.2d at 516, 115 LRRM at 4575.

[52]90 Cal. App. 2d 322, 202 P.2d 1059 (1949).

[53]*Id.* at 323-25, 202 P.2d at 1061.

[54]394 So.2d 678 (La. App. 1981).

[55]*Id.*

One state has extended the public policy doctrine in recognition of the importance of compliance with court orders to make child support payments. In *Greeley v. Miami Valley Maintenance Contractors, Inc.*,[56] the plaintiff alleged that he had been terminated because his wages had been garnished for child support payments pursuant to a court order. The Ohio Supreme Court recognized that an Ohio statute prohibited discrimination based on wage garnishments, and held that "[t]o allow an employer to bypass the obligation and escape a court's order to withhold would undermine the entire child support enforcement mechanism enacted by the General Assembly."[57]

The Limits of Public Policy

The judiciary has not hesitated to temper the harshness of the at-will rule of employment when important public interests have so demanded. However, the courts have also been careful not to overreact to the harshness of the at-will rule by modifying it at the mere suggestion of public policy implications. As the following cases demonstrate, the courts have refused to create public policy claims when the public health or safety is only marginally implicated.

Rights Unrelated to Employment

Even where a plaintiff contends that his discharge violated a legislative enactment, some courts have insisted that the constitution or statute in question set forth a general social policy in favor of all employees in the state regarding some aspect of the employment relationship. If the statute in question does not state a public policy applicable to employees, by virtue of their employment status, the court may refuse to create a cause of action based on the statute. For instance, in *Campbell v. Ford Industries*,[58] the employee alleged that he was discharged because he requested corporate information under a state statute that provides that stockholders have the right to examine the books and records of the corporation. The Oregon Supreme Court stated:

> [A]lthough there may be reasons of public policy why the stockholders of a corporation should have the right to examine its books and records, the primary basis for that right is not one of public policy, but the private and propriety interest of stockholders, as owners of the corporation. . . . It follows, in our opinion, that because the primary basis for the right of inspection of the books and records of a corporation by its

[56] 49 Ohio St. 3d 228, 551 N.E.2d 981, 5 IER Cases 257 (1990).

[57] *Id.*, 551 N.E.2d at 985, 5 IER Cases at 260.

[58] 274 Or. 243, 546 P.2d 141, 115 LRRM 4837 (1976). *But see* Bowman v. State Bank of Keysville, 229 Va. 534, 331 S.E.2d 797, 1 IER Cases 437, 119 LRRM 3095 (1985) (opposite result reached).

stockholders . . . is the protection of their private and proprietary interests as owners of the corporation, [and] any additional reasons of public policy as the basis for such a right are far less compelling, as a matter of "community interest," than the "community interest in having its citizens serve on jury duty. . . ."[59]

Distinguishing an earlier case in which a plaintiff was allowed to state a claim for serving on jury duty, the court stated that the conduct of the plaintiff in the previous case "related much more directly to her rights as an employee than did the conduct of [Campbell]. His demand to inspect corporate books and records was an attempt to exercise his rights as a stockholder, and had no direct relation to his rights as an employee."[60]

An attempt to borrow the privilege of using physical force in self-defense from the criminal law was rejected by the North Carolina Court of Appeals in *McLaughlin v. Barclays American Corp.*[61] The plaintiff alleged that he had been fired because he physically defended himself when assaulted by a subordinate. The court held that the principle of self-defense did not prevent the employer from terminating the plaintiff, and stated that "[w]ere we to recognize a cause of action in this case, every employee involved in an altercation would assert a self-defense justification. . . ."[62]

Constitutional Guarantees Against Government Action

In addition to the free speech cases discussed in the previous section, the courts have resisted attempts to apply other constitutional principles limiting government action to private sector employers. For example, the recent increase in the use of drug testing by many employers has prompted numerous challenges to such tests on the grounds that they constitute unreasonable searches under the Fourth Amendment to the United States Constitution, or that they violate the constitutional right of privacy. Most of these challenges have been rejected.

In *Jevic v. Coca-Cola,*[63] the plaintiff alleged that he had been refused employment based on a false positive test result which erroneously indicated the presence of drugs in a urine specimen. The court rejected the argument that the company's policy violated the Fourth Amendment or the right of privacy because those protections applied only to government action, not to the actions of private companies.[64]

---

[59]546 P.2d at 145-46.

[60]274 Or. at 249-51, 546 P.2d at 145-146, 115 LRRM at 4840.

[61]95 N.C. App. 301, 382 S.E.2d 836 (1989).

[62]*Id.*, 382 S.E. 2d at 840.

[63]5 IER Cases 765 (D.N.J. 1990).

[64]*Id.* at 770-772. *See also* Hershberger v. Jersey Shore Steel Co., 575 A.2d 944, 5 IER Cases 710 (Pa. Super. 1990) (same); Horne v. J.W. Gibson Well Serv., 5 IER Cases 69 (10th Cir. 1990) (no claim existed under Wyoming law).

Closely akin to the constitutional right of free speech discussed in the previous section is the right to petition the courts for redress, which is also set forth in the First Amendment. However, when employees bring lawsuits against their employers while still working for them, the duty of loyalty may be stretched to the breaking point. Lawsuits may not only be time-consuming and expensive, but they may also generate unwanted negative publicity for employers. In some contexts, lawsuits against employers are protected by statute. For example, Title VII permits employees to sue for discrimination short of termination, including failure to promote, and harassment in the workplace. Moreover, Title VII prohibits retaliation against employees who file such lawsuits while still employed.

Many employees who have sued their employers, in the absence of such statutory protection, have attempted to assert public policy causes of action on the basis that public policy should protect an employee's right to access to the courts, or to legal counsel. The courts have unanimously rejected such claims, based on the following reasoning:

> There is no question that the right to counsel and to free access to the courts are important public policies. However, these freedoms are usually expressed in terms of limitations on government, not on private parties. The invocation of the public interest in the effectuation of these policies to create new common law rights would be unprecedented; a party does not violate another party's right to counsel or to free access to the courts by taking measures, even though retaliatory and spiteful in nature which are lawfully available to him simply because resort to these measures somehow penalizes the other party for suing. . . . [Plaintiff's theory] would metamorphose the narrow [public policy] exception . . . into the monster that swallowed the employment-at-will rule. Whenever a dispute between an employer and an at-will employee threatens to culminate in the employee's discharge, the employee, simply by retaining an attorney and threatening to sue, could procure that which is unavailable to him through contract—employment security.[65]

In addition to the court's reservations about imposing concepts limiting government action upon private sector employers, the court also recognized that lawsuits by their nature are disruptive:

> [The employer] persuasively argues that inherent in the employment-at-will relationship it had with plaintiff was an understanding that the organization . . . functions more effectively in an atmosphere of trust and cooperation. . . . The rule advocated in the complaint ironically would penalize a company for discharging an at-will employee when the employment relationship has completely soured.[66]

---

[65]Kavanagh v. KLM Royal Dutch Airlines, 566 F. Supp. 242, 244, 115 LRRM 4266, 4267 (N.D. Ill. 1983) (applying Illinois law).

[66]*Id.* at 244, 115 LRRM at 4267-68.

Similar reasoning has prompted ten other jurisdictions to reject public policy claims advanced by employees who were discharged because they filed suit against their employers.[67]

Similarly, the courts have been hesitant to borrow the concept of the presumption of innocence, which is constitutionally guaranteed in criminal cases, to limit the discretion of private sector employers. In *Cisco v. United Parcel Services*,[68] the plaintiff alleged that he was unjustly accused of stealing property from customers, and that his employer forced him to resign under threat of termination. After he was tried and acquitted, the plaintiff alleged that his former employer refused to reinstate him. He argued to the Pennsylvania appellate court that terminating and refusing to rehire him violated the presumption of innocence, and a public policy against unwarranted stigmatization of criminal offenders who may have become law-abiding citizens. The court dismissed the case on the ground that the employer had a legitimate interest in protecting its reputation:

> [T]he employer, for a legitimate business reason, cannot risk [employing] someone under suspicion of having committed theft and trespass if the nature of its business is to enter onto the premises of others and to deliver parcels which belong to them.[69]

In contrast, in *Hunter v. Port Authority of Allegheny County*,[70] an employer refused to hire an individual who had been convicted thirteen years earlier of assault arising from a domestic dispute, and who had been unconditionally pardoned for that offense. A lower court upheld the employer's refusal to hire the individual for a bus driver position, on the ground that drivers needed to be able to deal with the public under stressful conditions without committing assaults. The Pennsylvania appellate court reversed, stating "that when a public employer denies employment to an individual because of his criminal record, the employer's denial of employment must be reasonably related to the furtherance of a legitimate public objective."[71] The appellate court instructed the lower court to review all of the circumstances of the case, including why the applicant was pardoned for the

---

[67]The following cases have rejected public policy claims brought by employees who sued their employers: Peoples Sec. Life Ins. Co. v. Watson, 81 Md. App. 420, 568 A.2d 835, 5 IER Cases 71 (1990); Abrams v. Echlin Corp., 174 Ill. App. 3d 434, 528 N.E.2d 429, 3 IER Cases 1191 (1988); Beam v. IPCO Corp., 883 F.2d 242, 2 IER Cases 1697 (7th Cir. 1988) (applying Wisconsin law); Clement v. Farmers Ins. Exch., 115 Idaho 298, 766 P.2d 768 (1988); Alexander v. Kay Findlay Jewelers, 208 N.J. Super. 503, 506 A.2d 379 (1986); Morgan Drive Away v. Brant, 489 N.E.2d 933, 1 IER Cases 961, 122 LRRM 2130 (Ind. 1986); Allen v. Safeway Stores, 699 P.2d 277, 120 LRRM 2987 (Wyo. 1985); Khanna v. Microdata Corp., 170 Cal. App. 3d 250, 215 Cal. Rptr. 860, 120 LRRM 2152, 1 IER Cases 1854 (1985); Buysse v. Paine, Webber, Jackson & Curtis, 623 F.2d 1244 (8th Cir. 1980) (applying Minnesota law); Daniel v. Magma Copper Co., 127 Ariz. 320, 620 P.2d 699, 115 LRRM 4326 (1980); DeMarco v. Publix Super Markets, 360 So. 2d 134, 115 LRRM 4784 (Fla. Sup. Ct. 1980).

[68]328 Pa. Super. 300, 476 A.2d 1340, 116 LRRM 2514 (1984).

[69]*Id.* at 308, 476 A.2d at 1344, 116 LRRM at 2517. *See also* Paca v. K-Mart Corp., 108 N.M. 479, 775 P.2d 245, 4 IER Cases 727 (1989) (no cause of action for dismissal based on implied accusation of embezzlement); Morris v. Hartford Courant Co., 200 Conn. 676, 513 A.2d 66 (1986) (no cause of action for allegedly negligent accusation of misappropriation of company funds).

[70]277 Pa. Super. 4, 419 A.2d 631 (1980).

[71]*Id.* at 17, 419 A.2d at 638.

assault. The holding of this case does not preclude employers from acting upon an employee's criminal record, but only requires that any adverse action be directly related to public objectives. Accordingly, the case applies the presumption of innocence in a limited fashion to the employment context.

In addition to the express constitutional guarantees of free speech and access to the courts, it has been argued that the United States Constitution impliedly guarantees a right of privacy. Most attempts to apply implied rights of privacy to private sector employment have not succeeded. For example, several jurisdictions have held that discharge for violation of an employer's policy against dating subordinates does not violate any right of privacy with respect to social relationships.[72] Laudable as adult education may be, a Kentucky appellate court rejected a claim in which the plaintiff alleged that he had been discharged because he was attending night law school, in violation of privacy rights to use his free time as he saw fit.[73]

Whistleblowing

The first branch of the public policy doctrine protects passive whistleblowers who refuse to commit illegal acts. Thus, the public policy doctrine in most jurisdictions protects the narrow category of passive whistleblowers. Active whistleblowers, who may object to their employers' practices inside or outside their organizations, have received varied treatment throughout the country. At this time, no separate branch of the public policy doctrine has been recognized for all whistleblowers under all circumstances. Rather, the courts have proceeded on a case-by-case basis to determine whether a particular whistleblower should be protected under the specific facts of each case. Because the common law continues to develop in this manner, there is currently no consensus among the jurisdictions of this country regarding the circumstances under which whistleblowers should or should not be protected. As might be expected, however, the courts have drawn distinctions between whistleblower cases based upon many of the same considerations reflected in the state statutes discussed in Chapters 3 and 4.

What May Be Complained About

The fundamental problem in all public policy cases is how judges should define what is in the public interest. In whistleblowing cases, the answer to this question determines the subjects about which

---

[72]Ward v. Frito-Lay, 95 Wis. 2d 372, 290 N.W.2d 536, 115 LRRM 4320 (1980); Crosier v. United Parcel Serv., 150 Cal. App. 3d 1132, 198 Cal. Rptr. 361, 115 LRRM 3585 (1983).

[73]Scroghan v. Kraftco, 551 S.W.2d 811, 115 LRRM 4769 (Ky. App. 1977).

whistleblowers may or may not legitimately complain. The nature of this problem was described by the Connecticut Supreme Court as follows:

> The issue then becomes the familiar common-law problem of deciding where and how to draw the line between claims that genuinely involve the mandates of public policy and are actionable, and ordinary disputes between employee and employer that are not. We are mindful that courts should not lightly intervene to impair the exercise of managerial discretion or to prevent unwarranted litigation. We are, however, equally mindful that the myriad of employees without the bargaining power to command employment contracts for a definite term are entitled to a modicum of judicial protection when their conduct as good citizens is punished by their employers.[74]

Criminal Activity

As noted previously, the courts have most readily accepted criminal laws as the strongest expression of public policy, and have protected passive whistleblowers who refuse to commit crimes. The judiciary has also been very protective of active whistleblowers who complain about allegedly criminal activity.

One of the first cases to protect an active whistleblower who complained about criminal activities was decided in 1978 by the West Virginia Supreme Court of Appeals. In *Harless v. First National Bank*,[75] the employee alleged that he was discharged in retaliation for his efforts to require his employer to comply with the state and federal consumer credit laws, which contained both civil and criminal penalties. The court reasoned:

> Here, the plaintiff's complaint refers to intentional violation . . . made by the defendants, which he endeavored to have stopped. This statutory provision is commonly known as the West Virginia Consumer Credit and Protection Act. [Citation omitted.] We need not discuss the act in detail in order to conclude that it represents a comprehensive attempt on the part of the legislature to extend protection to the consumers and persons who obtain credit in this State and who obviously constitute the vast majority of our adult citizens. . . . Not only did the Legislature regulate various consumer and credit practices, but it went further and established the right to civil action for damages on behalf of persons who have been subjected to practices that violate certain provisions of the act. In addition, criminal violations are sanctioned for certain willful violations. . . . We have no hesitation in stating that the Legislature intended to establish a clear and unequivocal public policy that consumers of credit covered by the Act would be given protection. Such manifest public policy should not be frustrated by a holding that an employee of a lending institution governed by the Act, who seeks to ensure that compliance is being made with the Act, can be discharged without being furnished a cause of action for such discharge.[76]

---

[74]Sheets v. Teddy's Frosted Foods, 179 Conn. 471, 427 A.2d 385, 387-88, 115 LRRM 4626, 4628 (1980).

[75]162 W. Va. 116, 246 S.E.2d 270, 115 LRRM 4380 (1978).

[76]*Id.* at 125-26, 246 S.E.2d at 275-76, 115 LRRM at 4384.

Similarly, in *Petrik v. Monarch Printing Corp.*,[77] Emil Petrik alleged that he came across a discrepancy in the employer's financial records in the course of his employment as vice president of finance. Petrick informed the president of the company, who requested that the plaintiff investigate the discrepancy. Petrik further alleged that at the end of his investigation it appeared that funds had been embezzled from the employer. He notified the president of the company that certain officers or employers of the company might have violated the criminal laws of Illinois. Petrik contended that he had been discharged in order to conceal the wrongdoing and in retaliation for his efforts to ensure that management complied with the requirements of the criminal law. The Illinois Appellate Court stated that, "it is apparent that Petrik's complaint involves something more than an ordinary internal dispute between an employee and his employer."[78] Other jurisdictions have also followed the rationale of *Harless* and *Petrik*.[79]

Given the strong public policies underlying the criminal law, it is not unexpected that one of the broadest forms of whistleblower protection arose in a case involving alleged criminal activities. In *Palmateer v. International Harvester Co.*,[80] a case decided by the Illinois Supreme Court, Ray Palmateer alleged that he was discharged for supplying information to local law enforcement authorities that another employee might be involved in petty theft, and for agreeing to assist in the investigation and trial of the employee as requested. The court stated:

> There is no public policy more basic, nothing more implicit in the concept of ordered liberty [citations omitted] than the enforcement of a state's criminal code. [Citations omitted.] There is no public policy more important or more fundamental than the one favoring the effective protection of the lives and property of citizens. [Citations omitted.] No specific constitutional or statutory provision requires a citizen to take an active part in the ferreting out and prosecution of crime, but public policy nevertheless favors citizen crime-fighters. Public policy favors the exposure of crime, and the cooperation of citizens possessing knowledge thereof is essential to effective implementation of that policy. Persons acting in good faith who have probable cause to believe crimes have been committed should not be deterred from reporting them by the fear of unfounded suits by those accused. . . . [Citations omitted.]
>
> Public policy favors Palmateer's conduct in volunteering information to the law-enforcement agency. Once the possibility of crime was reported, Palmateer was under a statutory duty to further assist officials when requested to do so.[81]

---

[77]111 Ill. App. 3d 502, 444 N.E.2d 588, 115 LRRM 4520 (1982).

[78]*Id.* at 508, 444 N.E.2d at 592, 115 LRRM at 4523.

[79]*See* Palmer v. Brown, 242 Kan. 893, 752 P.2d 685 (1988) (employee allegedly discharged for reporting Medicaid fraud); Adler v. American Standard Corp., 538 F. Supp. 572 (D.Md. 1982) (employee allegedly discharged for complaining to superiors about violations of federal antitrust, tax, and foreign corrupt practices laws).

[80]85 Ill. 2d 124, 421 N.E.2d 876, 115 LRRM 4165 (1981).

[81]*Id.* at 132-33, 421 N.E.2d at 879-80, 115 LRRM at 4168.

The principle that citizens should be encouraged to report violations of law is recognized in numerous contexts outside of the employment relationship. Several federal statutes provide rewards for persons who report illegal conduct to the proper authorities, the most familiar of which is the federal tax informer statute, which permits the Secretary of Treasury to reward an informant whose report leads to detection and punishment of any person who violates the tax laws. A similar but less well-known provision is contained in the customs laws.[82]

In the employment context, however, different considerations come into play. The tax and customs informer statutes encourage citizens to report allegedly illegal conduct of persons suspected of violating the federal tax or customs laws, who may not necessarily be co-workers. However, the rationale of *Palmateer* encourages informing upon one's co-workers. Because of the natural competitive tendencies in any workplace, an individual might have conflicting motives for bringing accusations of misconduct against co-workers, who might also happen to be competitors for pay raises or promotions. Moreover, workplaces may generate petty jealousies and animosities between co-workers, or between superiors and subordinates which might prompt unfounded recriminations. As discussed earlier in this chapter, the Ohio legislature was sufficiently concerned about improperly motivated complaints about co-workers that it required employees to report such complaints internally. As might be expected, whether employees should be protected for accusing co-workers of violating the law has been sharply debated in the cases. Several justices of the Illinois Supreme Court dissented from the *Palmateer* decision based upon similar reservations:

> It should be remembered that the plaintiff was not a unionized employee, but held a position in management. By assuming the role of a citizen crime-fighter, undertaking to ferret out crime for the police the plaintiff, through his spying, could seriously affect the labor relations of his employer. Also, his conduct, without consulting the proper management personnel, could impair the company's internal security program. In other words, the plaintiff here had taken it upon himself to become involved in crime fighting when it was neither required by law, nor by his employment, and obviously was against the wishes of his employer.[83]

In recognition of the complexities of the employment relationship, several jurisdictions have refused to follow the rationale of *Palmateer*, which involved an external whistleblower, in cases involving internal whistleblowers who do not make reports to law enforcement officials. For example, in *Vonch v. Carlson Companies*,[84] the plaintiff alleged

---

[82]The tax informer statute is codified at 26 U.S.C. §7623 (1988), and the regulations implementing the statute are found at 26 C.F.R. §301-7623-1. The customs informer statute is codified at 19 U.S.C. §1619 (1988).

[83]*Supra* note 80 at 142, 421 N.E.2d at 884, 115 LRRM at 4172.

[84]439 N.W. 2d 406, 4 IER Cases 789 (Minn. App. 1989).

that he was discharged because he complained that his supervisor's alleged travel and expense account improprieties amounted to theft and fraud. The court rejected this claim on the grounds that travel and expense improprieties were internal company matters which did not directly affect the public health or safety. Several other jurisdictions have followed this rationale.[85]

Two California decisions appear to limit the *Palmateer* rationale because of concerns regarding improperly motivated complaints. Those decisions refused to protect whistleblowers whose complaints were based upon speculation about criminal activities of fellow employees. In *Foley v. Interactive Data Corp.*,[86] discussed in detail in Chapter 2, the plaintiff alleged that he learned that his new supervisor was being investigated by the FBI for suspected embezzlement from the new supervisor's previous employer. The plaintiff alleged that he was discharged because he had voiced concern about the new supervisor and his past criminal conduct. As previously discussed, the court ruled that no public interest was involved in the case. Although not expressly stated, the court's reluctance to recognize a public policy claim appears to have been influenced by the possibility that the plaintiff's motives were suspect.

Similarly, in *Read v. City of Lynwood*,[87] Sandra Read was employed as the city's community development director, and reported directly to the city manager. Read contended that she had heard that a developer for a city project that was favored by the city manager had earlier attempted to bribe a city employee, and that she opposed the developer because she believed it to be the least qualified for the project. Read further alleged that she was informed that city employees were performing work for the city manager at his home on city time, and that the city manager frequently used erratic, volatile, and unpredictable methods of management, including undermining the authority of those in positions inferior to him. Read alleged that she met with the mayor and told him about her misgivings regarding the city manager's management abilities, and alleged that her position was eliminated in retaliation for voicing her concerns about the city manager to the mayor.

The court rejected the plaintiff's public policy claim because of the vague nature of the plaintiff's allegations of purported criminal conduct:

---

[85]Winters v. Houston Chronicle Publishing Co., 795 S.W.2d 723, 5 IER Cases 1185 (Tex. 1990) (alleged inventory theft and kickbacks); Leibowitz v. Bank Leumi Trust Co., 152 A.D. 2d 169, 548 N.Y.S.2d 513, 4 IER Cases 1786 (1989) (alleged fraud in loan documentation); Hineline v. Stroudsburg Elec. Supply, 384 Pa. Super. 537, 559 A.2d 566 (1989) (allegedly illegal video cameras used for surveillance); Mello v. Stop & Shop Cos., 402 Mass. 555, 524 N.E. 2d 105, 3 IER Cases 1105 (1988) (alleged inventory shortages and false claims based thereon).

[86]47 Cal. 3d 654, 254 Cal. Rptr. 211, 765 P.2d 373, 3 IER Cases 1729 (1988). *See also* Mello v. Stop & Shop Cos., *supra* note 85 (internal complaint about illegal activity not protected); Wiltsie v. Baby Grand Corp., 744 P.2d 432, 4 IER Cases 638 (Nev. 1989) (same).

[87]173 Cal. App. 3d 437, 219 Cal. Rptr. 26 (1985).

She alleges only that she heard the developer had at one time attempted to bribe a city employee. Nowhere is it alleged that the city manager or mayor participated in any way in the bribery attempt or that the developer was bribing or attempting to bribe them. Appellant hearing of an attempt proves nothing against anyone; nor does the fact the city manager and mayor favored appointment of this developer. . . . She alleges that she received "some information to the effect that" city employees were working on the city manager's home on city time. Receipt of information does not constitute proof of the misconduct alleged. . . . What this amounts to is an admission that she did not like the city manager's management approach. Such is her prerogative. However nowhere does she plead that any statute or public policy prevents termination of a probationary employee who voices his or her dissatisfaction with a superior's management style.[88]

The *Foley* and *Read* decisions suggest that the courts may not be receptive to whistleblowers who do not have direct personal knowledge of alleged criminal activities. Whistleblowers who do have personal knowledge of illegal conduct, because they also participated in it, are frequently excluded from protection by whistleblower protection statutes. Nevertheless, one Connecticut appellate court protected an employee who had committed criminal acts, but who later cooperated in an auditor's investigation to uncover the illegal scheme.[89] No other jurisdiction appears to have gone to this extreme to encourage reporting of crimes, and in view of the many statutes denying protection to participants in illegal activities, it may be that other jurisdictions will not protect such employees.

Violations of Noncriminal Laws

As is true in cases that have protected passive whistleblowers, the cases protecting active whistleblowers do not draw any distinctions between complaints about violations of criminal or civil laws. For example, in *Thompson v. St. Regis Paper Co.*,[90] the court recognized a cause of action on behalf of a plaintiff who alleged that he was discharged because he had implemented an accounting program in compliance with the Foreign Corrupt Practices Act of 1977 (FCPA). The plaintiff contended that his discharge was a warning to all other accounting personnel that they should not actively enforce the FCPA. Although no allegation of criminal conduct was alleged, the court decided that a public policy claim should be created.

A more complex set of facts was presented in *McQuary v. Bel Air Convalescent Home*,[91] where the employee was the director of nurses' training and education at a nursing home. The employee's aunt became a patient of the nursing home, and the aunt was accused by the

[88] *Id.* at 444, 445.

[89] Schmidt v. Yardney Elec. Corp., 4 Conn. App. 69, 492 A.2d 512 (1985).

[90] 102 Wash. 2d 219, 685 P.2d 1081, 1 IER Cases 392, 116 LRRM 3142 (1984).

[91] 69 Or. App. 107, 684 P.2d 21, 120 LRRM 3129 (1984).

administrator of the home of accidentally starting a fire. The employee threatened to report the administrator's purported abuse of her aunt to the state agency with jurisdiction over patient care, and was then fired by the administrator. Despite the overtones of overzealous family loyalty, the Oregon Court of Appeal reasoned:

> The evidence in this case would permit a jury to find that [the administrator] discharged plaintiff because she had threatened to report his actions to the Health Division and that she believed in good faith that his action violated her aunt's rights under the Nursing Home Patient's Bill of Rights. [Citations.] The Health Division is charged with protecting patients' rights under the act, and a report to it would be a societal obligation of a person who knows of violations. The legislature's desire to protect patients, which reflects a comparable concern on the part of the federal government, shows that the protection is an important public policy analogous to the performance of jury duty or the avoidance of defamation, policies which the Supreme Court has found to justify wrongful discharge claims.[92]

Because of the public interest in safe medical care, several other whistleblower claims involving allegations of unsafe medical or nursing care have been upheld.[93]

However, a federal court located in Illinois refused to protect an employee who complained internally about alleged violations of a statute which provided neither criminal nor civil penalties. In *Hicks v. Resolution Trust Corp.*,[94] the plaintiff was a bank officer responsible for compliance with the federal Community Reinvestment Act, and who complained that the bank was not complying with the Act. However, the Act contained no criminal or civil sanctions, but only allowed federal bank regulators to take the bank's compliance record into account in making regulatory decisions. The court dismissed the plaintiff's suit because it held that violations of the Act did not "pose a serious threat to the health and safety of Illinois citizens."[95]

The common law regarding the subjects about which whistleblowers may complain closely parallels the state protections for private sector employees. Many jurisdictions have created common-law protections for employees who report violations of federal, state, or local laws. However, as illustrated in the following sections, most jurisdictions have been reluctant to broaden the subjects of protected complaints beyond violations of statutes.[96]

---

[92]*Id.* at 110, 684 P.2d at 23, 120 LRRM at 3130.

[93]Hibbert v. Centennial Villas, Inc., 56 Wash. App. 889, 786 P.2d 309, 5 IER Cases 161 (1990) (recognizing cause of action of discharged nurse but dismissing claim for lack of specificity); McCool v. Hillhaven Corp., 97 Or. App. 536, 777 P.2d 1013, 4 IER Cases 1026 (1989) (recognizing cause of action for discharge because of complaints about patient abuse in convalescent home).

[94]736 F. Supp. 812, 5 IER Cases 772 (N.D. Ill. 1990).

[95]*Id.* at 818.

[96]The courts have generally insisted that the public policy relied upon by active whistleblowers be premised upon a statutory or constitutional provision that has allegedly been violated. Nevertheless, there may be some instances where an employee's complaint will be protected, even though he does not claim that any law has been violated, if the complaint is aimed at serving the interests of the public or of co-workers. For example, California has created a public policy claim on behalf of an employee who alleged that he had been dismissed because of his efforts to secure a reasonably smoke-free workplace for himself and other employees. In Hentzel

Product Safety

The safety of products in many industries is not regulated by criminal or civil statutes. Instead, the only remedy for individuals who are harmed by unsafe products may be a civil action for damages for any personal injuries they have suffered. Although there is undoubtedly public interest in the manufacture and distribution of safe products, that interest is sufficiently indirect that courts have generally refused to protect whistleblowers who complain about product safety.

One of the first cases to consider the claim of a whistleblower involved allegedly unsafe steel products. In *Geary v. United States Steel Corp.*,[97] which reached the Pennsylvania Supreme Court in

---

v. Singer Co., 138 Cal. App. 3d 290, 188 Cal. Rptr. 159, 115 LRRM 4036 (1982), the plaintiff alleged that his discharge contravened the policies expressed in several California labor statutes which require employers to provide safe work environments, and the California equivalent of the federal Occupational Safety and Health Act (CALOSHA). The defendant argued that the plaintiff could have sought relief under the antiretaliation provisions of CALOSHA, and therefore that CALOSHA either was the plaintiff's exclusive remedy, or imposed a requirement that plaintiff exhaust the administrative remedy provided in CALOSHA. Although the California Court of Appeal recognized that no private right of action existed under the federal OSHA, the court held that CALOSHA did not preclude an action for wrongful discharge and did not impose any exhaustion requirement. The court reasoned that because the public policy doctrine established by *Petermann, supra*, pre-dated the enactment of CALOSHA, the question was not whether a public policy claim should be created, but whether CALOSHA destroyed any preexisting common law remedies. Because the court found no legislative intent to destroy any preexisting remedies, the plaintiff was permitted to assert a public policy cause of action. *See also* Reed v. Municipality of Anchorage, 741 P.2d 1181, 4 IER Cases 1613 (1989) (Alaska OSHA not exclusive remedy); Skillsky v. Lucky Stores, Inc., 893 F.2d 1088 (9th Cir. 1990) (California public policy prevented discharge of employee by second employer based on workplace safety complaint to first employer).

At least one jurisdiction has refused to follow this rationale because, as discussed in Chapter 7, most jurisdictions have been hesitant to create a public policy remedy where a preexisting statute already provides one. Jones v. Industrial Electric-Seattle, 53 Wash. App. 536, 768 P.2d 520 (1989) (Washington workplace safety statute provided exclusive remedy for retaliatory discharge).

[97]456 Pa. 171, 319 A.2d 174, 115 LRRM 4665 (1974). The complaint of another employee was rejected in Percival v. General Motors Corp., 400 F. Supp. 1322 (E.D. Mo. 1975), *aff'd*, 539 F.2d 1126 (8th Cir. 1976), where the plaintiff was employed as the head of the Mechanical Development Department at the time of his termination. Plaintiff alleged that he was discharged because he took action both within and without the corporate structure to correct misleading statements made by the employer regarding its work on alternative power plants. Plaintiff contended that the company conveyed false and misleading information to stockholders in annual reports and flyers and to the general public in nationwide full-page newspaper advertisements. Plaintiff also contended that he was reprimanded for conveying truthful information to representatives of another corporation with whom General Motors was negotiating renewal of a joint venture in the development of an alternative power plant. Applying Missouri law, the court held that the plaintiff could not state a claim, stating:

> It should be kept in mind that as far as an employment relationship is concerned, an employer as well as an employee has rights; and it should also be kept in mind that a large corporate employer such as General Motors, except to the extent limited by statute or contractual obligations, must be accorded wide latitude in determining whom it will employ and retain in employment in high and sensitive managerial positions particularly where developments in the field of mechanical engineering are involved.

539 F.2d at 1130.

Another case involving safety of an employer's product was presented in Yaindl v. Ingersoll-Rand Co., 281 Pa. Super. 560, 422 A.2d 611, 115 LRRM 4738 (1980). Plaintiff was employed as manager of customer services and technical services engineer, and was asked by the company to travel to Italy to inspect certain pumps that the company had sold to an Italian steel company. Plaintiff analyzed the problem and submitted a report to management which recommended replacement of the pumps. The report antagonized the manufacturing manager, however, because it implicitly criticized the manufacturing operations. Plaintiff then accused the manufacturing manager of lying to another company official regarding inspection of the pumps prior to shipment to the Italian company. After a heated argument, no resolution of this issue was

1974, George Geary was a salesman who sold tubular products to the oil and gas industry. Geary alleged that he complained to a vice-president in charge of sales of tubular casing, designed for use under high pressure, that the product had not been adequately tested and constituted a serious danger to anyone who used it. Geary further alleged that as a result of his efforts the product was reevaluated and withdrawn from the market. The court stated that under exceptional circumstances it might recognize a cause of action where an employer's decision to discharge an employee was based on an improper motive. However, the court declined to recognize a cause of action for Geary for the following reasons:

> The facts alleged show only that there was a dispute over the merits of the new product; that Geary vigorously expressed his own point of view in the matter, bypassing his immediate superiors and taking his case to a company vice-president, and that he was ultimately discharged. There is nothing here from which we could infer that the company fired Geary for the specific purpose of causing him harm, or coercing him to break any law or otherwise to compromise himself. According to his own averments, Geary had already won his own battle within the company. The most natural inference from the change of events recited in the complaint is that Geary had made a nuisance of himself, and the company discharged him to preserve administrative order in its own house. . . . Geary asserts in his complaint that he was acting in the best interests of the general public as well as of his employer in opposing the marketing of a product which he believed to be defective. Certainly, the potential for abuse of an employer's power of dismissal is particularly serious where an employee must exercise independent, expert judgment in matters of product safety, but Geary does not hold himself out as this sort of employee. So far as the complaint shows, he was involved only in the sale of company products. There is no suggestion that he possessed any expert qualifications, or that his duties extended to making judgments in matters of product safety. In essence, Geary argues that his conduct should be protected because his intentions were good. No doubt most employees who are dismissed from their posts can make the same claim. We doubt that establishing a right to litigate every such case as it

---

achieved. Thereafter, plaintiff was transferred to another position which he refused to accept, and was then discharged. Plaintiff contended that his discharge was contrary to public policy because the pumps posed a serious safety hazard to people working nearby if they broke down. The court rejected this argument:

> We are unable, however, to discern any clear public policy that was threatened by appellant's discharge. . . . No indication of the specific hazards supposedly posed by the pumps at the [Italian] plant is to be found in the record, nor any instance of an injury caused by any pump sold by [the employer] to the Italian company or anyone else. Moreover, there is no evidence that [the employer] attempted to hide from [the Italian company], the defects in the pumps, or deny its responsibility for the defects. [Plaintiff] admits that his recommendations regarding repair of the pumps were, in general, accepted by [the employer], and that the defective pump rods were replaced within a reasonable time. . . .

Id. at 578-79, 422 A.2d at 620-21, 115 LRRM at 4745-46. Thus, the court viewed the case as presenting simply "an internal squabble concerning the manufacturing processes necessary to insure satisfactory performance of [the employer's] pumps. . . ." *Id.* at 579, 422 A.2d at 621, 115 LRRM at 4746. While the employee in *Yaindl* was in a position to make a judgment as to the safety of a product, the case did not involve the employer's attempt to cover up the fact that the product might have been defective. Rather, the court viewed the case as presenting a situation where the employee correctly pointed out a problem with the product, but voiced his opposition in such a way to disrupt the orderly management of the company.

arises would operate either in the best interests of the party or of the public.[98]

As noted above, one of the recurring themes in whistleblower cases is competition with co-workers. In this regard, the court noted:

> The problem extends beyond the question of individual competence, for even an unusually gifted person may be of no use to his employer if he cannot work effectively with fellow employees. Here, for example, Geary's complaint shows that he by-passed his immediate superiors and pressed his views on higher officers, utilizing his close contact with a company vice-president. The praiseworthiness of Geary's motives does not detract from the company's legitimate interest in preserving its normal operational procedures from disruption.[99]

The safety of pharmaceutical products was called into question in *Campbell v. Eli Lilly & Co.*[100] James Campbell was employed as a researcher by a manufacturer of pharmaceuticals. Campbell's attorney told the employer's staff counsel that Campbell had knowledge of various acts of misconduct by his superiors, and that Campbell questioned the safety of several of the drugs which he had researched. Campbell was placed on a paid leave of absence pending an investigation of his allegations. After the investigation was completed, Campbell reiterated his allegations of misconduct and contended that his work had saved the company approximately $500,000,000 in future product liability claims against the company. The employer concluded Campbell's allegations were false and discharged him. Campbell contended that his discharge violated public policy, in that the federal laws regarding manufacture of drugs required employers to submit all relevant data regarding drugs to the United States Food and Drug Administration (FDA). Campbell argued that if his discharge were allowed, other employees would be deterred from ensuring that the FDA obtained all relevant information. The Indiana appellate court rejected this argument because "[Campbell] has nowhere demonstrated a statutory source for the alleged right he claims to have exercised, nor has he demonstrated a statutory source for the duty he claims to have fulfilled."[101]

Unlike whistleblowers who can point to a specific law or regulation that has been violated, employees who complain about product safety may not be able to rely upon any statute. Because of judicial hesitance to intrude upon the legislative domain of defining public policy, whistleblowers who complain about product safety may not be protected if they cannot identify a law or regulation that is violated by the unsafe product.

---

[98]456 Pa. at 180-181, 319 A.2d at 178-79, 115 LRRM at 4668.

[99]*Id.* at 182-83, 319 A.2d at 179-180, 115 LRRM at 4669.

[100]413 N.E.2d 1054, 115 LRRM 4417 (1980).

[101]*Id.* at 1061, 115 LRRM at 4421.

Policy Disagreements

As a general rule, the courts have not created claims for whistleblowers whose complaints are based upon personal opinions regarding the way an organization is managed, rather than upon legal or ethical violations. For example, the plaintiff in *Rossi v. Pennsylvania State University*[102] alleged that he was discharged because he had complained that the department in which he worked was mismanaged. However, he did not claim that any law had been violated. The Pennsylvania appellate court refused to recognize a cause of action, stating:

> The question before us is whether there is a public policy against firing an employee who continuously complains about what he considers to be poor management of the unit in which he is an employee. . . . We think not. Initially this would have the unwise effect of transferring to the judicial forum the duty of evaluating the propriety of management decisions.[103]

Similarly, in *Schultz v. Industrial Coils, Inc.*,[104] the plaintiff was discharged for writing a letter criticizing the management practices of the officers of his employer to the editor of the local newspaper. The Wisconsin appellate court affirmed a summary judgment in favor of the employer, and stated:

> [A]n employer need not tolerate actions which undermine his or her authority, or are otherwise disruptive of office routine or employment routine or employment relations, in the name of a limited free speech interest.[105]

Good management includes not only deciding policy issues, but also providing leadership by setting an example of good behavior to be followed by others in an organization. An employee who felt that a superior who was having an extramarital affair was providing poor leadership was not protected by the Indiana courts in *Hillenbrand v. City of Evansville*.[106] The employee alleged that he was dismissed because he inadvertently observed a supervisor's extramarital activities. The court held that no public policy claim existed because the plaintiff was not required by any statute to monitor his supervisor's alleged misconduct.

---

[102] 340 Pa. Super. 39, 489 A.2d 828 (1985). Similarly, in Smith-Pfeffer v. Superintendent, Fernald School, 404 Mass. 145, 533 N.E.2d 1368, 4 IER Cases 289 (1989), the plaintiff, who was the director of a unit of a facility for the mentally retarded, was terminated because she disagreed with the way the facility was managed. The court rejected the plaintiff's claim on the ground that internal management disputes did not implicate public policy. *See also* Bourque v. Town of Bow, 736 F. Supp. 398 (D.N.H. 1990) (criticism of superior's shortcomings did not implicate public policy); Dicomes v. Washington, 113 Wash. 2d 612, 782 P.2d 1002, 4 IER Cases 1630 (1989) (disagreement regarding use of state funds did not rise to level of legal violation).

[103] 340 Pa. at 54, 489 A.2d at 836.

[104] 125 Wis. 2d 520, 373 N.W.2d 74 (1985).

[105] *Id.* at 526, 373 N.W.2d at 77.

[106] 457 N.E.2d 236, 115 LRRM 2219 (Ind. App. 1983).

Government or Private Sector Employment

Most public policy cases have been brought by employees in the private sector, perhaps because government employees may have statutory civil service remedies, while private sector employees may not. As discussed in Chapter 3, virtually any mismanagement in government affects the public interest because public monies may be squandered. Nevertheless, the courts have reached different conclusions in considering the definition of public policy in the context of government employment.

In *Rossi v. Pennsylvania State University*,[107] the Pennsylvania appellate court held that public policy was not directly implicated, even though the plaintiff complained about allegedly poor management, because of the absence of allegations of fraud or misuse of public funds. However, in *Vigil v. Arzola*[108] the New Mexico Court of Appeals created a public policy claim for an employee who alleged that he was dismissed for having complained about his employer's alleged personal use of federal and state funding, which rose above the level of negligent management.

Moreover, in *Pilcher v. Board of County Comm'rs*,[109] the plaintiff was a county employee who alleged that she was terminated because she opposed the hiring of a corrections employee who allegedly was unqualified, but who was hired due to political pressure. The court stated that public policy was implicated because "questionable hiring practices . . . ultimately would have a detrimental effect on the general welfare of the taxpayers of Wyandotte County."[110] Thus, the common-law protection for government whistleblowers may be broader than for private sector whistleblowers, in that complaints about mismanagement may be protected.

When, to Whom, How, and Why Complaints May Be Made

The previous section illustrates that the common law recognizes that the public interest in private sector employment is less direct than it is in government employment. This is also reflected in the state statutes protecting private sector whistleblowers. The common law also parallels the state whistleblower protection laws in striking a balance between the duty of loyalty and civic obligations.

Like most legislatures that have protected private sector whistleblowers, the majority of courts have also refused to protect private sector employees who fail to work within the internal channels of their organization. For example, in *Rozier v. St. Mary's Hospital*[111] the

---

[107]*Supra* note 102 at 54, 489 A.2d at 836.

[108]102 N.M. 689, 699 P.2d 613, 2 IER Cases 377 (1983).

[109]14 Kan. App. 2d 206, 787 P.2d 1204, 5 IER Cases 150 (1990).

[110]*Id.*, 787 P.2d at 1209, 5 IER Cases at 153.

[111]88 Ill. App. 3d 994, 411 N.E.2d 50, 115 LRRM 4391 (1980).

plaintiff informed a newspaper that other employees had improperly treated patients in the hospital and had been intoxicated on the job, but the plaintiff had not made any attempt to correct these circumstances within the channels of the hospital. The court implicitly held that a discharge of an employee for publicizing an internal dispute without making any good-faith efforts to resolve the dispute through proper channels was permissible.

Several courts have rejected claims of private sector employees who bypass internal channels by contacting the news media. The Wisconsin appellate courts have rejected two such claims. The first of these, the *Schultz v. Industrial Coils, Inc.*[112] decision discussed earlier in this chapter, involved a plaintiff who criticized his management in an open letter to the local newspaper. In the second case, the *Harman v. La Crosse Tribune*[113] decision also discussed earlier in this chapter, the court refused to protect an attorney who held a press conference urging prosecution of several employees of a client of his law firm. Similarly, a federal court applying New York law refused to protect an employee who gave a newspaper interview which resulted in adverse publicity for her employer.[114] In contrast to these cases involving private sector employment, a public sector employee who was terminated because the employer believed that she was responsible for a negative newspaper article was protected in *Pilcher v. Board of County Commissioners*.[115]

The majority of the decisions discussed in the preceding section protect active whistleblowers who complain internally, but who have not contacted an appropriate enforcement authority. Although not necessarily expressed in such terms, the rationale of these cases appears to be that loyal employees, who do not go outside their organizations, should not have less protection than employees who could be considered more disruptive by complaining outside their organizations.

An embryonic whistleblower was protected in *Johnston v. Del Mar Distrib. Co.*[116] in a manner similar to the state statutes discussed in chapters 3 and 4. The plaintiff in that case alleged that she was asked to mislabel a shipment of firearms, and that she was terminated after she contacted the federal Bureau of Alcohol, Tobacco & Firearms to determine whether the mislabeling was illegal. She had not yet complained about or refused to perform the mislabeling at the time she was terminated. The court reasoned as follows:

> It is implicit that in order to refuse to do an illegal act, an employee must either know or suspect that the requested act is illegal. In some cases it will be patently obvious that the act is illegal (murder, robbery, theft,

---

[112] *Supra* note 104.

[113] 117 Wis. 2d 448, 344 N.W.2d 536, 115 LRRM 3252 (1984).

[114] Boniuk v. New York Medical College, 535 F. Supp. 1353, 115 LRRM 4643 (S.D.N.Y. 1982).

[115] *Supra* note 109.

[116] 776 S.W.2d 768 (1989).

> etc.); however, in other cases it may not be so apparent. Since ignorance of the law is no defense to a criminal prosecution, it is reasonable to expect that if an employee has a good faith belief that a required act might be illegal, she will try to find out whether the act is in fact illegal prior to deciding what course of action to take. If an employer is allowed to terminate the employee at this point, the public policy exception announced in *Sabine Pilot* would have little or no effect. To hold otherwise would force an employee who suspects that a requested act might be illegal, to: (1) subject herself to possible discharge if she attempts to find out if the act is in fact illegal; or (2) remain ignorant, perform the act and, if it turns out to be illegal, face possible criminal sanctions.[117]

Whether an employee complained to an appropriate authority may be weighed in assessing if a whistleblower is acting from proper or improper motives. The common law has developed a requirement that an employee's complaint be made in good faith, which parallels similar requirements found in state statutes protecting private sector whistleblowers. For instance, the dissenting justices in *Sheets v. Teddy's Frosted Foods*, doubted the plaintiff's good faith by noting that "[t]he plaintiff, if he desired to protect the consumer, could have communicated, even anonymously, to the commissioner of consumer affairs his concerns . . . so as to invoke the statute's enforcement mechanisms."[118] Similarly, in *Campbell v. Eli Lilly & Co.*,[119] the plaintiff's allegations appeared to be an effort to obtain compensation for the money that the plaintiff had allegedly saved the employer in future lawsuits against it, instead of being a good-faith attempt to correct unsafe conditions. Even a dissenting justice, who would have recognized a cause of action on behalf of the plaintiff, stated that he did not appear to be a responsible whistleblower: "Campbell's deposition clearly established as a primary interest of his a desire to be rewarded for allegedly saving Lilly vast sums of money which they would have been compelled to pay in judgments had not his test results revealed the potential hazards of a certain drug."[120] Accordingly, the dissenting justice approved of the result rejecting the plaintiff's claim, on the separate ground that the plaintiff's complaints were made in bad faith. The court also imposed a good-faith requirement in *McQuary v. Bel Air Convalescent Home*,[121] the nursing home decision discussed earlier. The court held that the plaintiff was not required to prove that patient abuse had actually occurred, but only to prove that she had a good-faith belief that a patient had been abused.

Tort or Contract Damages

One of the most significant aspects of the recent public policy cases is that they permit the plaintiff to sue for tort damages, which

[117] *Id.* at 771.

[118] 179 Conn. 471, 482, 427 A.2d 385, 390, 115 LRRM 4626, 4630 (1980).

[119] *Supra* note 100.

[120] *Id.* at 1068, 115 LRRM at 4427.

[121] 69 Or. App. 107, 684 P.2d 21, 120 LRRM 3129 (1984).

exposes employers to damages for pain and suffering and other consequential losses, and to punitive damages in instances where employers have acted outrageously. It has been sharply debated whether the public policy cause of action should entitle a prevailing plaintiff to damages upon a contract theory, which would not include consequential or punitive damages in most jurisdictions, or on a tort theory, which would permit consequential and punitive damages.

With one exception, every jurisdiction has held that tort damages are available in public policy cases. One of the more thoughtful analyses of the legal underpinnings of public policy claims is contained in the California Supreme Court's opinion in *Foley v. Interactive Data Corp.*[122] The court explained that public policy causes of action were not dependent on an express or implied promise in the employment contract. Rather, "[w]hat is vindicated through the cause of action is not the terms or promise arising out of the particular employment relationship involved, but rather the public interest in not permitting employers to impose as a condition of employment a requirement that an employee act in a manner contrary to fundamental public policy."[123] Because the court characterized the source of the employer's duty not to require employees to perform illegal acts as arising from public policy, rather than from the employment contract, the court held that the tort measure of damages was available.

On the other hand, one jurisdiction has taken the position that the tort measure of damages is not recoverable in a public policy case. In *Brockmeyer v. Dun & Bradstreet*,[124] the plaintiff alleged that he was discharged after he was interrogated by his employer as to what he would say in an upcoming sexual harassment case, where the employee complaining of sexual harassment was the plaintiff's girlfriend. The plaintiff contended that the employer was upset because the plaintiff said that he would give testimony favorable to his girlfriend rather than to the company. The employer settled the sex discrimination case out of court before the plaintiff was required to give any testimony. The plaintiff contended that he was discharged because the employer was dissatisfied with his anticipated testimony in the harassment case. The Wisconsin Supreme Court stated that a narrow public policy exception should be adopted, but that the facts of the case before it did not merit its adoption. Although the plaintiff contended that he was discharged for refusing to commit perjury, the court stated:

> The record is devoid of any evidence demonstrating that Dun & Bradstreet asked Brockmeyer to lie. Admittedly, an inference can be drawn from this record that Dun & Bradstreet was concerned over the fact that Brockmeyer would tell the truth if asked to testify at proceedings concerning his former secretary's sex discrimination claim. This

---

[122] 47 Cal. 3d 654, 254 Cal. Rptr. 211, 765 P.2d 373, 3 IER Cases 1729 (1988).

[123] *Id.* at 667 n.7, 668, 254 Cal. Rptr. at 215 n.7, 216, 765 P.2d at 377 n.7, 378, 3 IER Cases at 1732 n.7, 1733.

[124] 113 Wis. 2d 561, 335 N.W.2d 834, 115 LRRM 4484 (1983).

> inference is a far cry from the allegation that Dun & Bradstreet wanted Brockmeyer to commit perjury. There is no clearly defined mandate of public policy against discharging an employee because his testimony may be contrary to an employer's interests. Such behavior may be indicative of bad faith, but it is not contrary to established public policies.[125]

On the issue of damages recoverable in public policy cases, the court held as follows:

> Those cases implying a contractual term of good faith dealing sounded in contract. Most, though not all of the public policy exception cases from other states were tort actions. The most significant distinction in our view between the two causes of action in wrongful discharge suits is in the damages that may be recovered. In tort actions, the only limitations are those of "proximate cause" or public policy considerations. Punitive damages are also allowed. In contract actions, damages are limited by the concepts of forseeability and mitigation. The remedies established by the majority of Wisconsin wrongful discharge statutes are limited to reinstatement and back pay, contractual remedy concepts. We believe that reinstatement and back pay are the most appropriate remedies for public policy exception wrongful discharges since the primary concern in these actions is to make the wronged employee "whole." Therefore, we conclude that a contract action is most appropriate for wrongful discharges.[126]

As Appendix D shows, eight jurisdictions have not yet created public policy causes of action. Assuming that those jurisdictions eventually will consider whether to create a public policy claim, one of the key issues will be whether to adopt the California or Wisconsin approach towards the measure of damages which may be recovered.

Retroactive Application

Although the law of the jurisdiction in which a public policy cause of action arises may permit awards of punitive damages, the courts may refuse to allow a plaintiff to recover punitive damages if, at the time the employer discharged the employee, the employer could not have known that its acts were in violation of public policy. Two of the principal rationales for awarding punitive damages are to punish defendants who knowingly violate the laws, and to deter defendants from committing similar wrongful acts in the future. The first rationale does not apply if the defendant did not know that its acts were wrongful at the time they were committed. Similarly, the deterrence rationale does not apply in such cases, because there is no reason to believe that the defendant will commit similar acts in the future when it knows that such acts are prohibited. Thus, the principal justifications for punitive damages are inapplicable in cases where

---

[125]*Id.* at 578-79, 335 N.W.2d 842-43, 115 LRRM at 4490.

[126]*Id.* at 575, 335 N.W.2d at 841, 115 LRRM at 4489.

defendants could not have known that their acts were wrongful at the time they acted.

The leading public policy case which refuses to apply punitive damages retroactively is *Nees v. Hocks*,[127] in which the Oregon Supreme Court created a cause of action for employees discharged for serving on juries. Prior to that decision, the rule in Oregon was that an employee could be discharged at will. The court stated:

> In our past cases the defendant knew his conduct was regarded as culpable and would give rise to a cause of action because of past judicial decisions or legislation. . . . Until the trial court's ruling in this case and our affirmance there was no judicial decision that an employer was liable if he discharged an employee because she served jury duty. As we earlier stated, the general rule known to employers and lawyers alike is that absent contract or statute, an employer can discharge an employee for any reason without incurring liability. If we held that punitive damages could be awarded in the present case we would be permitting the jury to punish defendants for conduct which they could not have determined beforehand was even actionable. The assessment of punitive damages has some of the same functions as the sanctions of criminal law. The sanctions of the criminal law cannot constitutionally be imposed when the criminality of the conduct is not capable of being known beforehand.[128]

Thus, even if the jurisdiction in which a public policy cause of action arises permits punitive damages, employers may successfully argue that punitive damages should not be retroactively applied because the employers could not have known that their acts were wrongful at the time that they acted.

The last decade has witnessed the emergence of a widely accepted common-law remedy for private sector whistleblowers as one aspect of the doctrine of wrongful discharge in violation of public policy. The present consensus is that protection should be extended only to private sector employees who complain about violations of law, as distinguished from waste or mismanagement. However, because this body of law continues to develop at a relatively slow pace, there is presently no consensus on many of the issues where balancing the duty of loyalty and civic obligations is required. Courts deciding these issues in the next decade at least will be able to draw upon the legislative attempts to achieve this delicate balance, as discussed in chapters 3 and 4.

---

[127] 272 Or. 210, 536 P.2d 512, 115 LRRM 4571 (1975). *See also* Clanton v. Cain-Sloan Co., 677 S.W.2d 441, 117 LRRM 2789 (Tenn. 1984) (no retroactive application of punitive damages).

[128] 272 Or. at 220-21, 536 P.2d at 516-17, 115 LRRM at 4575-76.

6

Protections of General Application

Most of the whistleblower protections discussed in chapters 3, 4, and 5 apply either to government or private sector employees, but not necessarily to both. The whistleblower protections discussed in this chapter are not limited to either government or private sector employees, but apply to both the public and private sectors. The first section discusses the protections for employees who disclose their employers' practices that may defraud the federal government. The second section of this chapter discusses the protections available for employees who protest their employers' practices that may violate federal civil rights legislation.

False Claims Reform Act of 1986

As mentioned in Chapter 1, the False Claims Act was amended in 1986 in order to increase detection and prosecution of false claims submitted to the federal government. The 1986 amendments increased the penalties imposed upon violators, and enacted protections for whistleblowers who participate in false claims actions. Those protections may apply to virtually all private and public sector employees. The 1986 amendments have spurred a tremendous amount of litigation. According to the United States Department of Justice, over 231 false claims lawsuits have been filed since 1986.[1] The Department of Justice has settled 21 of those cases for a total of $40 million, of which $4 million was paid to the individual plaintiffs.[2] Moreover, the total recovery obtained by the Department of Justice

---

[1]Hearing on Qui Tam Provisions of the False Claims Act Before the Subcomm. on Administrative Law and Governmental Relations of the House Comm. on the Judiciary, 101st Cong., 2d Sess. 2-4 (April 4, 1990) (statement of Asst. Atty. Gen. Stuart M. Gerson, U.S. Dept. of Justice).

[2]*Id.*

through settlements and judgments in all civil fraud cases, not limited to false claims actions, rose to $225 million in 1989.[3] With this marked increase in false claims and government fraud litigation, employers probably will face an increase in the number of whistleblower complaints brought by plaintiffs in false claims actions. The whistleblower protections contained in the 1986 amendments may be more easily understood in view of the history of the statute.

The 1863 False Claims Act

As first enacted in 1863, the False Claims Act provided a civil penalty of double the amount of damages suffered by the government, plus a $2,000 forfeiture for each false claim submitted.[4] In addition to enforcement actions by the federal government, the Act provided that any citizen could institute a lawsuit regarding a false claim on behalf of the government. An individual plaintiff who prosecuted the action to judgment was entitled to one-half of the damages recovered, and to costs of suit. Such an individual was denominated the "*qui tam*" plaintiff, which means that the plaintiff is suing in his own right "as well as" on behalf of the government.[5] However, the original False Claims Act provided no protection for employees who attempted to sue their own employers, which in practical terms forced employees to choose between the security of their jobs and the chance of making a recovery under the Act.

The 1943 Amendments

During World War II a number of lawsuits were commenced by individuals under the Act regarding fraud in defense procurement. Some actions by individuals appeared to be based solely upon information obtained through public reports of criminal indictments brought by the federal government. However, under the original Act the government had no power to take over prosecution of such lawsuits. Instead, a *qui tam* plaintiff's interest in the action was viewed as tantamount to a property right, which could not be divested if the government wished to settle with the defendant. This situation created a race to the courthouse between the government and potential *qui tam* plaintiffs, with the winner in control of the litigation.[6]

To address this problem, the Act was amended in 1943 in several respects. First, the amendments required dismissal of *qui tam* lawsuits based solely upon information within the possession of the gov-

---

[3]*Id.*

[4]The False Claims Act, as amended, is codified at 31 U.S.C. §§3729-3733 (1988).

[5]BLACK'S LAW DICTIONARY 1126 (5th ed. 1979).

[6]The history of the False Claims Act is contained in the legislative history of the False Claims Reform Act of 1986, S. REP. NO. 99-345, 99th Cong., 2d Sess., *reprinted* in 1986 U.S. CODE CONG. & ADMIN. NEWS 5226.

ernment. Second, the amendments required a *qui tam* plaintiff to serve a copy of the complaint upon the federal government, which then had 60 days in which to give written notice to the court whether it intended to prosecute the action. If the government took over the prosecution, the *qui tam* plaintiff was still eligible to receive up to 10 percent of the amount recovered either by judgment or by settlement. If the government elected not to do so, the *qui tam* plaintiff was eligible for a reasonable amount of the proceeds recovered, not to exceed 25 percent.

The 1986 Amendments

In recent years much publicity has appeared regarding charges of fraud in many government programs, including the areas of agricultural subsidies, welfare benefits, disaster relief programs, and defense procurement. In 1985 it was estimated that fraud accounted for as much as 1 to 10 percent of the federal budget of nearly $1 trillion, or $10 to $100 billion annually. Accordingly, in 1986 Congress passed the False Claims Reform Act (Reform Act) to strengthen the government's ability to recover amounts of which it has been defrauded.[7] The guiding principle underlying the 1986 amendments is that the detection and prosecution of fraud can be increased by raising the financial incentives for private citizens to sue on behalf of the government, and by providing protection for employees who fear reprisals if they take steps to report abuses. Thus, the 1986 amendments include a whistleblower protection clause which provides a civil remedy for discrimination in employment for having participated in a lawsuit under the act.[8]

Substantive Provisions

The Reform Act prohibits a wide variety of fraudulent activities. The most simple type of fraud prohibited is a false claim for payment for goods or services which were not actually provided to agents of the government, or to any government contractor or grantee. The statute makes it clear that submission of any false record or statement in support of a claim is also prohibited. Moreover, "reverse false claims," or attempts to avoid or decrease an obligation to the government, are also specifically outlawed.[9]

The penalties for violations of the Reform Act are serious. Violators are liable for treble damages, the costs of prosecution including

---

[7]Also in 1986, Congress passed the Program Fraud Civil Remedies Act of 1986 to address fraud in Department of Defense programs. Pub. L. No. 99-509, codified at 31 U.S.C. §3801-3812 (1988).

[8]31 U.S.C. §3730(h) (1988).

[9]*Id.* at §3729(a). All of the substantive provisions of the False Claims Reform Act are codified at 31 U.S.C. §§3729-3731.

attorneys' fees, and a civil penalty of up to $10,000 for each separate false claim. The courts are authorized to reduce the amount of damages, to a minimum of twice the loss suffered by the government, and to waive the civil penalty forfeiture provision if the violator confesses to having submitted a false claim within 30 days of its discovery and fully cooperates with any investigation. Some federal courts viewed the penalties under the original Act as quasi-criminal in nature, and required that a violation be proven by "clear and convincing" evidence, a higher standard than typically required to impose a civil penalty. To prevent such a judicial construction, the Reform Act specifically provides that violations need only be proven by a "preponderance of the evidence." To further enhance the likelihood of proving violations, the Reform Act expressly negates any requirement to prove specific intent to defraud the government. Instead, a defendant is liable if he either (1) has actual knowledge of the false claim, (2) acts in deliberate ignorance of the truth or falsity of a claim, or (3) acts in reckless disregard of the truth or falsity of a claim.

The statute permits any person, as well as the Attorney General, to file a lawsuit. The courts are in conflict over whether the Reform Act allows government employees to sue about information obtained in the course of the government employment.[10] If an individual commences an action, a copy of the complaint must be sent to the Attorney General, who then has up to 60 days in which to decide whether to prosecute the action himself or herself. The complaint must be kept under seal, and must not be served on the defendant, until the Attorney General advises the court of his or her intent.

If the Attorney General notifies the court that he or she intends to prosecute the action, the *qui tam* plaintiff has the right to continue as a party to the action, and has the right to oppose the Attorney General's decision to dismiss or settle the action by presenting evidence at a hearing. The court may approve dismissal or settlement over the objections of the *qui tam* plaintiff if the court determines that the resolution of the case is fair, adequate, and reasonable under the circumstances.[11] When the Attorney General takes over a *qui tam* action, the *qui tam* plaintiff is entitled to receive a minimum of 15 percent and a maximum of 25 percent of the proceeds. If the Attorney General elects not to prosecute the action, the financial rewards to a *qui tam* plaintiff are substantial. The court is required to award the *qui tam* plaintiff a minimum of 25 percent and a maximum of 30 percent of the proceeds from a judgment or settlement.

---

[10]In Erickson v. American Inst. of Bio. Sciences, 716 F. Supp. 908 (E.D. Va. 1989) the court held that a government employee had standing to sue under the Reform Act unless the lawsuit was based on publicly disclosed information. *But see* United States ex rel. LeBlanc v. Raytheon Co., 729 F. Supp. 170 (D. Mass.) (government employees do not have standing if suit based on information learned during government employment), *acq. in result*, 913 F.2d 17 (1st Cir. 1990).

[11]Gravitt v. General Elec. Co., 580 F. Supp. 1162 (S.D. Ohio) (court refused to approve unreasonable settlement), *app. dism'd.*, 848 F.2d. 190 (6th Cir.), *cert. denied,* 488 U.S. 901 (1988).

The drafters of the Reform Act recognized that the substantial financial incentives for citizens, arising from the provisions for treble damages and civil penalties, may lead to abuses. For example, it is conceivable that several citizens may attempt to prosecute separate *qui tam* actions arising from identical facts. The statute addresses this potential problem by creating a jurisdictional bar for actions based upon ongoing civil or administrative proceedings. The courts have rejected several lawsuits based on previous legal proceedings.[12] Another jurisdictional bar exists for actions against members of Congress, against members of the Judiciary, or against senior officials of the Executive Branch if the action is based on information already known to the government.

No similar jurisdictional bar exists for actions by *qui tam* plaintiffs acting in bad faith. Instead, if the court determines that a *qui tam* action is frivolous and was filed solely for vexatious reasons, the court may award the defendant its attorneys' fees and costs. Possibly out of concern for abusive lawsuits, one court has held that a nonprofit corporation, acting upon information supplied by an individual with no connection to the nonprofit, did not have standing to bring a *qui tam* action.[13]

Protection for Whistleblowers

While recognizing the potential for abuse, the Reform Act also recognizes that many conscientious citizens, acting from proper motives, may be deterred from participating in lawsuits because of fear of retaliation in their employment. The statute specifically prohibits discrimination against employees who disclose information regarding false claims to any government or law enforcement agency, or who participate in investigations or prosecutions of false claims. Thus, the Reform Act protects not only employees who are *qui tam* plaintiffs, but also protects employees who assist in investigations or testify in prosecutions of false claims. A stiff penalty is provided for violations of the whistleblower protection provision. A victim of retaliation may commence a civil action in the federal district court, and may be awarded reinstatement with restoration of seniority, two times the amount of backpay with interest, compensation for special

[12]United States ex rel. Dick v. Long Island Lighting Co., 710 F. Supp. 1485 (E.D.N.Y. 1989), *aff'd*, 912 F.2d 13, 54 Fed. Contract Cases 391 (2d Cir. 1990); United States v. Rockwell Int'l Corp., 730 F. Supp. 1031 (D. Colo. 1990); Houck v. Folding Carton Admin., 881 F.2d 494 (7th Cir. 1989). *See also* Boisjoly v. Mortan Thiokol, Inc., 706 F. Supp. 795 (D. Utah 1988) (no *qui tam* claim exists if the complaint alleges that the government was aware of the alleged fraudulent practices). However, several cases have allowed *qui tam* plaintiffs to sue if their allegations are only partially based on information in the public domain. United States ex rel. Stinson v. Provident Life, 721 F. Supp. 1247 (S.D. Fla. 1989); United States ex rel. LaValley v. First Nat'l. Bank of Boston, 707 F. Supp. 1351 (D. Mass. 1988).

[13]United States v. Rockwell Int'l Corp., *supra* note 12 at 1036. *But see* United States ex rel. Stinson v. Provident Life, *supra* note 12 at 1256-1258 (law firm allowed to file *qui tam* action based on information obtained during representation of client).

damages, and reasonable costs including attorneys' fees.[14] The legislative history of the Reform Act also makes it clear that an employee need not prove that his or her employer actually submitted a false claim, but only that the employee had a good-faith belief that a violation had been committed.[15]

The Reform Act creates sweeping new protections for both private and public sector employees who participate in false claims investigations and proceedings.[16] Moreover, most courts have held that the changes contained in the Reform Act are fully retroactive.[17] Unlike the CSRA, which creates an investigative and prosecutorial body to enforce its whistleblower protections, the Reform Act places the burden of enforcement upon individual whistleblowers.[18] While the lack of a special prosecutor may lessen the effectiveness of enforcement of the Reform Act, the threat of a federal district court action in which double damages, reinstatement, and attorneys' fees may be awarded may be an effective deterrent to retaliation against whistleblowers who aid in investigation and prosecution of false claims.

Title VII and Other Civil Rights Acts

The whistleblower protections discussed in chapters 3, 4, and 5 apply to conduct most commonly thought of as whistleblowing: the disclosure of practices that may present an imminent danger to the public welfare. In contrast, employee complaints regarding alleged violations of civil rights laws do not necessarily prevent immediate public harm, but may prevent harm only to individuals or classes of individuals who are victims of discrimination. For the present discussion, as noted in Chapter 1, the term whistleblowing has been defined broadly to include opposition to any legal violations, not necessarily those which present an immediate hazard to the public. Under this

---

[14]The whistleblower protection provisions of the False Claims Reform Act are set forth in 31 U.S.C. §3730(h).

[15]S. REP. NO. 99-345, 99th Cong., 2d Sess., *reprinted in* 1986 U.S. CODE CONG. & ADMIN. NEWS 5226, 5300.

[16]However, one court recently held that federal government employees are not protected by the whistleblower protection provisions of the Reform Act because the CSRA discussed in Chapter 3 is their exclusive remedy. Daly v. Department of Energy, 741 F. Supp. 202 (D. Colo. 1990).

[17]United States v. Rockwell Int'l Corp., *supra* note 12; United States ex rel. Stinson v. Provident Life, *supra* note 12; United States ex rel. LaValley v. First Nat'l Bank of Boston, *supra* note 12; United States v. Ettrick Wood Prods., 683 F. Supp. 1262 (W.D. Wis. 1988); United States v. Hill, 676 F. Supp. 1158 (N.D. Fla. 1987). *But see* United States v. Bekhrad, 672 F. Supp. 1529 (S.D. Iowa 1987) (increased penalties of Reform Act do not apply retroactively).

[18]The constitutionality of the Reform Act has been challenged on the ground that the statute impermissibly delegates prosecutorial power to individual citizens. *See* Comment, *The Standing of Qui Tam Relators Under the False Claims Act*, 57 U. CHI. L.R. 543 (1990); Comment, *The Constitutionality of Qui Tam Actions*, 99 YALE L.J. 341, 344, n.17 (1989). However, two published cases have held that the *qui tam* aspects of the Reform Act are constitutional. United States ex rel. Newsham v. Lockheed, 722 F. Supp. 607 (N.D. Cal. 1989); United States ex rel. Stillwell v. Hughes Helicopters, Inc., 714 F. Supp. 1084 (C.D. Cal. 1989).

definition, employee complaints about discriminatory practices in violation of civil rights legislation may be considered whistleblowing.

The employee protection aspects of Title VII and other civil rights legislation merit discussion in the context of whistleblowing for other reasons as well. Title VII, enacted in 1964, was one of the first laws apart from the NLRA specifically authorizing employees to testify against their employers, and specifically prohibiting retaliation for giving adverse testimony. Thus, Title VII was one of the first statutes to recognize that important social goals, such as the eradication of discrimination, may require that employees be protected for acting contrary to their employers' interests. Title VII protects employees who act as witnesses and "participate" in proceedings under Title VII, and employees who "oppose" discriminatory practices, including what has been defined as passive or active whistleblowing. In these respects, Title VII was a precursor of many of the whistleblower protection statutes discussed in chapters 3 and 4.

The federal courts have been interpreting the participation and opposition clauses of Title VII for over 25 years. Because many of the whistleblower protections discussed in chapters 3 and 4 were recently enacted, the courts have not had much opportunity to interpret the more recent statutes. Due to the similarity between conduct protected under Title VII as participation or opposition, and conduct protected under the more recent whistleblower protection laws, courts interpreting the recent whistleblower protection laws may turn to cases decided under Title VII for guidance.

Civil Rights Act of 1964 (Title VII)

Title VII outlaws discrimination in employment on the basis of race, color, religion, sex, or national origin. Unlawful sex discrimination also includes discrimination on the basis of pregnancy. Title VII sets up both administrative and judicial enforcement mechanisms. A person who believes that he or she has been retaliated against for protected activities must first file a charge of discrimination with the Equal Employment Opportunity Commission (EEOC) within 180 days after the alleged act of retaliation. The EEOC is required to investigate the charge and to attempt to conciliate the dispute, and may institute a civil action on behalf of the complainant.[19]

Title VII also permits an individual to institute litigation on his or her own behalf if the individual requests the right to do so, or if the EEOC has completed its administrative review. A civil action in federal district court may be commenced within 90 days after the individual has received notice from the EEOC of his or her right to sue.[20] The relief available in such an action includes reinstatement,

[19]42 U.S.C. §2000e-5 (1988).

[20]*Id.* at §2000e-5(f)(1).

back pay, attorneys' fees, or other equitable relief, but excludes compensatory or punitive damages.[21] The overwhelming weight of authority holds that no jury trial is available in Title VII cases, on the theory that Title VII "expressly authorizes only equitable remedies."[22]

To encourage employees to make appropriate complaints, Title VII prohibits employers from retaliating against employees who make charges of discrimination. To encourage co-workers to support employees who make appropriate complaints of discrimination, Title VII also contains broad protections for co-workers. The specific section of Title VII which prohibits retaliation provides as follows:

> It shall be an unlawful employment practice for an employer to discriminate against any of his employees or applicants for employment . . . because he has opposed any practice made an unlawful employment practice by this title, or because he has made a charge, testified, assisted, or participated in any manner in an investigation, proceeding, or hearing under this title.[23]

Section 704(a) thus protects both participation in proceedings to enforce Title VII, and opposition to unlawful practices, which is not precisely defined in Title VII itself.

The Participation Clause

The participation clause is typical of most of the whistleblower protection laws discussed in chapters 3 and 4, because employee participation in investigations and hearings is essential to effective enforcement of the law. The participation clause has been held to provide "exceptionally broad protection."[24] In addition to protecting employees who file complaints against their current employers, the participation clause has been construed to protect employees who filed discrimination claims against prior employers.[25] Moreover, employees who are potential witnesses,[26] spouses of persons who have previously filed charges of discrimination,[27] as well as employees who testify in Title VII hearings, have all been held to be protected by the participation clause. The rationale expressed by the courts for this extraordinarily broad protection is that the important national goal of eradicating discrimination requires that the law be construed in a way to encourage participation in antidiscrimination efforts, rather than to discourage such efforts.[28]

---

[21]*Id.* at §2000e-5(g); Shah v. Mt. Zion Hosp. & Medical Center, 642 F.2d 268, 27 FEP Cases 772 (9th Cir. 1981).

[22]Great Am. Fed. Sav. & Loan Ass'n v. Novotny, 442 U.S. 366, 375 (1979).

[23]42 U.S.C. §2000e-3(a) (1988).

[24]Pettway v. American Cast Iron Pipe Co., 411F.2d 998, 1006 n.18, 1 FEP Cases 752, 757 n.18 (5th Cir. 1969).

[25]Barela v. United Nuclear Corp., 462 F.2d 149, 4 FEP Cases 831 (10th Cir. 1972).

[26]EEOC v. Plumbers Local 189, 311 F. Supp. 464, 2 FEP Cases 529 (S.D. Ohio 1970).

[27]Kornbluh v. Stearns & Foster Co., 73 F.R.D. 307, 14 FEP Cases 847 (S.D. Ohio 1976).

[28]Smith v. Georgia, 684 F.2d 729, 29 FEP Cases 1134 (11th Cir. 1982).

It may not even be necessary to have filed a charge of discrimination for an employee to be protected under the participation clause. In one case, the participation clause was extended to protect an employee who had merely notified the employer of his intent to file a charge of discrimination.[29] These interpretations of the participation clause may create an anomalous situation where an employee who later files a frivolous charge of discrimination, and who files a second charge alleging retaliation, could lose on the first charge but prevail on the second charge of retaliation. This situation may arise because some courts do not require a plaintiff to prove that the original claim of discrimination was valid in order to prevail on a retaliation claim.[30]

Participation has also been construed to include conduct outside the hearing process. For instance, one court protected an employee who had obtained, from one of her company's clients, a memorandum issued by her superior which referred to her in a discriminatory manner.[31] Even though the employee's conduct did not involve testimony or providing evidence to the EEOC, the employee argued successfully that Title VII should also protect efforts to gather evidence or testimony to support a claim of discrimination. Thus, the participation clause may protect various forms of evidence gathering as well as testifying. Further, in cases analogous to the *Petermann* decision, employees who have refused to give testimony favorable to their employer have also been protected under the participation clause.[32]

The Opposition Clause

Most of the whistleblower protection laws contain clauses similar to the participation clause, in that they protect employees who make disclosures to outside authorities, and also testify in enforcement proceedings to enforce violations. Less typical of the whistleblower protection statutes discussed in chapters 3 and 4, however, is the category of conduct in opposition to unlawful practices. The term opposition could be defined narrowly as employees who testify in enforcement proceedings, or broadly as employees who make off-hand remarks to superiors in casual conversations.

The leading treatise regarding Title VII litigation has noted that three issues commonly arise in opposition cases: (1) whether broad or ambiguous complaints are protected; (2) whether the employee had a good-faith belief that the practice was unlawful; and (3) whether otherwise protected conduct may lose its protection because of the disruptive manner in which the opposition is carried out.[33] The courts

---

[29]Croushorn v. Board of Trustees, 518 F. Supp. 9, 30 FEP Cases 168 (M.D. Tenn. 1980).

[30]*See, e.g.*, Bradford v. Sloan Paper Co., 383 F. Supp. 1157, 8 FEP Cases 634 (N.D. Ala. 1974).

[31]EEOC v. Kallir, Phillips, Ross, Inc., 401 F. Supp. 66, 11 FEP Cases 241 (S.D.N.Y. 1975), *aff'd*, 559 F.2d 1203 (2d Cir.), *cert. denied*, 434 U.S. 920 (1977).

[32]*See, e.g.*, Smith v. Columbus Metro. Housing Auth., 443 F. Supp. 61, 17 FEP Cases 315 (S.D. Ohio 1977).

[33]B.L. SCHLEI & P. GROSSMAN, EMPLOYMENT DISCRIMINATION LAW 543 (2d ed. 1983).

have generally held that a wide variety of opposition activities are protected, regardless of whether employees specifically invoke the provisions of Title VII. For example, one court held that an employee's opposition to a practice which allegedly had an adverse effect upon women employees was protected, even though the employee did not specifically state that she believed that the practice violated Title VII:

> It requires a certain amount of sophistication for an employee to recognize that an offensive employment practice may represent sex or race discrimination that is against the law. Here, [plaintiff] argued from the outset that the collective bargaining agreement had a harsher impact on some of the women than it had on men.[34]

Using the definitions suggested in Chapter 1, in this case the opposition clause was construed to protect an active internal whistleblower.

Passive whistleblowers have also been protected under the opposition clause. One employee was protected when she refused to comply with her supervisor's order to falsify a black applicant's test score.[35] Further, the opposition clause was construed to protect a manager who had hired a black employee, and who was discharged after the employer began receiving bomb threats from the American Nazi Party regarding the black employee. Even though the manager had made no public statements regarding any of the employers' practices, the symbolic act of hiring the black employee was held to be protected.[36]

Once it is determined that opposition has occurred, the second common issue in such cases is whether the employee "opposed any practice made an unlawful employment practice" by Title VII. Most courts require only that the employee have a reasonable, good-faith belief that the employment practice in question violated Title VII.[37] However, some courts have required a plaintiff to prove that the practice which the employee opposed actually violated Title VII.[38]

The third issue in opposition cases is whether the opposition is carried out in such a disruptive manner that the conduct loses its statutory protection. In one case involving a small research foundation, an employee was held to have forfeited her protection under the opposition clause by unnecessarily disrupting the collegial atmosphere of the foundation. The disruption was caused by unfounded accusations by contacting newspaper reporters, and by threatening to file suit. In the context of a small collegial workplace, the court found that such disruptive conduct effectively destroyed the employee's abil-

---

[34]Gifford v. Atchison, Topeka & Santa Fe Ry., 685 F.2d 1149, 1157 (9th Cir. 1982).

[35]Tidwell v. American Oil Co., 332 F. Supp. 424, 3 FEP Cases 1007 (D. Utah 1971).

[36]EEOC v. St. Anne's Hosp., 664 F.2d 128, 27 FEP Cases 170 (7th Cir. 1981).

[37]*See, e.g.*, Parker v. Baltimore & Ohio R.R. Co., 652 F.2d 1012, 25 FEP Cases 889 (D.C.Cir. 1981); Payne v. McLemore's Wholesale & Retail Stores, 654 F.2d 1130, 26 FEP Cases 1500 (5th Cir. 1981); Berg v. LaCrosse Cooler Co., 612 F.2d 1041, 21 FEP Cases 1012 (7th Cir. 1980); Monteiro v. Poole Silver Co., 615 F.2d 4, 22 FEP Cases 90 (1st Cir. 1980).

[38]*See, e.g.*, EEOC v. C&D Sportswear Corp., 398 F. Supp. 300 (M.D. Ga. 1975); Winsey v. Pace College, 394 F. Supp. 1324 (S.D.N.Y. 1975).

ity to work cooperatively with her colleagues.[39] Of course, as noted in Chapter 2, complaints about illegal activity are by their nature disruptive, and some degree of disruption is the price of enforcing the law. However, disruption may be especially damaging in circumstances such as small, collegial work environments.

Sexual Harassment

Since 1986 one of the most frequent subjects of whistleblowing complaints has been sexual harassment on the job. Before that date, the courts had not clearly stated whether sexual harassment in the workplace was prohibited by Title VII. However, in *Meritor Savings Bank v. Vinson*[40] the Supreme Court held that sexual harassment may violate Title VII if an employee is required to submit to sexual advances as a condition of employment (*quid pro quo* harassment), or if an employee's work environment is intolerable because of offensive sexual conduct (hostile environment harassment). The *Meritor Savings Bank* decision has given rise to a unique set of rules regarding the protections for these whistleblowers.

Many of the whistleblower statutes discussed in the preceding chapters limit the topics about which whistleblowers may complain. In contrast, the only limitation upon the subject of complaints of sexual harassment is that the advances must be unwelcome in the sense that the employee did not invite or solicit the harassment.[41] Further, there is very little restriction upon when complaints about harassment must be made. Although a contemporaneous complaint about the harassment is viewed by the EEOC as strong evidence that the conduct was unwelcome, a valid complaint may be made as long as several months after the harassment occurred.[42]

There also are few restrictions regarding the persons to whom complaints about sexual harassment may be made. Because of a desire to protect whistleblowers from retaliation, complaints may be made either internally or directly to EEOC.[43] A good-faith requirement is imposed on employees in the sense that they are required to show that the offensive conduct was unwelcome. Title VII does not protect employees who willingly participate in conduct of a sexual nature, but who later claim in bad faith that their participation was coerced.[44]

---

[39]Hochstadt v. Worcester Found. for Experimental Biology, Inc., 545 F.2d 222, 13 FEP Cases 804 (1st Cir. 1976).

[40]477 U.S. 57, 54 USLW 4703, 40 FEP Cases 1822 (1986).

[41]Equal Employment Opportunity Commission, *EEOC Policy Guidance on Sexual Harassment* 2 (Oct. 17, 1988) [hereinafter "*Policy Guidance*"]. Although these guidelines do not have the force of law, the Supreme Court recognized that they "constitute a body of experience and informed judgment to which courts and litigants may properly resort for guidance. [Citations omitted.]" Meritor Savings Bank v. Vinson, *supra* note 40 at 65.

[42]*Policy Guidance, supra* note 41 at 2.

[43]*Id.*

[44]*Id.* at 3.

Age Discrimination in Employment Act

The Age Discrimination in Employment Act (ADEA) prohibits discrimination against employees, or applicants for employment, who have opposed any practice made unlawful by the ADEA, or who have made a charge, testified, assisted, or participated in an investigation, proceeding, or litigation under the ADEA.[45] Thus, the ADEA contains both opposition and participation clauses. At least one court has suggested that an employer may violate the ADEA retaliation provisions *before* a charge of discrimination has been filed under the ADEA by discriminating against an employee who has voiced continued opposition to an employer's act which constituted illegal age discrimination.[46]

The antiretaliation provisions of the ADEA have been broadly construed as well. For example, in *Wentz v. Maryland Casualty Co.*[47] an employee who had been placed on probation twice in 1983 for poor performance filed a charge of age discrimination with the EEOC on February 15, 1984. He was terminated the following day on the ground of poor performance, and sued for both age discrimination and retaliation for having filed an EEOC charge. The court found against the employee on the age discrimination claim, ruling that the probationary periods were justified by poor performance. However, the court also ruled that the employee was not precluded from pursuing a retaliation claim despite the absence of any discrimination on the basis of age.[48] This decision, and the Title VII cases, indicate that the courts may construe the ADEA and Title VII antiretaliation clauses very broadly so as not to inhibit the filing of charges of discrimination.

Reconstruction Era Civil Rights Acts

Several civil rights statutes that were passed after the Civil War for the primary purpose of discouraging violent activities by the Ku Klux Klan may also provide protection for whistleblowers. These statutes may duplicate the substantive protections provided under Title VII since they pertain primarily to racial discrimination. Nevertheless, different procedural aspects of these statutes may be attractive because the statute of limitations may differ from that under Title VII, and because there is no requirement of exhaustion of administrative remedies as under Title VII. Each of these statutes has peculiar features which limit their applicability to certain narrow categories of cases.

---

[45] 29 U.S.C. §623d (1988).

[46] Byers v. Follmer Trucking Co., 763 F.2d 599, 37 FEP Cases 1871 (3d Cir. 1985).

[47] 869 F.2d 1153, 49 FEP Cases 705 (8th Cir. 1989).

[48] *Id.* at 1155, 49 FEP Cases at 707.

Section 1981

The Civil Rights Act of 1866, also known as Section 1981, provides in relevant part:

> All persons . . . shall have the same right . . . to make and enforce contracts, to sue, be parties, give evidence, and to the full and equal benefit of all laws and proceedings for the security of persons and property *as is enjoyed by white persons* . . . (Emphasis added.)[49]

Section 1981 prohibits private as well as governmental acts of discrimination in employment, and creates rights and remedies independent of those established in Title VII.[50] However, Title VII has been held to be the exclusive remedy for federal government employees to whom Title VII applies.[51]

Because Section 1981 is phrased in terms of guaranteeing equal rights to all individuals as are enjoyed by "white persons," most courts have held that Section 1981 does not prohibit discrimination based upon sex,[52] ethnic or national origin,[53] or religious beliefs.[54] Rather, Section 1981 has been limited to prohibiting discrimination based on an individual's "nonwhite" status. Thus, Section 1981 may provide a cause of action to an individual allegedly retaliated against for opposing practices which discriminate against nonwhite individuals.[55]

However, in *Patterson v. McLean Credit Union*,[56] the Supreme Court limited Section 1981 to the making and enforcement of employment contracts, and held that Section 1981 did not provide a basis for a claim of racial harassment. If this decision is not legislatively overruled by proposed federal legislation[57] Section 1981 cannot be used as a basis for protecting whistleblowers who complain about race discrimination.

Sections 1985 and 1986

In contrast to the Civil Rights Act of 1866, which regulates private as well as governmental conduct, portions of the Civil Rights Act of 1871, known as sections 1983, 1985, and 1986, regulate only actions by state government. Section 1983 of the Act of 1871, also known as the Ku Klux Klan Act, applies by its terms only to actions "under color" of state law. While Section 1983 clearly applies to state agen-

---

[49]42 U.S.C. §1981 (1988).

[50]Johnson v. Railway Express Agency, 421 U.S. 454 (1975).

[51]Brown v. General Serv. Admin., 425 U.S. 820, 12 FEP Cases 1361 (1976).

[52]*E.g.*, Runyon v. McCrary, 427 U.S. 160 (1976).

[53]*E.g.*, Shah v. Mt. Zion Hosp., 642 F.2d 268, 27 FEP Cases 772 (9th Cir. 1981).

[54]*E.g.*, Manzanares v. Safeway Stores, 593 F.2d 968, 19 FEP Cases 191 (10th Cir. 1979).

[55]Goff v. Continental Oil Co., 678 F.2d 593, 29 FEP Cases 79 (5th Cir. 1982) (§1981 provided cause of action for black employee allegedly dismissed for having filed charges of race discrimination).

[56]491 U.S. ___, 57 USLW 4705, 49 FEP Cases 1814 (1989).

[57]*See, e.g.*, S. 2104, 101st Cong., 2d Sess. (1989).

cies,[58] public schools and universities,[59] and public hospitals,[60] it is not clear whether Section 1983 may be applied to private institutions which receive state assistance or which are regulated by the state. The United States Supreme Court requires not only that the private institution receive substantial financial assistance from a state, but also that there be a nexus between the state support and the allegedly discriminatory practices, such as a showing that the state was involved in the decision to implement such practices.[61]

The coverage of sections 1985 and 1986 is slightly broader and reaches narrow categories of private conduct. Section 1985 of the Ku Klux Klan Act prohibits conspiracies for the purpose of depriving any person or class of persons of "equal privileges and immunities under the laws," or for the purpose of preventing state authorities from securing for any persons the "equal protection of the laws."[62] Section 1986 makes liable any person who has knowledge of a conspiracy but neglects to prevent the commission of any acts pursuant to the conspiracy.[63] Although not expressly limited to actions "under color" of state law, as is Section 1983, for a century sections 1985 and 1986 were construed to prohibit only state action.[64] However, in its landmark 1971 decision in *Griffin v. Breckenridge*,[65] the Supreme Court held that these sections applied to purely private conspiracies, so long as such conspiracies were motivated by a racial or other class-based animus. If the conspiracy is not racially motivated, however, but is based on sex, religion, age, or commercial animus, sections 1985 and 1986 would probably not be applicable.

An attempt to premise a whistleblowing claim upon Section 1985 was rejected by the United States Court of Appeals for the Fourth Circuit. A group of employees of a state mental hospital contended that they had been discharged for both internal and external complaints regarding patient abuse, mismanagement, waste of funds, and racial discrimination. The court stated that a Section 1985 claim exists only where the class of persons discriminated against possesses the "discrete, insular and immutable characteristics comparable to those characterizing classes such as race, national origin and sex," and held that the whistleblowing employees did not possess such characteristics.[66] However, it is still an open question whether Section 1985

58Johnson v. Louisiana State Employment Serv., 301 F. Supp. 675, 1 FEP Cases 598 (W.D. La. 1968).

59Chance v. Board of Examiners, 458 F.2d 1167, 4 FEP Cases 596 (2d Cir. 1972).

60Chiaffitelli v. Dettmer Hosp., 437 F.2d 429 (6th Cir. 1971).

61Rendell-Baker v. Kohn, 457 U.S. 830 (1982) (privately owned school which received 90% of financial support through state and federal tuition plans not subject to §1983).

6242 U.S.C. §1985(3) (1988).

63*Id.* at §1986.

64Collins v. Handyman, 341 U.S. 651 (1951).

65Carpenters Local 610 v. Scott, 453 U.S. 825 (1983).

66Buschi v. Kirven, 775 F.2d 1240, 1257, 1 IER Cases 1726, 1739, 120 LRRM 3059, 3073 (4th Cir. 1985) (quoting Bellamy v. Mason's Stores, Inc., 368 F. Supp. 1025, 1028 (E.D. Va. 1973), *aff'd*, 508 F.2d 504 (4th Cir. 1974)). *See also* Taylor v. Brighton Corp., 616 F.2d 256 (6th Cir. 1980) (no §1985 claim for employees allegedly dismissed for complaints regarding OSHA violations).

may protect whistleblowers who are themselves members of minority groups.

As demonstrated by chapters 3 through 6, the decade of the 1980s marked a dramatic expansion in the protections available to whistleblowers in the public and private sectors. The following chapter will address the problems which may arise when those protections overlap or conflict with other laws.

7

Preemption and Related Issues

The whistleblower protections for private sector employees discussed in chapters 4, 5, and 6 suggest that there may be overlapping remedies available to whistleblowers. For example, whistleblowers who are union members may be able to challenge their discharges under collective bargaining agreements that require good cause for termination of employment. Many of the state statutes that protect private sector employees address the issue of remedies available to union employees under such good-cause provisions. As discussed in Chapter 4, the state statutes have addressed the availability of good-cause protection under collective bargaining agreements in three different ways. The first method, as exemplified by the New York and New Jersey statutes, requires employees to choose between the statutory and good-cause protections, with the election of one remedy being deemed a waiver of the other. The second method, which has been adopted under the Michigan statute, allows employees to seek protection under either the statute, the collective bargaining agreement, or both. The third method simply does not address the issue, and leaves to the courts the task of determining whether an election of remedies is required.

In addition to good-cause protections under collective bargaining agreements, whistleblowers may also attempt to obtain protection under the common-law doctrine of discharge in violation of public policy. As discussed in Chapter 1, one of the most compelling reasons for the creation of public policy causes of action was that, under the at-will rule, employees who were not covered by collective bargaining agreements, civil service rules, or civil rights legislation had no protection against discharge from employment. Under these circumstances, the courts did not hesitate to create a remedy where none had previously existed. However, the courts have been less willing to create public policy causes of action for employees who may already have remedies, either under labor legislation such as the NLRA, or under statutes prohibiting various forms of discrimination.

This chapter discusses the various problems caused by overlapping protections available to whistleblowers. The first section discusses the potential conflict between whistleblower protection laws and similar protections available under the NLRA; the second section discusses potential conflict with the protections under collective bargaining agreements; and the third section discusses potential conflict with preexisting statutory remedies.

Deference to the Jurisdiction of the National Labor Relations Board

As discussed in Chapter 4, the whistleblower protections created by state statutes or by the common-law public policy doctrine generally extend to employees who report violations of law. In some instances, whistleblowers who are union members may report their employers' violations of the NLRA, or of the collective bargaining agreements governing their employment. Alternatively, in nonunion workplaces, employees may be subjected to retaliation because their employers learn that they are making disclosures to unions, or to their co-workers, in an effort to organize those employers' work forces.

In these circumstances, special considerations come into play in order to support the authority of the National Labor Relations Board (NLRB) regarding union-management conflicts. Out of deference to the primary jurisdiction of the NLRB, the remedies created by state statutes or by the common-law public policy doctrine may be preempted by the jurisdiction of the NLRB. In order to understand why such preemption may occur, an overview of the doctrine of preemption may be helpful.

In our system of government, both the federal and state governments may regulate various aspects of our country's economic life. When the federal and state laws conflict, the Supremacy Clause of Article VI of the United States Constitution provides that federal laws take precedence over state laws:

> This Constitution, and the Laws of the United States which shall be made in Pursuance thereof . . . shall be the supreme Law of the Land; and the Judges in every State shall be bound thereby, any Thing in the Constitution or Laws of any State to the contrary notwithstanding.[1]

As noted in Chapter 1, during the 1930s the national consensus was that the interests of the country were best served by a creation of a uniform federal labor policy aimed at reducing labor unrest and economic disruption. To achieve this goal, Congress not only enacted the NLRA which protected the rights of employees to bargain collectively, but also established a single federal agency, the NLRB, to develop a

[1]U.S. CONST. art. VI, §2.

nationwide, uniform labor policy. As recognized by the Supreme Court in *Garner v. Teamsters Local 776*:

> Congress did not merely lay down a substantive rule of law to be enforced by a tribunal competent to apply law generally to the parties. It went on to confide primary interpretation and application of its rules to a specific and specially constituted tribunal and prescribed a particular procedure for investigation, complaint and notice, and hearing and decision, including judicial relief pending a final administrative order. Congress evidently considered that centralized administration of specially designed procedures was necessary to obtain uniform application of its substantive rules and to avoid these diversities and conflicts likely to result from a variety of local procedures and attitudes towards labor controversies. . . . A multiplicity of tribunals and a diversity of procedures are quite as apt to produce incompatible or conflicting adjudications as are different rules of substantive law. . . .[2]

In accordance with these principles, the federal courts have been extremely conscientious about protecting the primary jurisdiction of the NLRB to regulate labor controversies. It has been firmly established since the Supreme Court's decision in *San Diego Building Trades Council v. Garmon*[3] that the state courts may not regulate conduct which is either arguably prohibited or arguably protected by the NLRA. It has also been consistently held that if an employee's discharge possibly violates the NLRA, it may not be challenged in the courts. For example, in *Operating Engineers v. Jones,*[4] the plaintiff Jones was offered a supervisory position by the employer, and was discharged eight days later. Jones filed a charge with the NLRB contending that the Operating Engineers' Union, which provided the employer with the bulk of its employees, had improperly coerced the employer into discharging him because he was not a member of the Operating Engineers. Jones contended that his discharge violated a provision of the NLRA which made it unlawful for a union to coerce an employer in the matter of selecting the employer's representatives for the purposes of collective bargaining or the adjustment of grievances. Because Jones was a supervisory employee, in the normal course of affairs he might have been involved in the adjustment of grievances as a representative of the employer. The NLRB declined to prosecute the charge. Jones then filed suit in state court, against both the union and the company, alleging that the union had interfered with the contract of employment between Jones and the employer. The state court allowed Jones to proceed with his claim because, in its view, the state had a deep interest in protecting its citizens' contractual rights, and because the cause of action for interference with contractual rights was a tort cause of action unrelated to the concerns of the federal labor laws.

---

[2]346 U.S. 485, 490-91, 33 LRRM 2218, 2220-21 (1953).

[3]359 U.S. 236, 43 LRRM 2838 (1959).

[4]460 U.S. 669, 112 LRRM 3272 (1983). *See also* Amco Constr. Co. v. Freeman, 236 Kan. 626, 693 P.2d 1183 (1985) (NLRA preempted claim of employee discharged in retaliation for protesting wage rates on project).

The Supreme Court stated that the traditional approach to the question of whether the NLRA preempted state regulation was as follows:

> [Preemption turns upon] whether the conduct that the State seeks to regulate or to make the basis of liability is actually or arguably protected or prohibited by the NLRA. . . . When, however, the conduct at issue is only a peripheral concern of the Act or touches on interests so deeply rooted in local feeling and responsibility that, in the absence of compelling congressional direction, it could not be inferred that Congress intended to deprive the State of the power to act, we refuse to invalidate state regulation or sanction of the conduct. . . . The question of whether regulation should be allowed because of the deeply rooted nature of the local interest involves a sensitive balancing of any harm to the regulatory scheme established by Congress either in terms of negating the Board's exclusive jurisdiction or in terms of conflicting substantive rules, and the importance of the asserted cause of action to the State as a protection to its citizens.[5]

The Court held that Jones' common-law complaint was preempted because his cause of action was arguably prohibited by the NLRA's proviso forbidding unions to coerce employers in the selection of their representatives.

As demonstrated by this case, the preemptive effect of the jurisdiction of the NLRB is exceptionally strong. The Court ruled that the wrongful conduct need not actually violate the NLRA, but only need arguably violate the NLRA. Furthermore, as shown by the NLRB's refusal to prosecute Jones' allegations, the NLRB need not actually prosecute an alleged violation of the NLRA for preemption to exist. Whether Jones' complaint was meritorious, and whether the NLRB declined to prosecute his claim based on its view of the merits or for lack of resources, the need to support the authority of the NLRB required that Jones' state court action be dismissed. Thus, the preemption doctrine implicitly recognizes that while individual grievances such as Jones' may be meritorious, they may be sacrificed in the name of the larger goal of supporting the NLRB's jurisdiction.

An example of a deeply rooted state interest which is not preempted was presented in the Supreme Court's 1977 decision in *Farmer v. Carpenters*.[6] Farmer alleged that he belonged to the carpenters' union, which discriminated against him in job referrals from its hiring hall and subjected him to a campaign of personal harassment. Farmer filed suit in state court, claiming that the carpenters' union had intentionally engaged in conduct causing him severe emotional distress. Although such allegations might form the basis of an unfair labor practice charge with the NLRB, the court held that Farmer's complaint was not preempted because the focus of the state common-law claim was upon the abusiveness of the union's conduct, whereas the focus of the NLRA claim would simply be upon the question of

---

[5] 460 U.S. at 676, 112 LRRM at 3275.

[6] 430 U.S. 290, 94 LRRM 2759 (1977).

discrimination, with the abusiveness of the discrimination being immaterial.

Later cases suggest that the exception to the preemption doctrine carved out in *Farmer* is relatively narrow. In *Viestenz v. Fleming Cos.*,[7] Viestenz was interviewed by an independent security service which had been engaged by Fleming Companies to determine whether Viestenz was stealing company merchandise. Viestenz alleged that the investigator advised him that he could lose his job and be blackballed if he did not admit to the thefts, and that a court order could be obtained requiring him to submit to a polygraph test. Viestenz made restitution to Fleming and was discharged the next day. Viestenz believed that he was discharged, not for theft, but because he had previously reported Fleming for violations of its union contract. Viestenz sued in state court for wrongful discharge in violation of public policy, and for intentional infliction of emotional distress. The court held that Viestenz's public policy claim was preempted by a provision of the NLRA which prohibited discrimination on the basis of union activities, and held that the cause of action for intentional infliction of emotional distress was also preempted because the investigator's conduct was not so outrageous as to require state regulation.

Similar results have been reached in cases where the plaintiffs contended that they were dismissed for union-related activities. In *Sitek v. Forest City Enterprises*,[8] the plaintiff alleged that he was employed as director of security for an apartment complex, and that he was discharged because he refused to discourage employees under his supervision from joining a union. The plaintiff contended that he should be allowed to state a public policy claim based upon several Michigan statutes which made it unlawful for employers to interfere with or coerce employees in the exercise of their rights to join unions. The court noted that the NLRB had construed the NLRA to prohibit an employer from discharging a supervisor for refusing to commit unfair labor practices, or for failing to prevent unionization, and held that the public policy claim was preempted by the NLRA. The same result was reached in the decision of the California Court of Appeal in *Henry v. Intercontinental Radio, Inc.*[9] Henry alleged that he had been discharged from his position as station manager of a radio station because he had been working to increase wages for black employees, to improve working conditions, and to bring a union to the station. Henry filed a complaint in state court alleging several wrongful discharge theories including a public policy claim. The court held that the radio station's conduct was arguably prohibited by the NLRA, because the NLRB had ruled "that an employer will be held to have violated the Act when it discharges or otherwise discriminates against a supervisor for union-related factors on the theory that such conduct may

[7]681 F.2d 699, 110 LRRM 2935 (10th Cir.), *cert. denied*, 459 U.S. 972, 111 LRRM 2784 (1982).
[8]587 F. Supp. 1381 (E.D. Mich. 1984).
[9]155 Cal. App. 3d 707, 713, 202 Cal. Rptr. 328, 331 (1984).

have the effect of interfering, not with the right of supervisory employees who are not *per se* protected under the Act, but with the rights of non-supervisory employees who may suffer infringement in the exercise of their own rights under the Act."[10] Accordingly, Henry's complaint was dismissed as being preempted by the NLRA.

Viestenz, Sitek, and Henry all could be considered whistleblowers because they claimed that they were discharged for reporting contract violations, for opposing illegal requests, and for communicating with union organizers, respectively. However, these people probably would not be protected either under state whistleblower protection statutes, or under the public policy doctrine, because of the powerful preemptive effect of the jurisdiction of the NLRB. Because the preemption doctrine turns upon whether conduct is prohibited or protected under the NLRA, the NLRB's fluid interpretations of the Act will determine whether complaints will be preempted.[11]

Deference to Arbitrators Under Collective Bargaining Agreements

Another source of federal preemption of whistleblower protections arises when the interpretation of the terms of a collective bargaining agreement is required. In many instances, a whistleblower's complaint requires the interpretation of a collective bargaining agreement—as when, for example, employees are subjected to retaliation for having disclosed that their employers violated a particular provision of a collective bargaining agreement. If the provision is at all ambiguous, resolution of such employees' complaints may require interpretation of the ambiguous provision of the collective bargaining agreement.

Lawsuits regarding alleged violations of collective bargaining agreements are authorized by Section 301 of the NLRA.[12] Section 301 has been interpreted as expressing a federal policy requiring that collective bargaining agreements be construed according to a federal law which the courts must fashion from the policies underlying the national labor laws.[13] Moreover, the federal law which Section 301 authorizes to be created is paramount to any other regulation. In the Supreme Court's decision in *Teamsters v. Lucas Flour Co.*, the court stated "that in enacting section 301 Congress intended doctrines of

---

[10]*Id.* at 713, 202 Cal. Rptr. at 331.

[11]For broad overviews of the preemption doctrine which do not focus on whistleblower claims, *see* Cox, *Recent Developments in Federal Labor Law Preemption*, 41 OHIO ST. L.J. 277 (1980), and Comment, *Labor Law Preemption*, 71 CALIF. L. REV. 942 (1983).

[12]"Suits for violation of contracts between an employer and a labor organization representing employees in an industry affecting commerce . . . may be brought in any district court of the United States having jurisdiction of the parties. . . ." 29 U.S.C. §185(a) (1988).

[13]Textile Workers v. Lincoln Mills, 353 U.S. 448, 40 LRRM 2113 (1957).

federal labor law uniformly to prevail over inconsistent local rules."[14] As the *Lucas Flour* Court explained:

> [T]he subject matter of section 301 "is peculiarly one that calls for uniform law. . . ." [Citation omitted.] The possibility that individual contract terms might have different meanings under state and federal law would inevitably exert a disruptive influence upon both the negotiation and administration of collective agreements. Because neither party could be certain of the rights which it had obtained or conceded, the process of negotiating an agreement would be made immeasurably more difficult by the necessity of trying to formulate contract provisions in such a way as to contain the same meaning under two or more systems of law which might some day be invoked in enforcing the contract. Once the collective bargain was made, the possibility of conflicting substantive interpretation under competing legal systems would tend to stimulate and prolong disputes as to its interpretation . . . [and] might substantially impede the parties' willingness to agree to contract terms providing for final arbitral or judicial resolution of disputes.[15]

Furthermore, the federal courts have been extremely reluctant to allow state courts to interpret collective bargaining agreements because most such agreements require that disputes regarding their meaning be submitted to final and binding arbitration. Ever since the *Steelworkers* trilogy[16] decided by the Supreme Court in 1960, it has been established that the primary forum for resolution of disputes over collective bargaining agreements is final and binding arbitration before a neutral arbitrator mutually agreed upon by the union and the employer. As recently reaffirmed by the Supreme Court, litigation as a first resort is contrary to the central role of arbitration in our system of industrial self-government:

> [S]uit [should not] be brought directly in state court without first exhausting the grievance procedures established in the bargaining agreement. The need to preserve the effectiveness of arbitration was one of the central reasons that supported the court's holding in *Lucas Flour*. . . . The parties here have agreed that a neutral arbitrator will be responsible, in the first instance, for interpreting the meaning of their contract. Unless [the state court suit] is preempted, [the] federal right to decide who is to resolve contract disputes will be lost.[17]

Since the arbitration procedure provided by a collective bargaining agreement is a union member's exclusive remedy, an employee may pursue a court action only if the arbitration was flawed because the union failed to adequately represent the employee. The duty of a union to fairly represent its employees in arbitration proceedings was established by the Supreme Court in 1967 in *Vaca v. Sipes*, where the Court held:

---

[14]369 U.S. 95, 49 LRRM 2717 (1962).

[15]*Id.* at 103-104, 49 LRRM at 2721.

[16]Steelworkers v. Warrior & Gulf Navigation Co., 363 U.S. 574, 581, 46 LRRM 2416, 2419 (1960).

[17]Allis-Chalmers Corp. v. Lueck, 471 U.S. 202, 219, 1 IER Cases 541, 548, 118 LRRM 3345, 3352 (1985).

> [T]he exclusive agent's statutory authority to represent all members of a designated unit includes a statutory obligation to serve the interest of all members without hostility or discrimination toward any, to exercise its discretion with complete good faith and honesty, and to avoid arbitrary conduct. . . .[18]

If the union fails to fairly represent the employee in an arbitration or fails to take a grievance to arbitration, the employee may sue the union for breach of its duty of fair representation, and may sue the employer for breach of the collective bargaining agreement. Before filing suit, however, an employee must attempt to exhaust the contractual grievance procedure.[19]

Removal to Federal Court

Often a bargaining unit employee will sue in state court on a number of wrongful discharge theories, including breach of contract. Although no federal claim will appear on the face of the state court complaint, in substance these cases are essentially actions under *Vaca v. Sipes* for a union's breach of the duty of fair representation and an employer's breach of the collective bargaining agreement. These cases present two questions: whether a bargaining unit employee may assert state law claims even though he is protected by the "just cause" provision of a collective bargaining agreement, and whether the federal courts may exercise jurisdiction over a state court complaint which on its face may not appear to present a question of federal law, but which has been removed to federal court.

When confronted with such cases, the federal courts have invoked the "artful pleading" doctrine which allows the federal court to look behind the plaintiff's complaint to determine whether the plaintiff is subject to a collective bargaining agreement. If so, the court may find that the complaint actually is an action for breach of a collective bargaining agreement within the jurisdiction of the federal court. Thus, defendants have been permitted to remove such complaints from the state courts to the federal courts by asserting that such complaints are actually suits for breach of a collective bargaining agreement.

One of the leading cases adopting the artful pleading analysis is *Olguin v. Inspiration Consolidated Copper Co.*[20] Olguin was a bargaining unit employee subject to a collective bargaining agreement which gave the company the right to discharge employees for just cause, and which provided a grievance mechanism culminating in binding and final arbitration to resolve disputes over the discharge of employees. Olguin contended that he was discharged in retaliation for making complaints about mine safety and health, and filed an action

---

[18]386 U.S. 171, 177, 64 LRRM 2369, 2371 (1967).

[19]Republic Steel Corp. v. Maddox, 379 U.S. 650, 58 LRRM 2193 (1965).

[20]740 F.2d 1468, 1 IER Cases 399, 117 LRRM 2073 (9th Cir. 1984).

in the state court that included a public policy claim that his discharge violated the policy set forth in MSHA. The company removed the case to federal court on the ground that the lawsuit was in essence a suit for violation of a collective bargaining agreement within the meaning of Section 301. The court noted:

> The firmest of these historical doctrines [of federal question jurisdiction] is the well-pleaded complaint rule. The Supreme Court has repeatedly held that for federal question jurisdiction to exist a right or immunity created by the Constitution or laws of the United States must be an element, and an essential one, of the plaintiff's cause of action. . . . A plaintiff may not, however, avoid federal jurisdiction simply by omitting from the complaint federal law essential to his claim, or by casting in state law terms a claim that can be made only under federal law. Jurisdiction is determined on the basis of the well-pleaded complaint. A complaint that is "artfully pleaded" to avoid federal jurisdiction may be recharacterized as one arising under federal law. . . . Whether brought in state or federal court, however, a suit arising under a collective bargaining agreement is governed exclusively by federal law; this law displaces entirely any state cause of action for violation of contracts between an employer and a labor organization.[21]

Once the court determined that the plaintiff's claim was actually a claim arising under the collective bargaining agreement, the court noted that Olguin could not maintain a *Vaca v. Sipes* action unless he alleged that he had exhausted his remedies under the collective bargaining agreement, and that his union had failed to represent Olguin fairly throughout the grievance procedure. Because he had not exhausted his remedies and did not allege that the union had breached its duty of fair representation, the court dismissed all of Olguin's claims.[22]

Some courts have permitted plaintiffs to assert a public policy cause of action despite belonging to a collective bargaining unit, on the theory that the complaint was grounded on important local interests which would not interfere with federal labor policies. For example, in *Garibaldi v. Lucky Food Stores,*[23] the plaintiff alleged that he was discharged because he refused to deliver a load of spoiled milk, and further contended that the delivery of spoiled milk was prohibited by California law. The court recognized a public policy cause of action for the plaintiff, and held that his claim was not preempted:

> A claim grounded in state law for wrongful termination for public policy reasons poses no significant threat to the collective bargaining process; it does not alter the economic relationship between the employer and employee. The remedy is in tort, distinct from any contractual remedy

---

[21]740 F.2d at 1471-72, 1 IER Cases at 401-402, 117 LRRM at 2075-76.

[22]*See also* Fristoe v. Reynolds Metals Co., 615 F.2d 1209, 104 LRRM 3041 (9th Cir. 1980); Oglesby v. RCA Corp., 752 F.2d 272, 118 LRRM 2203 (7th Cir. 1985); Smith v. Greyhound Lines, Inc., 614 F. Supp. 558, 117 LRRM 2253 (W.D. Pa. 1984); Lamb v. Briggs Mfg., 700 F.2d 1092 (7th Cir. 1983); Portley v. Kaiser Hosp., 115 LRRM 2629 (N.D. Cal. 1983). The same result has been reached in cases interpreting the preemptive effect of the Railway Labor Act. *See, e.g.*, Schroeder v. Transworld Airlines, 702 F.2d 189, 113 LRRM 2051 (9th Cir. 1983).

[23]726 F.2d 1367, 1 IER Cases 354, 115 LRRM 3089 (9th Cir. 1984).

> an employee might have under the collective bargaining contract. It furthers the state's interest in protecting the general public—an interest which transcends the employment relationship.[24]

Thus, the court found that Garibaldi's case was similar to the exception to preemption carved out in the *Farmer* case, where the Supreme Court held that states may regulate the labor field if important local interests which do not conflict with the federal statutory scheme are involved.

Exceptions

Several exceptions to the preemptive effect of Section 301 have been carved out for employees asserting federal statutory rights under Title VII and under the Fair Labor Standards Act (FLSA). In *Alexander v. Gardner-Denver Co.,*[25] the plaintiff filed a grievance under a collective bargaining agreement alleging that he had been discharged because of race discrimination. The arbitrator found in favor of Gardner-Denver, and Alexander filed suit in federal court under Title VII. The Supreme Court held that Alexander could pursue his Title VII claim in spite of the fact that he had resorted to the arbitration procedure set forth in the collective bargaining agreement. Although the Court noted that the special expertise of arbitrators was in applying the industrial common law of the shop, the Court held that arbitrators had no special expertise in applying the "law of the land."[26] Moreover, Title VII vests final responsibility for enforcement of its provisions with the federal district courts to ensure the integrity of the remedies provided therein. The Title VII policy providing plaintiffs with a federal forum for their claims of discrimination would therefore be subverted if a bargaining unit employee were permitted to pursue his remedies only under the collective bargaining agreement. In the Court's view, this result did not do violence to the principle that contractual disputes should be resolved by arbitrators because a plaintiff claiming race discrimination was not presenting a contractual dispute.

A similar result was reached under the FLSA in *Barrentine v. Arkansas-Best Freight System,*[27] where the employees contended that they should be paid for conducting safety inspections of trucks before commencing any trips. The plaintiffs submitted their grievance to a committee established by the collective bargaining agreement to resolve such disputes, and lost. The plaintiffs then filed suit in federal court under the FLSA, contending that they should be paid for conducting the safety inspections. The court recognized the tension existing between the federal labor policy of encouraging arbitration of

---

[24]*Id.* at 1375, 1 IER Cases at 360, 115 LRRM at 3095.

[25]415 U.S. 36 (1974).

[26]*Id.* at 57.

[27]450 U.S. 728 (1981).

disputes on the one hand, and the federal policy of guaranteeing employees a minimum wage for certain work as reflected in the FLSA on the other, and held:

> Not all disputes between an employee and his employer are suited for binding resolution in accordance with the procedures established by collective bargaining. While courts should defer to an arbitral decision where the employee's claim is based on rights arising out of the collective-bargaining agreement, different considerations apply where the employee's claim is based on rights arising out of a statute designed to provide minimum substantive guarantees to individual workers.[28]

The court also rejected the employer's argument that the FLSA claim was preempted because it was based on a dispute over wages and hours—subjects at the heart of the collective bargaining process—because the FLSA was designed to give specific minimum protections to individual workers and was not directed at the collective interests of employees.[29] As in the *Alexander* case mentioned above, one factor underlying the court's decision was that "many arbitrators may not be conversant with the public law considerations underlying the FLSA."[30]

The foregoing principle of deference to the arbitration process was also an important factor in a recent Supreme Court ruling. In *Electric Workers v. Hechler*,[31] the Court held that an employee's complaint—purportedly based on state law—that her union breached its duty to provide a union member with a safe workplace was preempted by Section 301. Because the nature and scope of the union's duty to the plaintiff required reference to the applicable collective bargaining agreement, the court held that Section 301 preempted any state law claims. In that case, therefore, the whistleblower's concerns regarding the safety of her workplace were held to be within the exclusive province of an arbitrator to resolve.

When the whistleblowing activities of union employees do not require interpretation of a collective bargaining agreement, however, the doctrine of preemption under Section 301 may have no application, as illustrated by the Supreme Court's decision in *Lingle v. Norge Division of Magic Chef*.[32] Jonna Lingle filed a claim for workers' compensation benefits on December 5, 1984, and was terminated by Norge on December 11, 1984, for having filed a false compensation claim. Lingle filed a grievance challenging her termination under the just cause provision of the governing collective bargaining agreement, and eventually an arbitrator ruled in her favor. Lingle also filed a state court complaint alleging that she had been discharged in violation of public policy for having exercised her right to file a claim

---

[28]*Id.* at 737.
[29]*Id.* at 739.
[30]*Id.* at 743.
[31]481 U.S. 851 (1987).
[32]486 U.S. 399, 3 IER Cases 481, 46 FEP Cases 1553, 128 LRRM 2523 (1988).

under the Illinois workers' compensation laws. Norge argued that Lingle's claim was preempted by Section 301 because both the determinations of whether just cause existed for discharging Lingle, and whether Lingle was discharged in retaliation for having filed a workers' compensation claim, required consideration of the identical set of facts. The Supreme Court agreed that the identical facts would be considered by an arbitrator under a just-cause analysis, and by a state court under a public policy analysis. However, the Supreme Court rejected the idea that this premise logically required preemption of the public policy claim. Rather, the Court noted that a state court hearing Lingle's public policy claim would not be required to interpret the collective bargaining agreement; it would instead consider whether Lingle was retaliated against for having exercised workers' compensation rights, which was an entirely separate analysis. Because Lingle's state law claim did not require analysis of the collective bargaining agreement, the Court held that Section 301 preemption was not required.

The rationale of *Lingle* would appear not to be limited solely to retaliatory discharge claims based on exercise of workers' compensation rights, but seemingly would apply to all public policy claims that do not require interpretation of collective bargaining agreements. For example, many of the state whistleblower protection statutes discussed in Chapter 4 protect employees' rights to make disclosures to the appropriate authorities. Claims of wrongful termination by whistleblowers under those statutes would require the courts to consider whether the terminations were in retaliation for exercising the protected right to make disclosures, or were based on other permissible reasons. This analysis, like the analysis required in *Lingle*, would not necessarily require an arbitrator's interpretation of a collective bargaining agreement.

Therefore, the preemptive effect of Section 301 on claims of whistleblowers who are union employees may be relatively narrow. Whistleblower claims that require the interpretation of collective bargaining agreements will almost certainly be preempted in deference to the arbitration process. However, with almost equal certainty, under *Lingle* whistleblower claims that do not require such interpretation will not be preempted by Section 301.

Deference to Preexisting Statutory Remedy

The previous sections of this chapter have discussed the overlap of the NLRA, collective bargaining agreements, and other whistleblower protections, which arise primarily with respect to union employees. This section discusses the potential for whistleblower remedies, for either union or nonunion employees, to overlap because of the existence of other statutory remedies.

As discussed in chapters 1 and 5, most courts have felt compelled to create public policy causes of action in favor of whistleblowers in order to avoid the harsh consequences of the at-will rule. In most instances, the plaintiffs would have been without remedies if the court had not recognized causes of action on their behalf. However, in many cases plaintiffs attempt to assert public policy causes of action when a statutory remedy is already available. For instance, a plaintiff may attempt to allege a cause of action for opposing or complaining about race, sex, or age discrimination under a federal or state statute and, in addition, may ask the court to recognize a policy cause of action based upon the public policy against race, sex, or age discrimination expressed in the applicable statutes.

The majority of jurisdictions have rejected such attempts. Like cases involving the preemptive effect of the NLRA and Section 301, some of these decisions rest upon a legislative intent to preempt the field which is regulated. Other decisions have been based on the courts' reluctance to create a common-law remedy where a statutory remedy already exists. This second category of cases does not rely on a preemption analysis. Rather, the rationale for these decisions is that although the courts will exercise their inherent common-law authority to create a cause of action where none exists, the courts need not create duplicative remedies if the plaintiff already has a statutory remedy.

The vast majority of jurisdictions have rejected attempts to assert public policy claims based upon state antidiscrimination statutes.[33] A similar rationale has been followed in cases involving workplace safety. Several state courts have refused to create public policy causes of action on behalf of employees who alleged that they were discharged

---

[33]Conkwright v. Westinghouse Elec. Corp., 739 F. Supp. 1006 (D.Md. 1990) (no common-law action for age discrimination, applying Maryland law); Crews v. Memorex Corp., 588 F. Supp. 27, 120 LRRM 2679 (D. Mass. 1984) (same, applying Massachusetts law); Wolk v. Saks Fifth Ave., 728 F.2d 221, 1 IER Cases 361, 115 LRRM 3064 (3d Cir. 1984) (no public policy cause of action for sex discrimination because Pennsylvania statute provided exclusive remedy, applying Pennsylvania law); Wehr v. Burroughs Corp., 438 F. Supp. 1052 (E.D. Pa. 1977) (same); McCluney v. Joseph Schlitz Brewing Co., 489 F. Supp. 24, 115 LRRM 4227 (E.D. Wis. 1980) (no public policy claim for sex discrimination because Wisconsin statute provided exclusive remedy, applying Wisconsin law); Schroeder v. Dayton Hudson Corp., 448 F. Supp. 910, 115 LRRM 4365 (E.D. Mich. 1978) (no public policy cause of action for sex discrimination because Michigan sex discrimination statute provided exclusive remedy); Parets v. Eaton Corp., 479 F. Supp. 512 (E.D. Mich. 1979) (no public policy claim for national origin discrimination because Michigan antidiscrimination law provided exclusive remedy); Kelly v. Western Airlines, 115 LRRM 2110 (D. Utah 1983) (no cause of action for age discrimination under Utah law); Tarr v. Riberglass, Inc., 115 LRRM 3688 (D. Kan. 1984) (no public policy claim for age discrimination under Kansas law); Klages v. Sperry Corp., 118 LRRM 2463 (E.D. Pa. 1984) (same, applying Pennsylvania law); Bottijliso v. Hutchison Fruit Co., 96 N.M. 789, 635 P.2d 992, 118 LRRM 3095 (1981) (no public policy claim for discharge for filing workers' compensation claim where New Mexico workers' compensation statutes provide a remedy for discharge); Bonham v. Dresser Indus., 569 F.2d 187 (3d Cir. 1977) (no public policy claim for age discrimination because Pennsylvania age discrimination law provided exclusive remedy); Schwartz v. Michigan Sugar Co., 106 Mich. App. 471, 308 N.W.2d 459, 115 LRRM 4535 (1981) (no public policy claim for alleged discharge for reporting occupational safety hazards because Michigan occupational safety law provided exclusive remedy); Ohlsen v. DST Indus., 111 Mich. App. 580 (1982) (same); Yount v. Hesston Corp., 124 Ill. App. 3d 943, 464 N.E.2d 1214 (1984) (no public policy claim for discrimination on the basis of mental handicap because Illinois Human Rights Act provided exclusive remedy); Strauss v. A.L. Randall Co., 144 Cal. App. 3d 514, 194 Cal. Rptr. 520 (1983) (no public policy claim for age discrimination because California age discrimination law provided exclusive remedy).

for complaining about workplace safety because of the existence of a remedy under OSHA. For instance, in *Walsh v. Consolidated Freightways,*[34] the Oregon Supreme Court refused to create a cause of action on behalf of an employee who complained about noxious exhaust fumes because of the existence of a remedy under OSHA. This reasoning has also been followed in cases where employees claim that they were discharged in retaliation for attempting to obtain pension benefits. In *Witkowski v. St. Ann's Hospital of Chicago,*[35] the plaintiff alleged that she was discharged in order to prevent her from obtaining long-term disability benefits. The Illinois appellate court held that the plaintiff's exclusive remedy was contained in ERISA.

A minority of jurisdictions have recognized causes of action despite the existence of a statutory remedy. In *Holien v. Sears, Roebuck & Co.,*[36] the plaintiff alleged that she was discharged because she resisted her supervisor's sexual advances. The Oregon Supreme Court distinguished between discharge on the basis of subtle sex discrimination and discharge for resisting a supervisor's overt sexual advances. Because most sex discrimination is carried out in a subtle manner, without any blatant sexual comments or overtures, the court suggested that the exclusive remedy for discharge on the basis of sex discrimination, without more concrete evidence, would probably be the state statute. However, because the case before it was more in the nature of a traditional tort claim for assault because of the supervisor's overt physical advances, the court was of the opinion that the state antidiscrimination law was not the exclusive remedy for the obvious sexual overtures.

A different rationale was applied by the United States district court applying Massachusetts law, in *McKinney v. National Dairy Council.*[37] McKinney alleged that he had been discriminated against because of his age. Although Massachusetts law did not recognize a public policy cause of action, Massachusetts law did provide a cause of action for breach of an implied obligation of good faith and fair dealing. The court held that a discharge on the basis of age would violate the implied obligation of good faith and fair dealing inherent in the plaintiff's employment relationship. Thus, the theory of *McKinney* appears to be that in a cause of action based upon a contract, a discharge in violation of a statute would violate the implied term in the contract that all parties must abide by the applicable law. Accordingly, the *McKinney* court found the source of the plaintiff's claim to be in the contract between the parties rather than in the common-law public policy doctrine.

---

[34]278 Or. 347, 563 P.2d 1205, 115 LRRM 5045 (1977). *See also* Jones v. Industrial Electric-Seattle, 53 Wash. App. 536, 768 P.2d 520 (1989); Corbin v. Sinclair Mktg., Inc., 684 P.2d 265, 116 LRRM 3223 (Colo. App. 1984).

[35]113 Ill. App. 3d 745, 447 N.E.2d 1016 (1983). *See also* Felton v. Unisource Corp., 739 F. Supp. 1388 (D. Ariz. 1990).

[36]298 Or. 78, 689 P.2d 1292 (1984).

[37]491 F. Supp. 1108, 115 LRRM 4861 (D. Mass. 1980).

The general principle which may be distilled from the foregoing cases is that most jurisdictions will be reluctant to create new causes of action for plaintiffs who have a remedy available under either a state or federal statute. Moreover, the preexisting statutory remedy need not be a judicial remedy allowing recovery of tort damages. Most jurisdictions appear to be satisfied that an individual's rights have been sufficiently protected so long as a plaintiff has a "make-whole" remedy through an administrative framework with the opportunity for judicial review. Thus, the majority approach appears to avoid creating an overlap of common-law remedies for whistleblowers if a preexisting statutory remedy is already in place.

8

Litigating Whistleblower Cases

Whistleblowers who allege that they were victims of retaliation may be protected under one or several of the laws discussed in chapters 3, 4, 5, and 6. Some of these laws, including the Civil Service Reform Act which covers employees of the federal government, provide an administrative framework for resolution of whistleblower claims. In contrast, some whistleblowers may seek redress in the courts under the common law public policy doctrine, or union employees may seek protection through the arbitration mechanisms established by collective bargaining agreements. The exact elements of proof which employees and employers are required to show may vary under each particular law. Nevertheless, the substantive elements of whistleblower cases are generally similar, and will be discussed in this chapter. After outlining the substantive elements of whistleblower claims, this chapter will discuss procedural issues that may arise in whistleblower litigation.

One important assumption underlies the discussion in this chapter. It is assumed that whistleblowers will choose not to pursue frivolous claims, and that employers will choose not to defend claims where the employer actually did commit the violation complained of by the whistleblower, and the employer's decision to terminate the whistleblower was based solely on a desire for revenge. The premise underlying this assumption is that few whistleblowers or employers wish to have their frivolous or improper behavior publicized, which almost certainly results from litigation in proceedings open to the public. Moreover, depending upon the remedies provided by the law under which the whistleblower seeks protection, an employer's decision to defend a meritorious claim may result in an award of punitive damages. Therefore, this chapter assumes that some kind of settlement before trial will be reached if a whistleblower's claim is either clearly frivolous or clearly meritorious.

Based on this assumption, the following sections will discuss cases where the employer did not clearly commit the violation about which the whistleblower complained. It is also assumed that the employer's decision to terminate the whistleblower was not based solely on a desire to retaliate, but instead was at least partially based on legitimate business reasons.

Elements of Proof

This section will discuss the evidence that whistleblowers typically are required to present in order to carry their burden of proving a *prima facie* case, and the evidence that employers typically are required to present in order to rebut the whistleblowers' *prima facie* case. This evidentiary framework sets the boundaries for gathering evidence in discovery proceedings before trial, which are discussed later in this chapter.

The Whistleblowers' Prima Facie *Case*

Many of the whistleblower protection laws discussed in chapters 3, 4, and 5 are of relatively recent origin. Consequently, there are few precedents interpreting the proof requirements of most of those laws. In contrast, the antiretaliation provision of Title VII has been interpreted by judicial decisions for the last 25 years. Because retaliation claims under Title VII are similar to whistleblower cases, several courts that have interpreted other whistleblower protection laws have applied the evidentiary standards developed under Title VII in analyzing the whistleblowers' *prima facie* case.[1]

In order to prove a *prima facie* case that employees were terminated in retaliation for having opposed violations of Title VII, or for having participated in enforcing Title VII, employees must prove (1) that they engaged in conduct protected by Title VII, (2) that the employer took adverse action against them, and (3) that there was a causal connection between the protected conduct and the adverse action.[2]

The precise nature of the first element, that the employees engaged in protected conduct, will vary depending upon the whistleblower protection law in question. For example, Title VII protects the very broad categories of "opposition" to violations of Title VII or "participation" in enforcing violations, which includes many forms of conduct inside the whistleblowers' organizations. In contrast, the California whistleblower protection statute protects only active whistleblowers who actually report suspected violations to the appropriate

---

[1]Melchi v. Burns Int'l Sec. Servs., Inc., 597 F. Supp. 575 (E.D.Mich. 1984) (decided under Michigan Whistleblowers' Protection Act).

[2]*Id.*; Mackowiak v. University Nuclear Sys., Inc., 735 F.2d 1159 (9th Cir. 1984); Wentz v. Maryland Casualty Co., 869 F.2d 1153, 49 FEP Cases 705 (8th Cir. 1989).

authorities, and does not protect whistleblowers making internal reports within their organizations.[3] In addition, the majority of the state statutes that protect private sector whistleblowers, as described in Appendix B, require that whistleblowers' complaints be based on a good-faith belief that their employers had committed, or were about to commit, the suspected violations. In order to demonstrate their good-faith belief, whistleblowers would be required to present evidence of their employers' alleged misconduct, of the whistleblowers' knowledge of the laws that the employers allegedly violated, and of the efforts made by whistleblowers to verify the accuracy of their perceptions both of their employers' conduct and of the governing legal restrictions.[4]

The second element of proof is easily satisfied by whistleblowers whose employment has been terminated, which is the most severe form of adverse action. However, whistleblowers who have been subjected to retaliation short of discharge, in the form of unwanted transfers, lessening of job responsibilities or authority, demotion, or other adverse actions, may also be able to seek relief under whistleblower protection laws. For example, the majority of statutes protecting government and private sector whistleblowers prohibit not only termination of employment, but also lesser forms of harassment.[5]

At first glance the third element, which requires showing a causal connection between whistleblowing and retaliation, might appear more difficult to satisfy. Because few employers openly state that they are terminating employees solely because of their whistleblowing activities, direct proof of a causal connection is usually rare. Under many laws the existence of a causal connection may be proven by indirect evidence, such as the timing of the adverse action. For example, the existence of a causal connection may be established under many statutes simply by proving that the employer was aware of the whistleblowing, and that the adverse action occurred reasonably soon after an employee's whistleblowing activities, thereby permitting the inference of retaliatory motive from the timing of the adverse action.[6] The most extreme example of permitting indirect proof of a causal connection is found in the whistleblower protection statutes of Texas and South Carolina, which establish a rebuttable presumption that adverse actions taken six months or one year, respectively, after employees engage in whistleblowing, are motivated by a desire for retaliation.[7] Because many laws permit proof of a causal connection by means of inferences arising solely from the timing of adverse

---

[3]CAL. LAB. CODE §1102.5. (West 1989).

[4]*Supra* note 1 at 578.

[5]See the statutes summarized in Appendices A and B; *see also* Deford v. Secretary of Labor, 700 F.2d 281, 287 (6th Cir. 1983) (employee's evidence was sufficient to prove demotion was retaliatory).

[6]Couty v. Dole, 886 F.2d 147, 148 (8th Cir. 1989); Ellis Fischel State Cancer Hosp. v. Marshall, 629 F.2d 563, 566 (8th Cir. 1980), *cert. denied*, 450 U.S. 1040 (1981); Melchi v. Burns Int'l Sec. Servs., Inc., *supra* note 1 at 584.

[7]See Appendix B for a description of the Texas and South Carolina statutes.

action, whistleblowers may be able to satisfy the third element of proof more easily than might be anticipated.

Attempts to require whistleblowers to prove more than these bare elements have met with little success. For instance, in *Deford v. Secretary of Labor*,[8] the employer argued that whistleblowers should be required to prove that they disclosed unique evidence to the appropriate agency, or evidence that the employer had attempted to cover up damaging information. The court of appeals rejected this argument on the ground that the applicable statute was intended to protect employees who cooperate with regulatory agencies, whether or not the information they provide is novel or merely cumulative. The court also rejected the employer's argument that whistleblowers should be required to prove that they were treated differently than other employees, stating that "[a]n employer should not escape liability upon an otherwise valid claim, for example, solely because it chose to discriminate against three similarly situated employees rather than only one."[9]

As the foregoing discussion illustrates, the elements of whistleblowers' *prima facie* cases are not especially difficult to prove. In order to show that they engaged in protected conduct, they need only prove that they had a good-faith belief that their employers committed or were about to commit violations. Because the existence of good faith depends upon an individual's state of mind, this proof is almost exclusively available to whistleblowers. Moreover, most whistleblower protection laws do not require whistleblowers to prove, through evidence less readily available to whistleblowers, that their employers actually committed the violations about which the whistleblowers complained. The apparent justification for this aspect of the whistleblower protection laws is to encourage, rather than discourage, whistleblowing in close cases so that public dangers can be averted. Finally, many laws permit proof of a causal connection by means of inferences from the timing of the adverse action. This evidence is readily available to whistleblowers.

Defenses Available to Employers

The crucial issue in any whistleblower case is whether the adverse action taken by the employer was motivated by a desire to retaliate against the whistleblower for engaging in protected conduct, or for other legitimate business reasons. In most cases, the whistleblower contends that the employer's adverse action is prompted by a retaliatory motive, while the employer argues that its actions were based upon proper business reasons which have no relation to the whistleblower's protected conduct. Thus, many whistleblower cases

---

[8]700 F.2d 281 (6th Cir. 1983).

[9]*Id.* at 286.

eventually require the judge, jury, or arbitrator to decide whether the employer truly made its determination for legitimate reasons, such as poor performance, or because of a desire to retaliate against the whistleblower. When employers defend whistleblower cases on the ground that their decisions were based on proper motives, those cases have been come to be known as "mixed motive" cases.

Mixed Motives

The leading case establishing the legal standards for evaluating "mixed motive" cases is the Supreme Court's decision in *Mount Healthy City School District Board of Education v. Doyle.*[10] Doyle was an untenured school teacher whose contract was not renewed by the Board of Education. Doyle alleged that his contract was not renewed because he complained to a radio station regarding a dress code for school teachers. The dress code had been recently issued because of a perceived nexus between teacher appearance and public support for bond issues. Doyle alleged that his comments to the radio station were constitutionally protected, and could not be the basis of the refusal to renew his contract. However, the school board contended that he was discharged because he had a history of unprofessional activities which included not only the dress code incident, but also included making an obscene gesture to students while he was acting as supervisor of the school cafeteria. The Supreme Court established the following framework for evaluating these competing positions:

> Initially, in this case, the burden was properly placed upon respondent to show that his conduct was constitutionally protected, and that this conduct was a substantial factor—or, to put it in other words, that it was a motivating factor in the Board's decision not to rehire him. Respondent having carried that burden, however, the district court should have gone on to determine whether the Board had shown by a preponderance of the evidence that it would have reached the same decision as to respondent's re-employment even in the absence of the protected conduct.[11]

The *Mount Healthy* case establishes a "but for" causation test. If the school board would have refused to renew Doyle's contract even if he had not complained to the radio station, then the school board would not be held liable. However, if the school board would have renewed Doyle's contract despite the obscene gesture incident, and if he had not made the comments to the radio station, then the school board would be liable. This standard has been applied under most statutes.[12]

Disruptive or Disloyal Manner of Protest

In some cases companies may terminate whistleblowers because they made their allegations in an unduly disruptive fashion. Even

---

[10]429 U.S. 274, 1 IER Cases 76 (1976).

[11]*Id.* at 287, 1 IER Cases at 80.

[12]*See, e.g.,* Ellis Fischel State Cancer Hosp. v. Marshall, *supra* note 6 at 566.

though the whistleblowers' job performance was satisfactory, and they would not have been terminated if they had not engaged in whistleblowing, the employers may decide to terminate the whistleblowers because of the disruptive manner or demoralizing effect of their protests. These are not mixed motive cases because the employer admits that the whistleblowing conduct was the reason for the discharge. Rather, the issue in these cases is whether the whistleblowing conduct, which would be legally protected if carried out in a reasonable manner, might lose its protected status by being carried out in an unduly disruptive or disloyal fashion.

For example, in *Hochstadt v. Worcester Foundation for Experimental Biology,*[13] referred to briefly in Chapter 6, the court held that an employee's complaints of sex discrimination, which were protected by Title VII of the Civil Rights Act of 1964, were so disruptive to the collegial atmosphere of a small research foundation that the complaints lost their statutory protection. The court stated:

> The district court was entitled to find that [plaintiff's] constant complaints to colleagues damaged relationships among members of the cell biology group and sometimes even interfered with laboratory research. Even if justified, they occurred upon some occasions when the employer was entitled to expect her full commitment and loyalty. [Title VII] does not afford an employee unlimited license to complain at any and all times and places.[14]

These principles developed under Title VII were applied to uphold the discharge of a whistleblower in the nuclear power industry in *Dunham v. Brock.*[15] William Dunham was employed by Brown & Root as a quality assurance inspector at the Comanche Peak power plant. Dunham complained to the Nuclear Regulatory Commission in early 1983 that he was being harassed by his supervisor, who was eventually reassigned to another job. After the reassignment Dunham still believed that he was being harassed, and continued to voice his concerns. In August 1983 Dunham attended a meeting between the quality assurance department and another department, in which several attendees felt that Dunham acted in an argumentative and counterproductive manner. Dunham's new supervisor decided to counsel Dunham, and scheduled a meeting to discuss Dunham's behavior. When Dunham was handed a counseling report at the meeting, he made an obscene remark and invited the supervisor to terminate him because he would not change his behavior. After considering it only for a few moments, the supervisor terminated Dunham for insubordination. Rejecting the argument that the counseling meeting and report

---

[13]545 F.2d 222, 13 FEP Cases 804 (1st Cir. 1976). For other cases holding that the unreasonable manner of protests is unprotected, *see* Rollins v. Florida, 868 F.2d 397, 49 FEP Cases 763 (11th Cir. 1989); Payne v. McLemore's Wholesale & Retail Stores, 654 F.2d 1130, 1137, 26 FEP Cases 1500, 1507 (5th Cir. 1981), *cert. denied*, 455 U.S. 100 (1982); Whatley v. Metropolitan Atlanta Rapid Transit Auth., 632 F.2d 1325, 1329, 24 FEP Cases 1148, 1151 (5th Cir. 1980); Pendleton v. Rumsfeld, 628 F.2d 102, 108, 22 FEP Cases 733, 738 (D.C. Cir. 1980).

[14]545 F.2d at 233, 13 FEP Cases at 812.

[15]794 F.2d 1037 (5th Cir. 1986).

were a "set-up" intended to provoke him into intemperate behavior, the court upheld the Secretary of Labor's ruling that approved the discharge because of the extreme nature of Dunham's response.[16]

The principle that an employee's conduct may be so disloyal or disruptive that the conduct loses its protected status is also recognized under other statutes. In a case under the NLRA, *NLRB v. Electrical Workers (IBEW) (Jefferson Standard)*, employees who were picketing, an activity generally protected by the NLRA, were held to have abused their right to picket by disparaging the employer's business practices and products. The Supreme Court stated that "[t]here is no more elemental cause for discharge of an employee than disloyalty to his employer," and held that the employees' disparaging statements justified their discharge.[17] Accordingly, even in the absence of poor job performance or other justification, the disruptive manner in which disclosures are made may constitute sufficient reason for adverse action against whistleblowers.

Disproving a Whistleblower's Good Faith

Because most whistleblower protections require that whistleblowers prove that their protests were made in good faith, employers may also attempt to prove that the protests were improperly motivated. Technically, such an attempt would constitute a rebuttal of one element of a whistleblower's *prima facie* case rather than constituting an affirmative defense.

As noted above, the evidence of a whistleblowers' good faith is in most cases solely within their control. Just as employers rarely articulate their intent to retaliate against whistleblowers, it is equally rare for whistleblowers to admit that their protests are made for improper reasons. Accordingly, companies may have difficulty in proving that protests were not made in good faith. Nevertheless, employers may be able to raise serious questions regarding the good faith of whistleblowers in some situations. For example, as pointed out by the

---

[16] *Id.* at 1041.

[17] 346 U.S. 464, 472, 33 LRRM 2183, 2189 (1953). This principle is also recognized in arbitration decisions interpreting collective bargaining agreements that require "just cause" for termination. In Southwestern Elec. Power Co., 84 LA 743 (1985), the arbitrator held that there was just cause to discharge an employee who filed suit against the company and a number of its officials personally, alleging that the company permitted unsafe working conditions. The arbitrator noted that "the suit prompted wide media attention," and held:

> [B]y seeking monetary damages not only from the Company but from five supervisors as well, the [employee] demonstrated his objective of disparaging and harming not only [the employer] but individual officials as well . . . [T]he Employee's actions constituted a direct affront to managerial authority and did so in such a manner as to adversely affect the Employer-Employee relationship. How could the filing of a lawsuit against [the Company] and five Company officials, charging irresponsible and dangerous practices and claiming $1,500,000 in damages, be construed as anything but a direct confrontation with Management?

Id. at 748-49.

Similarly, in Forest City Publishing Co., 58 LA 773 (1972), the arbitrator held that "just cause" existed for termination of a newspaper reporter who published an article disparaging the newspaper that employed him, and stated that the issue presented by the case was the following: "Can you bite the hand that feeds you, and insist on staying for future banquets?" *Id.* at 783.

legislative history of the Civil Service Reform Act, employees who knew that they were about to be disciplined or terminated for poor performance may attempt to pass themselves off as whistleblowers in order to delay or stop the impending disciplinary action. Serious doubts about good faith may be raised by proof that employees knew of the impending disciplinary action before they became whistleblowers. Similarly, the Wisconsin whistleblower protection statute provides that employees who stand to gain monetarily because of their whistleblowing activity are not protected. If employers can prove that whistleblowers received money for their disclosures, the Wisconsin statute would not protect them.

Shift in Burden of Proof

Whether an employer defends a whistleblower case on the basis of the mixed motive or manner of protest grounds, the question arises as to how the judge, jury, or arbitrator should evaluate the evidence produced by whistleblowers and by employers. Most courts deciding whistleblower cases have adopted the allocation of burden of proof that has been developed by the Supreme Court in cases under Title VII of the Civil Rights Act of 1964.[18] In *McDonnell Douglas Corp. v. Green*,[19] the Supreme Court established that the employee bears the ultimate burden of proving that he was terminated wrongfully.

If the employee is able to establish a *prima facie* case as outlined above, the employer then bears the burden of coming forward with evidence that the true reason for the adverse action was a legitimate reason. This requirement does not impose any burden of proof on the employer, but merely imposes a duty to articulate a legitimate reason for the discharge. Thus, if a whistleblower can prove a *prima facie* case, the employer must then come forward with evidence that its decision was based upon a legitimate business reason rather than upon the employee's whistleblowing activity.[20]

If the employer successfully articulates a legitimate reason for the adverse action, the burden then is upon the whistleblower to prove that the articulated reason is a pretext designed to mask the employer's improper motive.[21] Thus, after all of the evidence is in, the question for the trier of fact is whether the employee has carried his ultimate burden of proving that the employer's articulated reason was not the honest reason for the discharge, but instead was a pretext to hide an illegitimate reason for the discharge, and that the adverse action would not have taken place in the absence of the protected

---

[18]*But see* Consolidated Edison Co. of N.Y. v. Donovan, 673 F.2d 61, 62 (2d Cir. 1982) (NLRB evidentiary standards applied under which employer bears burden of proving a legitimate reason for the adverse action).

[19]411 U.S. 792, 802-07, 5 FEP Cases 965, 969-71 (1973).

[20]*Id.*

[21]*Id.*

conduct. Using the example of the *Mt. Healthy* case, it was Doyle's burden to prove that the school board's stated reason for failing to renew his contract was a pretext, and that Doyle's contract would have been renewed absent his comments to the radio station. In the *Dunham* case, it was Dunham's burden to show that his employer's stated reason, his insubordination, was a pretext.

Administrative Investigations

Whistleblower cases may generate two kinds of administrative investigations for which both whistleblowers and their employers must be prepared. First, in the case of an active whistleblower who complains externally to the appropriate government agency, the agency may start an investigation into whether the employer committed the alleged violation. Second, even if there is no administrative investigation into the alleged violation, many of the federal whistleblower protection laws that provide an administrative remedy for retaliation against whistleblowers, as set forth in Appendix C, require administrative agencies to investigate complaints of retaliation. Moreover, several of these statutes require the agency to attempt to resolve the complaints informally during the course of the investigation, before the complaints are adjudicated in formal adversary proceedings. This section will first discuss the importance of administrative investigations into the merits of the violations complained of by whistleblowers, and second, will discuss the administrative procedures used by the Department of Labor for resolving complaints of retaliation against whistleblowers.

Investigations Regarding Alleged Violations

Assume that an employee reports to the U.S. Environmental Protection Agency (EPA) that his or her employer is discharging toxic chemicals into nearby waters in violation of applicable federal restrictions. Before the employer has had time to discipline or discharge the whistleblower, the EPA may begin an investigation into whether its regulations have been violated. If the whistleblower is eventually terminated by the employer, the result of this investigation may be extremely important in any litigation regarding the propriety of the termination. If the EPA investigation concludes that the alleged violations actually did occur, the whistleblower will wish to use the EPA's findings as evidence of his or her good faith. If the EPA concludes that no violations occurred, the employer will wish to use the EPA's findings as evidence of the employee's lack of good faith. Such reports may be admissible in evidence under the "official records" exception to the hearsay rule.[22] Because the EPA in theory is a disinterested party regarding the dispute between the whistleblower and the employer, the EPA's findings may be given much weight by the judge, jury, or arbitrator who decides the whistleblower's retaliation claim.

For these reasons, both whistleblowers and employers may wish to exert themselves as much as possible to obtain a favorable result in the investigation. Both should cooperate fully with the investigative agency, and should provide as much information as possible in favor of their position. To avoid any appearance of impropriety employers should, if possible, probably refrain from taking adverse action against whistleblowers until any administrative investigation is concluded.

Employers should conduct an immediate internal investigation into the alleged violation while memories are fresh. In some instances, the government agency may not have adequate resources to conduct a thorough investigation of its own, may not believe the complaint to be serious enough to warrant investigation, or may not conduct an investigation because it believes it has enough information to determine whether the complaint is true or untrue. In any case, consideration should be given to preparing a report for submission to the agency, even if no investigation is planned, to ensure that the employer's side of the story is considered. Further, government agencies may be subject to intense media or political pressures to act quickly on whistleblower complaints. Because agencies may be pressured to reach a decision without an investigation or before hearing the employer's version, it may be essential to provide as much information to the agency as possible before it makes any findings.

Investigations Regarding Alleged Retaliation Against Whistleblowers

Many federal whistleblower protection statutes are enforced by the U.S. Department of Labor (DOL), as was generally discussed in Chapter 4. This section will discuss in detail how whistleblowers and employers may wish to approach DOL investigations of complaints of retaliation.

The DOL is required by statute to investigate and adjudicate complaints of retaliation within 90 days after filing.[23] Almost immediately after the DOL receives a complaint, an investigator from the Wage & Hour Division of the DOL will attempt to interview the whistleblower and those persons whom the whistleblower has identified as having knowledge regarding the complaint.[24] Bearing in mind

---

[22]*See, e.g.*, FED. R. EVID. 803(8); CAL. EVID. CODE §1280 (West 1966 & Supp. 1990).

[23]29 C.F.R. §24.6(b).

[24]The Wage and Hour Administrator is required to issue a determination within 30 days after filing of a complaint of retaliation. 29 C.F.R. §24.4(d)(1).

that this investigator will be preparing a report to serve as the basis for the Wage & Hour Administrator's decision as to the merits of the complaint, it is critical that the investigator be given the whistleblower's side of the story in as detailed and organized a fashion as possible. This is especially important in cases where the whistleblower's complaint is technically complex, because every effort must be made to educate the DOL investigators, who in some instances may have little technical training regarding the subject matter of the complaint. In order to do this, whistleblowers must gather all pertinent information into presentable form, which often consists of a detailed affidavit. Similarly, employers must interview all personnel with pertinent information, collect and review all documents bearing on the issues, and formulate a logical position for presentation to the investigator.

Once the investigator arrives at the employer's premises, every effort to cooperate with the investigator's reasonable requests should be made to avoid the appearance of preventing the investigator from developing adverse information. Because the investigator is operating under extreme time pressures, and may not have sufficient time to understand fully many of the issues involved, the investigator's subjective perceptions of whether the employer is hindering the investigation may be a significant factor in the investigator's recommendations. The investigator may ask to interview a large number of employees, and within reason, such requests should be honored.

It should be emphasized that usually the investigator has heard only the whistleblower's side of the story, and that the investigator will probably request to interview persons who the employee has identified as individuals most likely to corroborate his or her story. Accordingly, the investigator may not request to interview many witnesses whose testimony would be highly favorable to the employer. Thus, the employer must ensure that the investigator interviews as many favorable witnesses as possible.

After the investigation is completed, the Wage & Hour Administrator reviews the investigator's report and issues a determination as to whether the employee was subjected to improper retaliation. Either party may appeal the determination, within five days, to the Chief Administrative Law Judge of the DOL.[25] A complete adversarial hearing will be held on the complaint before an Administrative Law Judge (ALJ), whose decision is forwarded for review to the Secretary of Labor.[26] If either party is dissatisfied with the ruling of the Secretary, an appeal may be taken to the U.S. court of appeals in the circuit where the retaliation allegedly occurred.[27] Litigation of hearings before an ALJ from the DOL will involve many of the considerations discussed in the following section.

---

[25] *Id.* at §24.4(d)(2).
[26] *Id.* at §24.6.
[27] *Id.* at §24.7.

Litigating a Whistleblower Case

Because a whistleblower case may arise in a wide variety of administrative and judicial proceedings, the particular litigation procedures applicable in each forum may differ significantly. In order to illustrate the types of common problems which may arise in any whistleblower case, this section will focus on a civil action for wrongful discharge under the public policy doctrine.

Issues at the Pleading Stage

The first issue facing a whistleblower is where to file the complaint. In most instances, whistleblowers will have the option of filing in either state or federal court under the applicable rules of jurisdiction and venue. Assuming that the employee has decided to sue in state court, there are a number of issues that the employer must decide within a short time after service of the complaint.

Removal to Federal Court

Chances are that the whistleblower has sued the employer in state court because that forum is viewed as the most receptive to his complaint. However, there may be some options to move the case to a forum more favorable to the employer. One of the first issues that should be looked into is whether the case may be removed to federal court under federal removal jurisdiction, which permits a defendant to move a case from state to federal court if the plaintiff could have originally filed the case in federal court.[28] In order to remove a case, the defendant must take certain procedural steps within 30 days after service of the complaint.[29]

The two general bases for federal jurisdiction are diversity of citizenship,[30] and the presence of a question "arising under" federal law.[31] Diversity of citizenship is present when the plaintiff and the defendant are citizens of different states. For purposes of federal jurisdiction, a corporation is deemed to be a citizen of the state of its incorporation and of the state where its principal place of business is located.[32] Thus, if a corporate defendant is sued in a state other than its state of incorporation and where its principal place of business is located, and if the plaintiff is not a citizen of either of those states, the defendant may remove the case to the federal district court for the district in which the state court is located. Depending on how many federal districts a state is divided into, removal of the case may change

[28] 28 U.S.C. §1441 *et seq.*

[29] *Id.* at §1446.

[30] *Id.* at §1332.

[31] *Id.* at §1331.

[32] *Id.* at §1332(c).

the venue from one part of the state to another area more favorable to the defendant.[33]

The second general category of cases which may be removed are those which present questions "arising under" federal law. As discussed in Chapter 7, the complaint may be an attempt to "artfully plead" a federal cause of action in the guise of a state law claim and the complaint may be removable to federal court. In addition, a complaint filed in state court may contain one federal claim, such as a claim under the Age Discrimination in Employment Act, along with numerous state law causes of action. The federal removal statutes may permit removal of such complaints under the federal courts' pendent jurisdiction if all of the causes of action arise out of the same facts.[34]

The advantages or disadvantages of removal to federal district court will vary depending on the particular characteristics of the federal and state courts in question. In general, the federal courts draw their jurors from a multi-county pool instead of a single county pool as do most state courts. Most federal courts assign one case to one judge for all purposes, while some state courts are organized such that different judges decide different issues in the case. Also, the federal courts may have different caseloads than the state courts.

Change of Venue

Another method of obtaining a different forum, while remaining within the state court system, is by a motion for change of venue. Most state codes allow a defendant to obtain a change of venue if the plaintiff has brought suit in a county where the defendant cannot legally be sued.[35] However, the right to obtain a change of venue may be waived if not exercised within the time for responding to the complaint.

Some grounds for requesting a change of venue, however, are so fundamental that they may be raised at later points in the proceeding. For instance, under California law a motion to change venue on the grounds that an impartial trial cannot be obtained, or for the convenience of witnesses, may be made after the time for responding to the complaint has passed.[36] If a change of venue is requested on the ground that a fair trial cannot be had, such a motion may require factual support in the form of a survey of potential jurors on the relevant issues, or of newspaper or other media reports about the case.

---

[33]For example, California is divided into the Northern (San Francisco), Central (Los Angeles), Eastern (Sacramento), and Southern (San Diego) Districts. 28 U.S.C. §84 (1988). Because the number of districts is vastly smaller than the number of California counties, more often than not removal of a case to federal court will result in a change in the county in which the action is tried.

[34]Mine Workers v. Gibbs, 383 U.S. 715, 61 LRRM 2561 (1966).

[35]*See, e.g.*, CAL. CIV. PROC. CODE §396b (West 1973 & Supp. 1990).

[36]*Id.* at §397.

Cross-Complaints

Another issue that must be decided quickly is whether any cross-complaint should be filed against the employee for having misappropriated trade secrets or customer lists, or for having committed any other improprieties. Many state codes of procedure require that such cross-actions arising out of a single set of occurrences be filed at the same time as a responsive pleading to the complaint.[37] Thus, any possible grounds for an appropriate cross-complaint against an employee must be investigated early in the lawsuit.

It should be emphasized that only meritorious cross-complaints should be filed. Cross-complaints which are asserted merely as tactics to harass plaintiffs may expose defendants to sanctions. For example, in *Hudson v. Moore Business Forms*,[38] the employer cross-complained on the theory that the plaintiff had breached a duty of loyalty by rejecting opportunities to remain employed by the defendant, by accepting special termination payments, and by filing an action for wrongful discharge. The court rejected the defendant's cross-complaint and imposed sanctions against the defendant's counsel for $15,000, the amount of attorneys' fees expended by the plaintiff to defeat the cross-complaints.[39] Although these sanctions were imposed pursuant to Rule 11 of the Federal Rules of Civil Procedure, many states have analogous statutes on which sanctions for an ungrounded cross-complaint may be premised.[40]

Discovery by Whistleblowers

The most important evidence from an employee's standpoint is proof of retaliatory motive. As discussed earlier in this chapter, direct evidence of improper motivation is rare. Accordingly, employees must develop whatever circumstantial evidence regarding motive there may be. For example, whistleblowers may wish to confirm, in sworn discovery responses, the suspicious timing of adverse action. Alternatively, employees may wish to depose several supervisors in the hope of obtaining inconsistent testimony regarding their motives, so that it can be inferred that an unstated retaliatory motive existed.

Some of the most powerful evidence whistleblowers may obtain is evidence regarding whether the violation reported by the whistleblower actually occurred. If a whistleblower can demonstrate that the violation actually occurred, and that the employer reacted immediately in anger by firing the whistleblower rather than deliberating

[37]*See, e.g., id.* at §426.30.
[38]609 F. Supp. 467, 478 (N.D. Cal. 1985).
[39]*Id.* at 484.
[40]*See, e.g.,* CAL. CIV. PROC. CODE §128.5 (West 1982 & Supp. 1990).

carefully, such evidence might support an inference of retaliatory motive.[41]

Finally, whistleblowers may wish to obtain favorable testimony from co-workers if possible. Because of the controversial nature of whistleblower cases, it may be difficult to persuade other employees to become involved as witnesses. If favorable testimony can be obtained from a company's own employees, the testimony may not only constitute an admission binding upon the company,[42] but may also be highly persuasive to a jury.

Discovery by Employers

In many instances an employer may become aware of a potential whistleblower problem before a lawsuit is filed. As soon as it becomes apparent that a whistleblower problem is likely to arise, even before a lawsuit is filed, an employer should begin gathering whatever information is needed to defend itself. An immediate comprehensive internal investigation is important for several reasons. If the investigation reveals that the whistleblower's complaints are serious and well-taken, the employer will be able to obtain favorable publicity by taking quick corrective action on the complaints. If the investigation reveals that the complaints are unfounded, the employer may also obtain favorable publicity by demonstrating its concern regarding the alleged problems.

From a litigation standpoint, it is crucial to interview potential witnesses while their memories are fresh and clear. Many whistleblower cases involve differences of professional opinion on highly detailed technical or scientific questions, and it may be difficult for witnesses to recall the factual details supporting their conclusion that the whistleblower's complaint was or was not well-taken. It is essential to obtain the precise factual basis for any disagreement with a whistleblower because, if the case is ever tried before a jury, the jury is not likely to be impressed by conclusory statements that the whistleblower's complaints were baseless in the absence of a concrete explanation. Moreover, if the employer is a medium to large-sized corporation, it is likely that many witnesses will transfer from one location to another while the case is pending, and it may be difficult to locate and interview relevant witnesses.

In addition to gathering information within the possession of the employer and its personnel, it is also critical to gather as much information about the whistleblower as possible from third-party witnesses. Because employees may not be entirely straightforward about their background, it is often more fruitful to obtain discovery from third-party witnesses before taking the deposition of employees.

---

[41]*See, e.g.*, Dunham v. Brock, 794 F.2d 1037, 1039 (5th Cir. 1986).

[42]*See, e.g.*, FED. R. EVID. 804(b)(3).

As in any employment-related case, the plaintiff's job history is highly relevant. For instance, it may be that an irresponsible whistleblower has a history of unfounded internal complaints to previous employers that were never publicized. To ascertain whether this is the case, the personnel records of previous employers should be obtained, and where appropriate, the testimony of individuals who had contact with the plaintiff in previous jobs should also be obtained. It is valuable to obtain this information before deposing the plaintiff, because in some cases an employee may refuse to provide such information. If this happens, the employer may never discover highly damaging information in the whistleblower's job history. Moreover, the plaintiff may be confronted with such information and forced to admit, deny, or otherwise explain any adverse information. If the employee has not been prepared to handle questions about prior employment, some detrimental admissions or inconsistent statements may be obtained.

A whistleblower's employment history may also reveal previous complaints of alleged improprieties to government law enforcement agencies. It may be possible to obtain whatever information such agencies possess through the Freedom of Information Act.[43] In the case of an individual who has been discharged by numerous prior employers, the plaintiff may have complained to government agencies that enforce antidiscrimination laws, such as the federal Equal Employment Opportunity Commission, or an analogous state agency. The Freedom of Information Act may also permit an employer to obtain such complaints.

Some whistleblower cases involve differences of professional opinion among physicians, lawyers, accountants, engineers, or other professionals, as discussed in Chapter 5. A whistleblower may have had contact with a professional society promulgating standards relevant to the whistleblower's complaints, in an effort to persuade the society to adopt the whistleblower's point of view, or simply to obtain information about the applicable standards. It may be useful to ascertain whether the plaintiff has had any contact with a professional society, in order to prove whether the employee had a good-faith belief in the merits of his complaints. If it can be shown that the appropriate professional group had rejected the plaintiff's viewpoint, but that the plaintiff still pursued his or her views, this information may be very helpful.

In some cases an employer may suspect that the plaintiff's complaints are not made in good faith, but instead are politically motivated and supported by a particular political group. In such cases, the employer should ascertain the timing and substance of the plaintiff's contacts with the political group. This may entail obtaining documents from the political organization itself as well as from individual members or employees of the organization.

---

[43] 5 U.S.C. §552 *et seq.* (1988).

In addition to discovery regarding the substance of the whistleblower's complaints, substantial discovery should also be taken regarding the employee's alleged damages. As discussed in Chapter 5, most state court public policy claims are asserted as tort causes of action. In tort actions, employees may contend that they are entitled not only to damages for lost wages and employment benefits, but also to damages for mental pain and suffering. If the plaintiff asserts a claim for mental or emotional suffering, the employer may be permitted discovery into the plaintiff's medical or psychological history. Such information may be relevant if it can be shown that the asserted emotional damages are simply part of a history of preexisting difficulties.

It may also be permissible to obtain a psychiatric examination of the plaintiff prior to trial based on the same rationale. For example, Rule 35 of the Federal Rules of Civil Procedure provides that, for good cause shown upon noticed motion, the court may order a party to submit to a physical or mental examination if the party's physical or mental condition is in controversy. Many state codes of procedure permit physical or mental examinations in similar circumstances.[44] It is within the discretion of the court to decide whether such an examination is permitted. Whistleblowers may also claim that various individuals were witnesses to their emotional suffering, including members of the immediate family, co-workers, and neighbors. It may be necessary to take the depositions of the plaintiff's spouse and other persons designated by the employee, to determine the extent of the plaintiff's alleged emotional distress.

Summary Judgment

It may be possible to obtain summary adjudication of all or part of a whistleblower case. For example, in a case in which the company admits that the whistleblower's termination was based on the disruptive manner of the disclosure, the only issue may be whether the whistleblowing conduct actually was disruptive enough to warrant disciplinary action. If discovery establishes that an employer's evidence of disruptiveness is extremely weak or nonexistent, a whistleblower may wish to seek summary judgment on the ground that the evidence regarding disruptiveness is insufficient as a matter of law to support termination. Otherwise, as discussed earlier in this chapter, it probably would be very difficult for whistleblowers to obtain summary judgment on the issue of retaliatory intent because that issue depends upon inferences regarding state of mind which may require live testimony.[45] By the same token, in rare circumstances a whistleblower's *prima facie* case may be so weak—for instance if the evidence regard-

---

[44]*See, e.g.,* CAL. CIV. PROC. CODE §2032 (West 1983 & Supp. 1990).

[45]*See, e.g., id.* at §437c(e) ("[S]ummary judgment shall not be denied on the grounds of credibility . . . [except] where a material fact is an individual's state of mind or lack thereof. . . .").

ing the timing of the alleged retaliation is extremely flimsy—that an employer may wish to seek summary judgment.

Even if total summary judgment is not possible, most jurisdictions permit partial summary adjudication of issues for the purpose of simplifying litigation.[46] As mentioned earlier in this chapter, a key issue in whistleblower cases is whether the alleged violations disclosed by whistleblowers actually occurred. If so, whistleblowers will argue that this evidence demonstrates their good faith, and if not, employers will argue that it demonstrates lack of good faith. Consequently, if the evidence on this point is sufficiently clear, whistleblowers and employers may wish to seek summary adjudication of this issue. Whatever ruling is made on such a motion may have a significant effect on the attitudes of the parties towards settling the litigation on reasonable terms.

Considerations at Trial

Many whistleblower cases present a classic confrontation between an individual "David" standing up to a corporate "Goliath" allegedly involved in conduct harmful to the public. Because the natural tendency of many jurors would be to sympathize with the individual rather than with a large corporation, the employer must make every effort during the trial to avoid the appearance of overreaching. This may be exceedingly difficult because the employer's defense may be that the whistleblower is either incompetent, a chronic complainer, or a vexatious litigant. The delicate task is to develop these defenses without giving the appearance of personally attacking the plaintiff. Most strategic and tactical decisions should be governed by this fundamental need to avoid the appearance of overreaching.

From the standpoint of whistleblowers, this natural emotional advantage must not be squandered. As discussed in Chapter 2, the strong duties of loyalty expected of employees may cause jurors to react negatively to a whistleblower perceived as acting in a way that unnecessarily damaged co-workers or companies. The courtroom demeanor of whistleblowers and their counsel should take this potentially negative reaction into account.

Whistleblower cases present jury selection problems even more delicate than those in the typical case involving an individual plaintiff and a corporate defendant. Not only is the corporate defendant faced with the typical "deep pocket" problems, but the company also often stands before the jury accused of social wrongdoing beyond its mistreatment of the plaintiff. To select jurors who can objectively consider such emotional issues, a substantial amount of time should be devoted to developing profiles of acceptable and unacceptable jurors. In addition, in some jurisdictions attorneys may obtain basic background data regarding jurors (e.g., residence, occupation, marital status) from

---

[46] *See, e.g.*, FED. R. CIV. P. 56(d); CAL. CIV. PROC. CODE §437c(f) (West 1973 & Supp. 1990).

consultants who obtain lists of jurors from the courts on the day of trial. This information can be invaluable if the jurisdiction in which the case is tried does not permit extensive *voir dire* examination by attorneys. Substantial effort should also be devoted to developing an extensive set of *voir dire* questions if attorneys are permitted to conduct such examination.

In many cases either party may wish to introduce evidence regarding marginally relevant but highly prejudicial matter. For example, in a case regarding a whistleblower's complaints about toxic waste, the whistleblower's counsel might ask the following question: "Isn't the problem you complained about the same problem that exists at the Love Canal?" Even if the company's counsel objects to the question, and the objection is sustained, the damage already will have been done because the jurors will have the spectre of the Love Canal in the back of their minds. To prevent such occurrences, counsel for either party should consider whether to make motions *in limine*, which are pretrial motions usually made in the judge's chambers, to prevent any such questions being asked. This mechanism may not be expressly recognized in codes of civil procedure or of evidence, but is commonly recognized in most jurisdictions.[47] The purpose of such a motion is to address admissibility of the inflammatory evidence outside the presence of the jury so that improper questioning can be avoided. Whistleblower cases call for a great deal of foresight and creativity in anticipating inflammatory but irrelevant matter that may be interjected, and these matters should be thoroughly pretried by way of motions *in limine*.

For example, if a government agency has investigated the whistleblower's disclosures and concluded that they were well-founded, the plaintiff may attempt to introduce the reports as evidence of a good-faith belief in the truth of the disclosures. If the report does not support the whistleblower, the company will contend that the employee did not have a good-faith belief. Depending on the agency's findings, either party may wish to make a motion *in limine* to prevent reference to the report at trial. In addition, companies may wish to introduce evidence that they are firmly committed to encouraging responsible whistleblowers, including evidence regarding written personnel policies setting up mechanisms for employee complaints, or statistics on the number of complaints processed through such mechanisms. Whistleblowers may wish to seek exclusion of such evidence.

As discussed in this section, the issues involved in litigating whistleblower claims can be wide-ranging, and can require large investments of time, effort, and money. Moreover, such litigation may have unpleasant side-effects, such as negative publicity for either party, or discovery into individual or corporate matters usually considered private. The following chapter will discuss how costly and, in some cases, how unnecessary litigation might be avoided.

---

[47] *See, e.g.*, R. KEETON, TRIAL TACTICS AND METHODS 200-201 (2d ed. 1973).

9

Avoiding Whistleblower Litigation

In the United States today it is a truism that litigation is costly. Even simple commercial disputes between rational business persons can escalate into protracted legal battles, which accounts in part for the rising interest in alternative dispute resolution in recent years.[1] This truism is especially applicable to whistleblower litigation, which has all of the emotional undercurrents arising from the conflicting legal and ethical duties discussed in Chapter 2.

In addition to the highly charged emotional nature of whistleblower cases, the stakes involved may be very high for both whistleblowers and their companies. Individuals who have had their employment terminated, and companies that have had their practices publicly questioned, may view litigation as the only means of restoring their tarnished reputations.[2] Companies also may be greatly concerned that the atmosphere of their workplaces will become marked by suspicion and secrecy if companies do not attempt to stop unfounded whistleblowing. Although difficult to quantify, the reputational and other intangible aspects of whistleblower cases may make the stakes at issue much higher than the monetary amounts that are sought as damages. These considerations suggest that both whistleblowers and employers should attempt to resolve their differences short of litigation whenever possible.

Responsible Whistleblowing

As suggested in Chapter 2, employees may wish to avoid adverse reaction by their employers by attempting to resolve perceived prob-

---

[1]*See, e.g.*, FEDERAL LITIGATION GUIDE (various eds., Mathew Bender 1989) at Chapter 50, "Alternative Dispute Resolution."

[2]M. GLAZER & P. GLAZER, THE WHISTLEBLOWERS: EXPOSING CORRUPTION IN GOVERNMENT AND INDUSTRY 133-166 (1989).

lems in an informal manner before reporting to outside agencies. If no solution is reached internally, employees may wish to select carefully among various potential recipients of complaints, and to make their disclosures in a nonsensational way. One persistent theme in the various whistleblower cases discussed in the preceding chapters is that whistleblowing is not an absolute, unqualified right which may be exercised at any time, in any place, and in any manner. Rather, legal considerations and common sense suggest that whistleblowing should be conducted so as to preserve and maintain constructive relationships with co-workers and companies.

Another persistent theme in literature authored by whistleblowers is the value of consulting with as many knowledgeable persons as possible before blowing the whistle.[3] Because of the complex thicket of legal and ethical considerations involved in deciding whether to blow the whistle, it is exceedingly difficult to expect one individual to perceive and to evaluate clearly all facets of a particular problem.[4] This is not to suggest that conscience should not be the final guide; it is simply to suggest that conscience should not be the sole guide along a thorny path.

Creating a Climate That Discourages Improper Conduct

Many participants in the Conference on Professional Responsibility referred to in Chapter 1 stated that the decision to "blow the whistle" stems from employees' perceptions that it would be futile to seek to change alleged improprieties from within their organizations. In some cases, employees may believe that management is already committed to an improper course of conduct and will not listen to internal dissent, while in other cases employees may believe that the process of seeking change internally would be too slow to prevent an allegedly hazardous course of conduct. Moreover, employees may believe that internal mechanisms for expressing dissent are ineffective or merely a sham. If internal mechanisms are perceived to be inadequate, employees may believe that management has intentionally made them so in the hope of suppressing dissent, while giving the appearance of being receptive to complaints.

Because of these attitudes of mistrust, the chief objective of companies in either preventing or handling whistleblower complaints must be to gain the trust of employees. Employees may be less likely to complain outside their organizations if they believe that their companies have effective internal mechanisms for expressing dissent and achieving change. If internal mechanisms are perceived as mean-

---

[3]Several individual whistleblowers have detailed their experiences in WHISTLEBLOWING: LOYALTY AND DISSENT IN THE CORPORATION (A. Westin, ed. 1981). *See also* GLAZER & GLAZER, *supra* note 2 at 167-205.

[4]D. CALLAHAN & S. BOK, ETHICS TEACHING IN HIGHER EDUCATION 277-295 (1980).

ingful, it is less likely that employees will view the mechanisms as attempts to co-opt dissenters, and less likely that an atmosphere of distrust will result. Internal mechanisms for complaints may also aid employers in whistleblower litigation. Some courts that have refused to recognize a cause of action for alleged whistleblowers appear to have relied on the fact that the employee did not exhaust existing internal channels for complaints. However, if no such channels exist, employers obviously will not be able to argue that employees have failed to exhaust them.

As an important first step to gaining the trust of employees, companies should strongly articulate their insistence upon compliance with applicable law. Whether justified or not, employees may view a company's silence regarding compliance with governing law as a conscious decision not to encourage compliance. Accordingly, employers may wish to establish policies which expressly require employees to comply with applicable laws. One of the more prominent policy statements of this kind is the Code of Ethics for Government Service, which governs the conduct of all federal government employees. The Code of Ethics was originally promulgated in 1958, and provides as follows:

> Any person in Government service should:
>
> I. Put loyalty to the highest moral principles and to country above loyalty to persons, party, or Government department.
> II. Uphold the Constitution, laws, and regulations of the United States and of all governments therein and never be a party to their evasion.
> III. Give a full day's labor for a full day's pay; giving earnest effort and best thought to the performance of duties.
> IV. Seek to find and employ more efficient and economical ways of getting tasks accomplished.
> V. Never discriminate unfairly by the dispensing of special favors or privileges to anyone, whether for remuneration or not; and never accept, for himself or herself or for family members, favors or benefits under circumstances which might be construed by reasonable persons as influencing the performance of governmental duties.
> VI. Make no private promises of any kind binding upon the duties of office, since a Government employee has no private word which can be binding on public duty.
> VII. Engage in no business with the Government, either directly or indirectly, which is inconsistent with the conscientious performance of governmental duties.
> VIII. Never use any information gained confidentially in the performance of governmental duties as a means of making private profit.
> IX. Expose corruption wherever discovered.
> X. Uphold these principles, ever conscious that public office is a public trust.[5]

The Code is required to be posted on prominent areas of all federal government buildings.[6] In addition to requiring compliance with all

---

[5]Pub. L. No. 96-303, 94 Stat. 855, *reprinted* in 5 U.S.C. §7301 app. (1988).
[6]*Id.*

applicable laws, the Code encourages government employees to adhere to high ethical standards. Finally, the Code imposes a duty upon employees to "[e]xpose corruption wherever discovered," which strongly recommends that employees become whistleblowers if circumstances so require.

Mere promulgation of policies such as the Code of Ethics, however, is not necessarily sufficient to encourage responsible whistleblowing. One study of federal government employees, who were covered by the Code of Ethics, concluded that most employees who observed but did not report wrongdoing failed to do so because they did not believe that corrective action would be taken.[7] Thus, any ethics policy must also contain assurances that it will be effectively implemented.

Several elements might be added to policies such as the Code of Ethics to encourage employees to report improprieties.[8] First, it may be prudent to provide a means for employees to seek informal clarification of company policies or laws. If employees are reluctant to make reports because they are unsure whether particular conduct is improper, such a mechanism might encourage appropriate reports and discourage unfounded reports. Accordingly, companies may wish to designate one or more departments, such as human resources, security, or internal audit, as departments where clarification of laws or policies may be obtained.

A second important element is to provide more than one channel for employee disclosures. Companies that only permit employees to complain to their immediate supervisors may run the risk of discouraging complaints about such supervisors. Furthermore, the existence of multiple channels for complaints may increase the likelihood that employees will view at least one of the channels as being effective.

One of the most important elements of any policy is an assurance that no retribution will be taken for responsible disclosures. If companies do not expressly state that retribution will not be tolerated, employees may conclude that the companies consciously refrain from doing so. A policy which encourages disclosures but does not prohibit retaliation may not be taken seriously. Similarly, assurances that disclosures will be treated confidentially to the extent possible may decrease fears of retribution.

Finally, the policy should specify what penalties may be imposed for violations of applicable laws. As mentioned previously, even if employees are shielded from retaliation, they may be reluctant to disclose wrongdoing if they think that no corrective action will be taken.[9] To emphasize that legal or other violations will be taken seriously, companies may wish to specify that violators will be subject

---

[7]Miceli & Near, *The Relationship Among Beliefs, Organizational Position, and Whistleblowing Status*, 27 ACAD. MGMT. J. 687, 703-04 (1984).

[8]For an example of a policy regarding whistleblowing, see K. DECKER, EMPLOYEE PRIVACY FORMS AND PROCEDURES 299-300 (1988).

[9]Miceli & Near, *supra* note 7 at 703-04.

to discipline, up to and including discharge. Companies may also wish to involve whistleblowers in the resolution of their complaints. For example, a whistleblower might be appointed as one member of an *ad hoc* committee to resolve his or her complaint. Even if the whistleblower's proposed resolution is not adopted, at least he or she will have had a voice in the process.

Effectively Implementing Policies Against Improper Conduct

There are many different methods of implementing policies against improper conduct. Selection of the appropriate method depends upon the size and nature of the employer. These methods will be discussed in the following section. In order to determine which methods may be more or less effective, companies may wish to attempt to identify areas within their organizations which are potential sources of improper conduct or of whistleblower complaints. Once potential trouble spots have been identified, a program for effectively implementing policies can be tailored to specific employers.

Many companies have some divisions which are subject to greater governmental regulation than other divisions. For example, some divisions may be subject to environment, government contracts, or antitrust regulations more than other divisions. In such cases, it might be prudent to focus educational and implementation efforts more sharply on the more strictly regulated divisions. Companies may also consider using compliance reviews as a tool for early resolution of whistleblower complaints. This may require not only reviews of documentation, but also confidential interviews of employees by third persons from other departments or divisions.

Similarly, many companies have quality control or quality assurance departments, whose functions are to call into question the fitness of the work product of other departments. It might be anticipated that more potential whistleblower disclosures will be generated from quality control or quality assurance departments, which suggests that companies might wish to devote more attention to employee concerns in those departments. Finally, it has been suggested—although by no means established—that white-collar crime is more likely to occur in financially troubled organizations that are pressured to cut corners.[10] If some departments are under more pressure than others, companies may wish to focus their preventive efforts on those departments.

In addition to attempting to identify institutional sources of conflict which may lead to whistleblowing, companies may also wish to attempt to identify the types of individuals who are more likely than

---

[10]Braithwaite, *White Collar Crime*, 22 ANN. REV. SOC. 1, 6 (1985).

others to become whistleblowers. It has been hypothesized that whistleblowers may tend to be individuals at lower levels who feel powerless to effectuate change within their institutions.[11] Depending upon whether this generalization fits a particular organization, employers may wish to devote most of their efforts to persuading lower-level employees that their legitimate concerns will be taken seriously. Using these considerations as background, the following section will discuss various methods for resolving potential whistleblower complaints.

Open-Door Policy

At the informal end of the spectrum, a simple open-door policy can be implemented. This means that employers would permit employees to bring complaints to the attention of their supervisors at any time, either orally or in writing. In order for such a policy to be effective, however, each supervisor must be cautioned to be receptive to complaints to avoid creating a perception that complaints will not be taken seriously. Such policies usually also provide that employees may take their grievances through the chain of command if they believe that their grievances have not been properly resolved. The advantages of an open-door policy are that complaints can be discussed and resolved informally without creating an unduly adversarial atmosphere, and that such a system does not require creation of a special department but instead relies upon supervisors already in place. On the negative side, employees may perceive such a system to be ineffective if all supervisors do not take the policy seriously.

Ombudsman

In the middle of the spectrum would be an ombudsman system where companies designate an individual as the person to whom complaints should be directed. In order for an ombudsman to be credible, however, the work duties of the designated individual should be reduced so that a significant share of the individual's time can be allocated to responding to complaints. Moreover, the individual should be relatively senior in the organization or otherwise respected so that the individual will be perceived as someone with enough credibility to make necessary changes. One of the advantages of such a system is that the responsibility for responding to complaints rests with one person rather than with each supervisor. This lends an air of professionalism to the office of ombudsman. Such a system, however, also requires the individual to spend a large portion of otherwise productive time on complaint resolution, thus reducing the contribu-

---

[11]Farrell & Peterson, *Patterns of Political Behavior in Organizations*, 7 ACAD. MGMT. REV., 403, 406 (1982).

tion that the individual might make to the employer. In addition, the system may contribute to an adversarial atmosphere unless employees are required to attempt to informally resolve their disputes with their supervisors prior to resorting to the ombudsman.

Grievance Procedure

The most formal method of providing an internal channel for dissent would be to establish a grievance procedure that results in a hearing on the grievance, to be adjudicated by a person from the company who is not involved in the dispute. Employees may perceive such a system to be superior because, under the previous two methods, no formal hearing is required where both sides have an opportunity to present their side of the story, and to rebut the other side's version. However, such a procedure requires a vastly greater investment of time and resources, and may simply be impractical in smaller workplaces.

Regular Organizational Meetings

In some instances whistleblowing may be caused by a lack of communication within an organization. For example, employees may become suspicious of wholly innocent activities because they have insufficient information. To prevent whistleblowing occasioned by misunderstanding, companies may consider requiring departments that are likely to generate whistleblowing activity to hold regular meetings so that misunderstandings are avoided. Further, some surveys indicate that employees are most likely to be reassured by informal, face-to-face discussions with supervisors rather than by more formal activities.[12]

Ethics Training

The legal and ethical duties of employees who are considering whether to disclose improprieties are often in conflict, as discussed in Chapter 2. Many individuals who have become whistleblowers have stated that the decisions to make their disclosures were exceptionally difficult, and that they felt the need to discuss whether they should make their disclosures with several other persons before doing so.[13] The complex legal and ethical dilemmas faced by whistleblowers have prompted two commentators to recommend that case studies of whistleblowers be studied in professional schools.[14]

---

[12]*Personnel Management* (BNA 1989), Employee Relations: Communication, p. 243:301-306.

[13]*See, e.g.*, WHISTLEBLOWING: LOYALTY AND DISSENT IN THE CORPORATION (A. Westin ed. 1981).

[14]D. CALLAHAN & S. BOK, *supra* note 4 at 277-295.

Companies may wish to take this proposal one step further by conducting ethical training for their employees. Rather than being an academic discussion of abstract problems, such training could take the form of case studies that address concrete problems which may arise in companies. The use of case studies would allow individual companies to tailor these programs to their own specific needs. Training may help to demonstrate the seriousness with which the companies view ethical problems, which may help to encourage legitimate whistleblowing. By the same token, training may help to discourage unfounded whistleblowing by educating employees regarding their ethical responsibilities to other persons in their organizations. Perhaps most importantly, training may create an atmosphere where employees feel comfortable in working out informal solutions to prevent potential violations, rather than allowing violations to occur for fear of discussing them.

Consultants

Some internal disagreements, which may lead to whistleblowing, may be incapable of informal resolution between the disputing individuals or departments. One commentator has suggested that consultants—either from disinterested organizations within the company or from outside companies—be used to attempt to resolve such situations.[15] It is possible to avoid potential whistleblowing by calling in a disinterested third party who listens to the competing viewpoints and then attempts to forge a solution. The advantage of bringing in disinterested consultants on an *ad hoc* basis, rather than having one company official designated as an ombudsman, is that employees may have more faith in the impartiality of a fresh observer than in an official who routinely attempts to resolve disputes.

Limits on Complaints

Whichever method of allowing internal dissent is implemented, it may be advisable to limit complaints to significant issues regarding public health and safety. No internal mechanism should be permitted to become an outlet for petty matters or other insignificant issues, because such a development would detract from the importance of the mechanism. Accordingly, some limits on the nature of complaints to be resolved by the procedure should be imposed. One method of limiting the nature of complaints, taken from some whistleblower protection statutes, might be to require that the employee have a good-faith belief that an immediate and significant danger to the public health and safety would result if a particular course of conduct is followed.

---

[15]F. Elliston, J. Keenan, P. Lockhart, & J. van Schaick, Whistleblowing: Managing Dissent in the Workplace 31-32 (1985).

Arbitration

Even if all informal efforts to resolve whistleblower complaints have failed, it may be possible to avoid costly litigation in the courts by means of alternative means for dispute resolution. Depending upon the circumstances in each company, it may be possible to obtain the agreement of employees to arbitrate any disputes arising out of their employment including whistleblower complaints.

Arbitration has gained favor in recent years as the dockets of the state and federal courts have become increasingly congested. Several recent Supreme Court decisions have gone so far as to suggest that arbitration is favored as a matter of judicial policy.[16] If an employee has agreed to be bound by an arbitration agreement, it may be possible to obtain a court order compelling arbitration of whistleblower complaints under the Federal Arbitration Act.[17] However, in general, arbitration agreements will only be enforced if they are not unconscionable or oppressive.[18] To avoid such situations, companies may wish to avoid coercing employees to sign arbitration agreements, and to avoid the appearance that such agreements are merely formalities without any real significance. Moreover, companies may wish to affirmatively emphasize the importance of the arbitration agreement in the hiring process.[19]

There is no easy solution for avoiding whistleblower litigation. Whatever policies or procedures are implemented to encourage early and informal resolution of potential violations, there is always the risk that employees may perceive that well-intentioned policies are not fully carried out in practice. Thus, the spirit in which potential whistleblowing problems are resolved is equally if not more important than the letter of policies and practices. If management is able to create a climate that encourages responsible whistleblowing, much whistleblower litigation may be avoided.

---

[16]Rodriguez de Quijas v. Shearson/American Exp., Inc., 490 U.S. 477 (1989); Shearson/American Exp., Inc. v. McMahon, 482 U.S. 220 (1987); Mitsubishi Motors Corp. v. Soler Chrysler-Plymouth, 473 U.S. 614 (1985).

[17]9 U.S.C. §2 (1988). *But see* Nicholson v. CPC Int'l, Inc., 877 F.2d 221, 49 FEP Cases 1678 (3d Cir. 1989) (court denied order compelling arbitration of age discrimination claim); Utley v. Goldman Sachs & Co., 883 F.2d 184, 50 FEP Cases 1087 (1st Cir. 1989), *cert. denied*, 493 U.S. ___, 58 USLW 3449 (court denied order compelling arbitration of discrimination claim under Title VII); Swenson v. Management Recruiters Int'l, Inc., 858 F.2d 1304 (8th Cir. 1988), *reh'g denied*, 872 F.2d 264, *cert. denied*, 493 U.S.___, 58 USLW 3216 (1989) (same).

[18]*See, e.g.*, Tonetti v. Shirley, 173 Cal. App. 3d 1144, 219 Cal. Rptr. 616 (1985) (agreement requiring arbitration of termination of stock broker not enforced as unconscionably favoring employer); Graham v. Scissor-Tail, Inc., 28 Cal. 3d 807, 171 Cal. Rptr. 604, 623 P.2d 165 (1981) (arbitration agreement between concert promoters and musicians not enforced).

[19]*See, e.g.*, Sarchett v. Blue Shield, 43 Cal. 3d 1, 233 Cal. Rptr. 76, 729 P.2d 267 (1987), *modified*, 43 Cal. 3d 316b (1987) (arbitration can be waived if arbitration provision is not clearly stated in contract and communicated to employee after dispute arises).

Appendix A

State Statutes Protecting Public Sector Employees

This appendix summarizes the state statutes which protect whistleblowers employed in the public sector. These statutes may be found in the BNA Labor Relations Reporter Manual, State Laws, Volumes 4 and 4A.

STATE	COVERAGE	PROTECTED CONDUCT	NATURE OF VIOLATION	REMEDY	OPPORTUNITY TO CORRECT
ALASKA, Alaska Stat. §§39.90.100 *et seq.* (1989)	State or local government employees	Employee who reports, or is about to report, violation to a public body where employee has reasonable belief.	Violation of any law or regulation, danger to public health and safety, gross mismanagement, waste, abuse of authority, or a matter for investigation by the office of the ombudsman.	Civil action, damages including punitive damages; civil fine not to exceed $10,000.	Employer may require employee to give notice prior to initiating a report; however, employee is not required to give prior notice if reasonably believes it would not result in prompt action; the activity is already known to the employer; an emergency is involved, or fears reprisal or discrimination.
ARIZONA, Ariz. Rev. Stat. Ann. §38-531 *et seq.* (1989)	State or local government employees	Employee who reports violation to attorney general, legislature, governor, county attorney, or federal, state or local law enforcement agency.	Violation of any law, or mismanagement, gross waste of monies, or abuse of authority.	Administrative hearing; violators shall be suspended up to 30 days or dismissed.	N/A
CALIFORNIA, Cal. Gov't Code §§10540 *et seq.* (West 1989)	Employees of state government or state universities	Employee who reports violation to Joint Legislative Audit Committee, Auditor General, or university officers.	Violation of state or federal law or regulation, economic waste, or gross misconduct, incompetency, or inefficiency.	Administrative hearing before State Personnel Board, or if no action by Board, civil action for compensatory and punitive damages and attorneys' fees.	N/A

STATE	COVERAGE	PROTECTED CONDUCT	NATURE OF VIOLATION	REMEDY	OPPORTUNITY TO CORRECT
COLORADO, Colo. Rev. Stat. §§24-50.5-101 *et seq.* (1989)	State employees	Employee who discloses information to any person or testifies before any committee of the general assembly.	Any practice, including waste of public funds, abuse of authority, or mismanagement.	Administrative hearing for employees in state personnel system; civil action for reinstatement, backpay, and other relief.	Employees must make good-faith effort to provide information to supervisor, member of general assembly, or appointing authority before disclosure.
DELAWARE, Del. Code Ann. tit. 29, §5115 (1989)	State employees	Employee who reports to state Office of Auditor of Accounts.	Violation of state or federal law or regulation.	Civil action within 90 days, damages available not specified.	N/A
FLORIDA, Fla. Stat. Ann. §112.3187 (West 1989)	State or local government employees, or employees of contractors with state or local government.	Employee who discloses violation to state or federal agency with authority to investigate the violation.	Violations of any federal, state, or local law or regulation that presents a substantial and specific danger to the public health, safety, or welfare; or malfeasance, misfeasance, or neglect of duty by an agency.	After exhausting administrative remedies, employees may bring civil actions for reinstatement, backpay and attorneys' fees.	N/A
ILLINOIS, Ill. Ann. Stat. ch. 127, para. 63b119c.1 (Smith-Hurd 1989)	State employees	Employee who discloses violation.	Violation of law, rule, or regulation; mismanagement, gross waste of funds, abuse of authority, substantial and specific danger to public health and safety.	Administrative hearing.	N/A
INDIANA, Ind. Code Ann. §4-15-10-4 (West 1989)	State employees	Employee who reports violation in writing, unless employee knows of falsity.	Violation of state or federal laws or regulations, misuse of public resources.	Administrative appeal.	Employee must disclose to supervisor and give reasonable time to correct.

IOWA, Iowa Code §§79.28 *et seq.* (1989)	State employees	Disclosure of information to member of General Assembly, legislative service bureau, legislative fiscal bureau, caucus staff of General Assembly, where employee has reasonable belief.	Violation of law or rule, mismanagement, gross abuse of funds, abuse of authority, or substantial and specific danger to public health and safety.	None provided.	N/A
KANSAS, Kan. Stat. Ann. §75-2973 (1988)	State employees	Reporting of violation to any person, agency, or organization, unless employee knows of falsity or recklessly disregards falsity.	Violation of state or federal law, rules or regulations.	None provided.	Statute specifically prohibits any requirement of prior disclosure to supervisor.
KENTUCKY, Ky. Rev. Stat. Ann. §§61.101 *et seq.* (Baldwin 1989)	State employees	Employees who report violations to judicial, legislative, or enforcement agencies; employees bear burden of providing by clear and convincing evidence that they were about to make protected disclosures.	Violation of any state or federal law or regulation, or mismanagement, waste, fraud, or endangerment of public health or safety.	In addition to administrative remedies, employees may bring a civil action for reinstatement and punitive damages.	Employers may not require notice prior to disclosure of information.
MARYLAND, Maryland Ann. Code art.64A, §§12F *et seq.* (1983)	State employees	Disclosure of violation which employee reasonably believes to exist.	Violation of any law, rule, regulation; gross mismanagement; gross waste of funds; abuse of authority; substantial and specific danger to public health & safety.	None provided.	N/A
MISSOURI, Mo. Rev. Stat. §105.055 (1989)	State employees	Employees who disclose violations to state auditor or member of legislature.	Violation of any law or regulation, mismanagement, gross waste of funds, abuse of authority, or a substantial and specific danger to public health or safety.	Administrative hearing which may result in suspension up to 30 days, or forfeiture of position in cases of willful or repeated violations.	Employers may not require employees to give notice prior to disclosure of information.

STATE	COVERAGE	PROTECTED CONDUCT	NATURE OF VIOLATION	REMEDY	OPPORTUNITY TO CORRECT
NEW HAMPSHIRE, N.H. Rev. Stat. Ann. §98-E:1 (1988)	State employees	Public discussion and giving of opinions on all matters concerning the state and its policies.	All matters concerning the state and its policies.	N/A	N/A
NORTH CAROLINA, N.C. Gen. Stat. §§126-84 *et seq.* (1989)	State employees	Employees who report, or are about to report, violations to supervisor or other appropriate authority, where employee has reasonable belief.	Violation of state or federal law or regulation, fraud, misappropriation of state funds, or a danger to public health and safety.	Civil action for injunction, reinstatement, back wages, actual damages, punitive damages for willful retaliation, and attorneys' fees.	Statute specifically provides that notice be given to supervisor or other appropriate authority.
OKLAHOMA, Okla. Stat. tit. 74, §§841.7 *et seq.* (1989)	State employees	Disclosure of, or offer to disclose, information to any member of legislature, legislative committee, administrative hearing, or court of law.	Any information.	Administrative hearing and appeal before Ethics and Merit Commission, supervisor forfeits job and eligibility for state employment for five years.	N/A
OREGON, Or. Rev. Stat. §240.316(5) (1983)	State employees and employees of public corporations	Disclosure of violations.	Violation of laws, rules, or improper actions or inefficiency of superior officers or fellow employees; gross waste of funds, abuse of authority, specific danger to public health & safety.	Administrative hearing.	N/A

PENNSYLVANIA, 43 Pa. Cons. Stat. §§1421 *et seq.* (1989)	State or local government employees	Employees who disclose violations to superiors, or appropriate federal, state or local agencies; employees must prove by preponderance of evidence that they were about to make disclosures.	Violations which are not technical or minimal of any federal or state law or regulation, or of code of ethics designed to protect interest of public or employer.	Civil action for reinstatement and actual damages, including attorneys' fees; civil fine not to exceed $500; suspension of violator for up to six months.	N/A
SOUTH CAROLINA, S.C. Code Ann. §§8-27-10 *et seq.* (Law Co-op 1988)	State or local government employees	Employees who disclose violations to appropriate public bodies; rebuttable presumption that adverse action within one year of disclosure was motivated by intent to retaliate.	Violation of any federal or state law or regulation, or criminality, corruption, waste, fraud, gross negligence, or mismanagement.	Civil action for reinstatement and damages, including 25% of public funds saved up to $2,000.	N/A
TENNESSEE, Tenn. Code Ann. §§49-50-1401 *et seq.* (1989)	State education employees	Employee who discloses violation to State Department of Education, legislator, or employee of the department or legislature, or testifies before any committee of the General Assembly.	Knowing or willful falsifications to state officials, law enforcement agencies, or judiciary; waste or mismanagement of public education funds.	Civil action for injunction, reinstatement, back wages, seniority rights, actual damages, and attorneys' fees.	N/A
TEXAS, Tex. Rev. Civ. Stat. Ann. art. 6252-16a (Vernon 1989)	State employees	Employee who reports violation to law enforcement agency in good faith; employee has burden; rebuttable presumption of violation if act of discrimination occurs within 90 days of report.	Violation of state or federal statute or rule, or local ordinance or rule.	Civil action within 90 days; reinstatement, backpay, costs, attorneys' fees, punitive damages, and actual damages.	N/A

STATE	COVERAGE	PROTECTED CONDUCT	NATURE OF VIOLATION	REMEDY	OPPORTUNITY TO CORRECT
UTAH, Utah Code Ann. §67-21-1 (1986)	State or local government employees	Report in any fashion including verbal, written, broadcast or otherwise, of violation, unless employee has reason to know that report is false; employee has burden by clear and convincing evidence to show he was intending to make report.	Violation of federal, state, or local law or rule, or waste of public funds, property, or manpower.	Civil action within 90 days, reinstatement, backpay, costs, attorneys' fees, and civil fine.	Employee must give employer formal notice and allow reasonable time for correction, or conform with reasonable administration procedures for reports.
WASHINGTON, Wash. Rev. Code §42.40.010 (1989)	State employees	Report to State Auditor regarding violation, where employee has good-faith belief.	Violation of any state law or rule; abuse of authority; gross waste of public funds; or substantial and specific danger to public health and safety.	No exhaustion of administrative remedies required; civil action within two years; attorneys' fees; no other available damages specified.	N/A
WEST VIRGINIA, W. Va. Code §§6C-1-1 *et seq.* (1989)	State or local government employees	Employees who report violations to superiors or to appropriate public bodies; employees must prove by preponderance of evidence that they were about to make disclosures.	Violations which are not technical or minimal of any federal or state law or regulation, or of code of ethics designed to protect interest of public or employer.	Civil action for reinstatement and actual damages, including attorneys' fees; civil fine not to exceed $500; suspension of violator for up to six months.	N/A
WISCONSIN, Wis. Stat. Ann. §§230.80 *et seq.* (West 1988)	State employees	Disclosure of criminal activity to law enforcement agency; disclosure of violation to any person; unless employee anticipates that disclosure is likely to result in receipt of anything of value by employee's immediate family.	Violation of any state or federal statute, rule or regulation; mismanagement, abuse of authority, substantial waste of public funds, or a danger to public health and safety.	Administrative remedy or civil action; no available damages specified.	Employee must disclose information in writing to supervisor, or ask commission to which government agency report should be made.

Appendix B

State Statutes Protecting Private Sector, or Both Private and Public Sector Employees

This appendix summarizes the state statutes which protect whistleblowers employed in the private sector, or in both the private and public sectors. These statutes may be found in the BNA Labor Relations Reporter Manual, State Laws, Volumes 4 and 4A.

STATE	COVERAGE	PROTECTED CONDUCT	NATURE OF VIOLATION	REMEDY	OPPORTUNITY TO CORRECT
CALIFORNIA, Cal. Lab. Code §1102.5 (West 1989)	Private sector employees	Employee, with reasonable cause to believe violation has occurred, who makes report to government or law enforcement agency.	Violation of federal or state statute or regulation.	Misdemeanor penalty.	N/A
CONNECTICUT, Conn. Gen. Stat. Ann. §631-51m (West 1989)	Private sector employees	Employee reports or testimony to public body of violation unless employee knows it to be false.	Violation of federal, state, or local statutes, regulation, or ordinance.	After exhaustion of administrative remedies, civil action within 90 days; reinstatement, backpay, costs, and attorneys' fees.	N/A
	State or local government employees	Report of violation to public body unless employee knows it is false.	Corruption, unethical conduct, violation of state or federal law, gross waste, mismanagement, abuse of authority, danger to public health and safety.	Administrative complaint with state employee Review Board.	N/A
HAWAII, Haw. Rev. Stat. §378-61 (1988)	Private and public sector employees	Employees who disclose violations to public bodies.	Violations of state or federal laws or rules.	Civil action for reinstatement, backpay, actual damages and attorneys' fees; civil fine of up to $500.	N/A

STATE	COVERAGE	PROTECTED CONDUCT	NATURE OF VIOLATION	REMEDY	OPPORTUNITY TO CORRECT
LOUISIANA, La. Rev. Stat. Ann. §2027 (West 1989)	Private and public sector employees	Complaints or reports regarding violations of environmental laws of state, federal or local authorities, unless employee has deliberately violated environmental laws.	Environmental violations.	Civil action, treble damages, costs, attorneys' fees, backpay, and emotional distress damages.	N/A
MAINE, Me. Rev. Stat. Ann. tit.26, §§831 *et seq.* (1989)	Private sector employees	Employee, with reasonable cause, who reports or gives information concerning violation; employee bears burden by a preponderance of evidence.	Violation of state or federal law or regulation.	After exhaustion of administrative remedies, civil action within 90 days, reinstatement, backpay, costs, attorneys' fees, and civil fine.	Employee unprotected unless first discloses to supervisor, and gives opportunity to correct, unless futile.
	State employees	Employee giving information to legislative committee.	Any information.	Civil action within 120 days, reinstatement, backpay, costs, attorneys' fees, and civil fine.	N/A
	Public utility employees	Employee giving information to legislative committee or Public Utilities Commission, unless it is a trade secret or corporate strategy.	Any information unless it is a trade secret or corporate strategy.	After exhaustion of administrative remedies, civil action within 90 days, reinstatement, backpay, costs, attorneys' fees, and civil fine.	N/A
MICHIGAN, Mich. Comp. Laws. Ann. §§15.361 *et seq.* (West 1989)	Private and public sector employees	Employee who reports, or is about to report, suspected violation, unless employee knows of falsity; employee has burden by clear and convincing evidence.	Violation of federal, state, or local statute or regulation.	Civil action within 90 days, reinstatement, backpay, costs, attorneys' fees, and civil fine.	N/A

MINNESOTA, Minn. Stat. Ann. §§181.931 *et seq.* (West 1989)	Private and public sector employees	Employee who reports violation to employer or to any governmental body or law enforcement official; employee's identity shall not be disclosed without employee's consent; employer required to give written notice of reason for termination.	Violation of any federal or state law or rule.	Civil action for equitable relief and all damages recoverable at law, including attorneys' fees.	N/A
NEW HAMPSHIRE, N.H. Rev. Stat. Ann. §§275-E:1 *et seq.* (1988)	Private and public sector employees	Employee who reports violation in good faith, or who participates in an investigation by a governmental entity; employee may refuse to execute any directive which is a violation of a state or federal law or rule.	Violation of federal, state, or local law or rule.	After exhaustion of workplace remedies, hearing before the commissioner of labor for reinstatement, seniority rights, fringe benefits, and injunction.	Employee required to give prior notice to employer and reasonable opportunity to correct unless futile.
NEW JERSEY, N.J. Stat. Ann. §§34:19-1 *et seq.* (West 1987)	Private and public sector employees	Employee who reports violation to supervisor or to public body; employees may refuse to participate in violations of law, fraudulent activity, or conduct incompatible with clear mandate of public policy.	Violation of any law or regulation.	Civil action for reinstatement, backpay, punitive damages and attorneys' fees; civil fine up to $1000 for first violation and up to $5000 for subsequent violations.	Employees required to give written notice to supervisors, unless employees reasonably believe that violation is known to supervisors, reasonably fear physical harm, or in emergencies.
NEW YORK, N.Y. Lab. Law §740 (McKinney 1989)	Private sector employees	Employee who discloses or threatens to disclose violation, or gives information to a public body, or refuses to participate in violation.	Violation of state, federal, or local statute or regulation which creates substantial and specific danger to the public health and safety.	Civil action within one year; reinstatement, backpay, costs, and attorneys' fees; employer can get attorneys' fees if no basis for action; filing action waives rights under collective bargaining agreement.	Employee must disclose to supervisor and give reasonable opportunity to correct before disclosure.

STATE	COVERAGE	PROTECTED CONDUCT	NATURE OF VIOLATION	REMEDY	OPPORTUNITY TO CORRECT
NEW YORK (cont'd)	Public sector employees	Employee who discloses violation to a government body in good faith.	Violation of federal, state or local law, rule or regulation, or danger to public safety or health.	Administrative hearing; reinstatement and backpay.	Employee must disclose to employer and allow reasonable opportunity to correct unless imminent threat to public safety.
OHIO, Ohio Rev. Code Ann. §§4113.51 *et seq.* (Baldwin 1989)	Private and public sector employees	Employees who disclose violations to supervisors or appropriate public officials.	Violation of any federal or state law or regulation which is either criminal or likely to cause imminent risk of physical harm to persons or a hazard to public safety.	Civil action for reinstatement, backpay and attorneys' fees.	Employees required to give immediate oral notice followed by written report, to which employers must respond within 24 hours; if violation is not corrected employees may report to appropriate public officials.
RHODE ISLAND, R.I. Gen. Laws §§36-15-1 *et seq.* (1989)	State or local government employees	Employee, with reasonable belief, who reports or is about to report violation, unless employee knows of falsity; providing information to public body; employee has burden by clear and convincing evidence.	Violation of state, federal or local statute or regulation.	Civil action within three years; reinstatement, backpay, costs.	N/A
RHODE ISLAND, R.I. Gen. Laws §36-15-9 (1989)	Private and public sector employees	"	Violation of laws regarding toxic waste.	"	N/A

TENNESSEE, Tenn. Code Ann. §50-1-304 (Supp. 1990)	Private sector employees	Employee who refuses to participate in, or remain silent about, illegal activities; employees' off-duty use of non-regulated agricultural products.	Violation of state or federal civil or criminal code, or regulation intended to protect public health and safety.	Civil action for wrongful discharge; if employee files frivolous or abusive lawsuit, court may impose sanctions including attorneys' fees.	N/A
WISCONSIN, Wis. Stat. Ann. §§101.01 *et seq.* (West 1990)	Private sector employees	Employees who complain or report violations to Department of Industry, Labor and Human Resources.	Violations of state laws regarding wages, hours, child labor, workplace safety and discrimination.	Administrative hearing, (30 days to file complaint), back pay, reinstatement, or compensation in lieu of reinstatement, and education or training programs.	N/A

Appendix C

Federal Statutes Protecting Employees

This appendix sets forth the federal environmental, workplace safety, civil rights, and public health statutes that protect employees who report violations of these statutes.

Statute	Responsible Agency	Substantive Protection	Procedures and Remedies
Age Discrimination in Employment Act (ADEA), 29 U.S.C. §621 *et seq.* (1988). Section 623 contains the antiretaliation provision.	Equal Employment Opportunity Commission (EEOC)	Retaliation prohibited for "opposing" unlawful practice, testifying, "participating" or assisting in enforcement proceedings.	Administrative investigation (complaint must be filed with EEOC within 180 or 300 days of alleged discrimination), which may result in prosecution by EEOC or by employee in U.S. District Court (suit must be filed within 2 years, or 3 years for willful violations). Damages include reinstatement, backpay, liquidated damages for willful violations, and attorneys' fees.
Asbestos Hazard Emergency Response Act of 1986, 15 U.S.C. §2641 *et seq.* (1988). Section 2651 contains the antiretaliation provision.	Department of Labor	Retaliation prohibited for reporting asbestos in schools to any person, including state or federal government.	Administrative investigation (90 days to file complaint), action may be brought by Secretary of Labor on employee's behalf in U.S. District Court. Damages include reinstatement and backpay.

Statute	Responsible Agency	Substantive Protection	Procedures and Remedies
Asbestos School Hazard Detection Act of 1980, 20 U.S.C. §3601 *et seq.* (1988). Section 3608 contains the antiretaliation provision.	None	Retaliation prohibited, by state or local educational agencies receiving federal assistance to remove asbestos, against employees who bring asbestos problem in schools to attention of public.	None
Clean Air Act (CAA), 42 U.S.C. §7401 *et seq.* (1988). Section 7622 contains the antiretaliation provision.	Department of Labor	Retaliation prohibited for commencing proceedings, or for testifying, assisting, or participating in enforcement proceedings.	Administrative hearing before ALJ (30 days to file complaint), review by Secretary of Labor, appeal to U.S. Court of Appeals. Damages include reinstatement, backpay, compensatory damages, and attorneys' fees.
Comprehensive Environmental Response, Compensation and Liability Act of 1980 (CERCLA), 42 U.S.C. §9601 *et seq.* (1988). Section 9610 contains the antiretaliation provision.	Department of Labor	Retaliation prohibited for providing information to state or federal government, filing or testifying in enforcement proceedings.	Administrative investigation by Secretary of Labor (30 days to file complaint), including opportunity for public hearing, appeal to U.S. Court of Appeals. Damages include reinstatement, backpay, and attorneys' fees.

Statute	Responsible Agency	Substantive Protection	Procedures and Remedies
Department of Defense Authorization Act of 1984, 10 U.S.C. §1587 (1988).	Department of Defense	Retaliation prohibited against civilian employees of Department of Defense for disclosing violations of laws, rules, or regulations, or mismanagement, gross waste of funds, abuse of authority, or substantial and specific danger to public health or safety.	Administrative investigation by Secretary of Defense, who has authority to correct adverse employment actions.
Department of Defense Authorization Act of 1987, 10 U.S.C. §2409 (1988).	Department of Defense	Retaliation prohibited against employees of defense contractors who disclose substantial violations of law relating to defense contracts to Members of Congress or authorized representatives of Departments of Defense or Justice.	Administrative investigation by Inspector General of Department of Defense (no time limit for complaint), who is required to submit a report to the Secretary of Defense. No damages provided.
Employee Retirement Income Security Act (ERISA), 29 U.S.C. §§1001 *et seq.* (1988). Section 1140 contains the antiretaliation provision.	None	Retaliation prohibited for giving information, or testifying in any inquiry or proceeding.	Civil action in U.S. District Court for reinstatement, backpay, and attorneys' fees.

Statute	Responsible Agency	Substantive Protection	Procedures and Remedies
Energy Reorganization Act of 1974 (ERA), 42 U.S.C. §5801 *et seq.* (1988). Section 5851 contains the antiretaliation provision.	Department of Labor	Retaliation prohibited for commencing proceedings, or for testifying, assisting, or participating in enforcement proceedings.	Administrative hearing before ALJ (30 days to file complaint), review by Secretary of Labor, appeal to U.S. Court of Appeals; Damages include reinstatement, backpay, compensatory damages, and attorneys' fees.
Equal Employment Opportunity Act, (Title VII), 42 U.S.C. §§2000e *et seq.* (1988). Section 2000e-3(a) contains the antiretaliation provision.	Equal Employment Opportunity Commission	Retaliation prohibited for "opposing" unlawful practice, or testifying, participating, or assisting in enforcement proceedings.	Administrative investigation (180 or 300 days to file charge with EEOC), which may result in prosecution by EEOC or by employee in U.S. District Court (within 90 days of notice of right to sue). Damages include reinstatement, backpay, and attorneys' fees.
Fair Labor Standards Act (FLSA), 29 U.S.C. §215(a)(3) (1988).	U.S. District Court or State Court	Retaliation prohibited for filing complaint, testifying in proceedings, or serving on industry committee.	Civil action in state or federal court for reinstatement, backpay, an equal amount of liquidated damages, and attorneys' fees.

Statute	Responsible Agency	Substantive Protection	Procedures and Remedies
Federal Employers' Liability Act (FELA), 45 U.S.C. §51 *et seq.* (1988). Section 60 contains the antiretaliation provision.	None	Retaliation prohibited for providing information regarding death or injury of employee.	Civil action in U.S. District Court for reinstatement and backpay.
Federal Mine Safety & Health Act (FMSHA), 30 U.S.C. §801 *et seq.* (1988). Section 815 contains the antiretaliation provision.	Federal Mine Safety & Health Review Commission	Retaliation prohibited for commencing proceedings, or for testifying or assisting in enforcement proceedings.	Administrative hearing before ALJ (60 days to file complaint), review by Federal Mine Safety & Health Review Commission, appeal to U.S. Court of Appeals. Damages include reinstatement, backpay, and attorneys' fees.
Federal Water Pollution Control Act of 1972, 33 U.S.C. §1251 *et seq.* (1988). Section 1367 contains the antiretaliation provision.	Department of Labor	Retaliation prohibited for commencing proceedings, or for testifying, assisting, or participating in enforcement proceedings.	Administrative hearing before ALJ (30 days to file complaint), review by Secretary of Labor, appeal to U.S. Court of Appeals. Damages include reinstatement, backpay, compensatory damages, and attorneys' fees.

Statute	Responsible Agency	Substantive Protection	Procedures and Remedies
Hazardous Substances Release Act, 42 U.S.C. §9601 *et seq*. (1988). Section 9610 contains the antiretaliation provision.	Secretary of Labor	Retaliation prohibited for providing information, proceedings, or for testifying in enforcement proceedings.	Administrative hearing (30 days to file complaint), appeal to U.S. Court of Appeals. Damages include reinstatement, backpay, compensatory damages, and attorneys' fees.
International Safe Containers Act, 46 U.S.C. §1501 *et seq*. (1988). Section 1506 contains the antiretaliation provision.	Department of Labor	Retaliation prohibited for reporting existence of unsafe container to Secretary of Transportation.	Administrative investigation by Secretary of Labor (60 days to file complaint), who may file action in U.S. District Court for reinstatement and backpay.
Jurors' Employment Protection Act, 28 U.S.C. §1861 *et seq*. (1988). Section 1875 contains the antiretaliation provision.	U.S. District Court	Retaliation prohibited for jury service in federal courts.	Employees may apply to the U.S. District Court, which may appoint counsel for employees. Damages include reinstatement and backpay.
Longshoremen's & Harbor Workers' Compensation Act, 33 U.S.C. §901 *et seq*. (1988). Section 948a contains the antiretaliation provision.	U.S. Department of Labor Benefits Review Board	Retaliation prohibited for having sought workers' compensation, or for testifying in proceedings.	Administrative hearing before ALJ. Damages include reinstatement and backpay.

Statute	Responsible Agency	Substantive Protection	Procedures and Remedies
Migrant Seasonal and Agricultural Worker Protection Act, 29 U.S.C. §1801 *et seq.* (1988). Section 1855 contains the antiretaliation provision.	Department of Labor	Retaliation prohibited against migrant workers who, with just cause, file or testify in proceedings, or who exercise any other right under the Act.	Administrative investigation by the Secretary of Labor (180 days to file complaint), who may bring a civil action in U.S. District Court for reinstatement, backpay, and other damages.
Occupational Safety & Health Act, 29 U.S.C. §651 *et seq.* (1988). Section 660 contains the antiretaliation provision.	Occupational Safety & Health Administration	Retaliation prohibited for filing complaint, testifying in enforcement proceedings, or exercise of any other rights under OSHA (includes limited right to refuse to work).	Administrative investigation (30 days to file complaint), action may be brought by agency on employee's behalf in U.S. District Court. Damages include reinstatement and backpay.
Public Health Service Act, 42 U.S.C. §201 *et seq.* (1988). Section 300a-7 contains the antiretaliation provision.	None	Retaliation prohibited for refusal to participate in sterilization, abortion, or research, on religious or moral grounds.	None

Statute	Responsible Agency	Substantive Protection	Procedures and Remedies
Railroad Safety Authorization Act of 1978, 45 U.S.C. §421 *et seq.* (1988). Section 441(a) contains the antiretaliation provision.	National Railroad Adjustment Board	Retaliation prohibited for complaints regarding enforcement of federal railroad safety laws, testifying in enforcement proceedings, or refusal to work under hazardous conditions; identity of employees who make disclosures required to be kept confidential.	Administrative investigation which must be completed within 180 days. Damages include reinstatement, backpay, and punitive damages not to exceed $20,000.
Safe Drinking Water Act, 42 U.S.C. §300f *et seq.* (1988). Section 300j-9 contains the antiretaliation provision.	Department of Labor	Retaliation prohibited for commencing proceedings, or for testifying, assisting, or participating in enforcement proceedings.	Administrative hearing before ALJ (30 days to file complaint), review by Secretary of Labor, appeal to U.S. Court of Appeals. Damages include reinstatement, backpay, compensatory damages, and attorneys' fees.

Statute	Responsible Agency	Substantive Protection	Procedures and Remedies
Solid Waste Disposal Act, 42 U.S.C. §6901 *et seq*. (1988). Section 6971 contains the antiretaliation provision.	Department of Labor	Retaliation prohibited for commencing proceedings, or for testifying, assisting, or participating in enforcement proceedings.	Administrative hearing before ALJ (30 days to file complaint), review by Secretary of Labor, appeal to U.S. Court of Appeals. Damages include reinstatement, backpay, compensatory damages, attorneys' fees, and costs.
Surface Mining Control & Reclamation Act, 30 U.S.C. §1201 *et seq*. (1988). Section 1293 contains the antiretaliation provision.	Secretary of Interior	Retaliation prohibited for filing complaint or testifying in enforcement proceedings.	Administrative hearing (30 days to file complaint), review in U.S. Court of Appeals. Damages include reinstatement, backpay and attorneys' fees.
Surface Transportation Assistance Act of 1978, 49 U.S.C. §2301 *et seq*. (1988). Section 2305 contains the antiretaliation provision.	Department of Labor	Retaliation prohibited for filing a complaint or instituting any proceeding relating to violations of motor vehicle safety rules or refusing to operate unsafe vehicle.	Administrative investigation by Secretary of Labor (180 days to file complaint), appeal to U.S. Court of Appeals following a hearing. Damages include reinstatement, back pay, compensatory damages, and attorneys' fees.

Statute	Responsible Agency	Substantive Protection	Procedures and Remedies
Toxic Substances Control Act, 15 U.S.C. §2601 *et seq*. (1988). Section 2622 contains the antiretaliation provision.	Department of Labor	Retaliation prohibited for commencing proceedings, or for testifying, assisting, or participating in enforcement proceedings.	Administrative hearing before ALJ (30 days to file complaint), review by Secretary of Labor, appeal to U.S. Court of Appeals. Damages include reinstatement, backpay, compensatory damages, and attorneys' fees.

Appendix D

Common-Law Protections for Whistleblowers

This appendix sets forth a state-by-state analysis of whether the courts of the jurisdiction in question have held, or stated in *dicta*, that they would recognize a public policy cause of action, and whether the public policy theory of that jurisdiction has been held to protect whistleblowers. At this writing, 43 of 51 jurisdictions have recognized public policy claims. Twenty-two jurisdictions have interpreted the public policy doctrine to protect whistleblowers under varying circumstances.

Alabama:	No public policy exception has been created. *Jones v. Ethridge*, 497 So.2d 1107 (Ala. 1986) (upholding right of employer to discharge employee for refusing to commit a crime); *French v. Beatrice Foods Co.*, 854 F.2d 964, 3 IER Cases 1321 (7th Cir. 1988) (upholding right of employer to discharge employee for cooperating with auditors).
Alaska:	Alaska courts have not rejected a public policy exception, but as of yet they have generally encompassed it within the implied covenant of good faith and fair dealing. *Knight v. American Guard & Alert, Inc.*, 714 P.2d 788 (Alaska 1986) (claim for breach of covenant of good faith was recognized for security officer who claimed he was fired in retaliation for informing pipeline operator of alcohol use and drug abuse of another security officer); *Luedtke v. Nabors Alaska Drilling, Inc.*, 768 P.2d 1123, 4 IER Cases 129 (Alaska 1989) (discharge of employees for failing to submit to urine analysis screening upheld although court recognized strong public policies supporting employee privacy).
Arizona:	Arizona courts have adopted the public policy exception and have indicated its protection should be extended to whistleblowers. *Wagenseller v. Scottsdale Memorial Hosp.*, 147 Ariz. 370, 710 P.2d 1025, 1 IER Cases 526 (1985) (public policy claim recognized based on indecent exposure laws for employee who refused to "moon" co-workers in skit on company outing); *Vermillion v. AAA Pro Moving & Storage*, 146 Ariz. 215, 704 P.2d 1360, 119 LRRM 2337 (1985) (claim recognized for employee allegedly dis-

missed for refusing to participate in theft); *Wagner v. Globe*, 150 Ariz. 82, 722 P.2d 250, 1 IER Cases 501 (1986) (claim stated by employee terminated from the police force because he refused to conceal the illegal arrest and detention of a citizen and was instrumental in having the citizen brought before a magistrate. The court stated that whistleblowing activity which serves a public purpose should be protected and remanded the case).

Arkansas: Arkansas has recognized the public policy exception and has extended that protection to whistleblowers in some circumstances. *Sterling Drug, Inc. v. Oxford*, 294 Ark. 239, 743 S.W.2d 380, 3 IER Cases 1060 (1988) (public policy claim recognized for employee who blew the whistle on employer overcharging the government). *But see Smith v. Southern Starr*, 700 F. Supp. 1026, 4 IER Cases 663 (E.D. Ark. 1988) (no public policy exception recognized in claim of wrongful discharge based on age discrimination).

California: California has recognized a public policy exception which protects whistleblowers under limited circumstances. *Tameny v. Atlantic Richfield Company*, 27 Cal. 3d 167, 164 Cal. Rptr. 839, 610 P.2d 1330, 1 IER Cases 102 (1980) (public policy claim stated by employee who refused to engage in antitrust violations); *Garcia v. Rockwell Int'l Corp.*, 187 Cal. App. 3d 1556, 232 Cal. Rptr. 490 (1986) (employee can maintain a tort action for retaliatory discipline against employer where disciplinary action but not discharge, has been taken against the employee in retaliation for the employee's whistleblowing activities); *Semore v. Pool*, 217 Cal. App. 3d 1087, 266 Cal.Rptr. 280, 5 IER Cases 129 (1990) (claim stated by employee who refused to submit to drug testing). *But see, Foley v. Interactive Data Corp.*, 47 Cal.3d 654, 254 Cal.Rptr. 211, 3 IER Cases 1729 (1988) (public policy claim stated if claim is based on firmly established policy which benefits the public generally; however, no claim recognized for employee who was allegedly discharged for reporting prior criminal investigation of co-employee); *Luck v. Southern Pacific Transp. Co.*, 218 Cal. App. 3d 1, 267 Cal. Rptr. 618, 5 IER Cases 415 (1990) (no tort claim recognized for employee who refused to submit to drug testing applying *Foley* criteria).

Colorado: Colorado has adopted a limited public policy exception, which applies to whistleblowers only if the alleged misconduct is covered by a statute. *Lampe v. Presbyterian Medical Center*, 41 Col. App. 465, 590 P.2d 513, 155 LRRM 4313 (1978) (no public policy claim for a nurse concerned about possible ethical violations; *dicta* stating that public policy might be recognized in an appropriate case); *Cronk v. Intermountain Rural Elec. Ass'n*, 765 P.2d 619, 3 IER Cases 1049 (Colo. App. 1988) (public policy claim recognized for public utility employees who refused to testify untruthfully before regulatory commission); *But see Corbin v. Sinclair Mktg., Inc.*, 684 P.2d 265, 116 LRRM 3223 (Colo. App. 1984) (public policy exception is not available when a statute provides the employee with a wrongful discharge remedy).

Connecticut: Connecticut has recognized the public policy exception, and has extended its protection to whistleblowers in some cases. *Sheets v. Teddy's Frosted Foods, Inc.*, 179 Conn. 471, 427 A.2d 385, 115 LRRM 426 (1980) (public policy claim recognized for employee who complained about food packaging violations); *Girgenti v. Cali-Con Inc.*, 15 Conn. App. 130, 544 A.2d 655 (1988) (public policy claim stated by discharged theater employee allegedly fired after he called police and emptied theater because he feared there was an intruder in the projection room).

Delaware: No public policy cause of action has been recognized. *Asher v. E.I. DuPont Inst. of the Nemours Found.*, 1987 WL 14876 (Del. Super. 1987) (no public policy exception recognized for employee who was allegedly discharged based on age discrimination).

District of Columbia: No public policy cause of action is recognized by the District of Columbia courts. *Ivy v. Army Times Publishing Co.*, 428 A.2d 831, 115 LRRM 4549 (D.C. 1981) (employee discharged for truthful testimony against employer). *But see Alder v. Columbia Historical Soc'y*, 690 F. Supp. 9, 3 IER Cases 614 (D.D.C. 1988) (federal court recognized public policy exception for employee who was allegedly discharged for opposing employer's discriminatory treatment of co-worker).

Florida: No public policy cause of action has been recognized except in limited circumstances. *Ochab v. Morrison, Inc.*, 517 So.2d 763, 3 IER Cases 672

(Fla. App. 1987) (no public policy exception recognized for employee who refused to violate alcoholic beverage statute); *Hartley v. Ocean Reef Club, Inc.*, 476 So.2d 1327 (Fla. App. 1985) (at-will employee failed to state cause of action for wrongful discharge when he was fired for allegedly refusing to participate in employer's violation of environmental statutes and regulations). *But see Smith v. Piezo Technology*, 427 So.2d 182, 117 LRRM 3378 (Fla. 1983) (limited public policy exception for discharge in retaliation for filing workers' compensation claim).

Georgia: No public policy cause of action is recognized. *Evans v. Bibb Co.*, 178 Ga. App. 139, 342 S.E.2d 484 (1986) (discharge of employee who filed workers' compensation claim upheld); *Burke v. Georgia Power Co.*, 115 LRRM 4062 (S.D.Ga. 1983) (no public policy claim recognized for employee who was discharged after initiating lawsuit against employer).

Hawaii: Hawaii has recognized the public policy exception, and in some cases it has extended that protection to whistleblowers. *Parnar v. Americana Hotels, Inc.*, 65 Haw. 370, 652 P.2d 625, 115 LRRM 4817 (1982) (public policy claim recognized for employee discharged to prevent employee from participating in an antitrust investigation); *Morishige v. Spencecliff Corp.*, 720 F. Supp. 829, 4 IER Cases 1271 (D.Haw. 1989) (public policy exception may apply to employee who is allegedly discharged due to objections to employer's violation of liquor laws and building codes).

Idaho: Idaho has recognized a public policy exception. *Jackson v. Minidoka Irrigation Dist.*, 98 Idaho 330, 563 P.2d 54 (1977) (*dicta* stating that public policy exception would be created in appropriate case); *MacNeil v. Minidoka Memorial Hosp.*, 108 Idaho 588, 701 P.2d 208, 122 LRRM 2043 (1985) (employer may be liable for wrongful discharge when the motivation for discharge contravenes public policy).

Illinois: Illinois has recognized the public policy exception and has extended its protection to whistleblowers in some circumstances. *Kelsay v. Motorola, Inc.*, 74 Ill.2d 172, 384 N.E.2d 353 (1979) (a public policy claim recognized for employee discharged for filing workers' compensation claim); *Palmateer v. International Harvester Co.*, 85 Ill.2d 124, 421 N.E.2d 876, 115

LRRM 4165 (1981) (claim recognized for employee's whistleblowing activities in aiding criminal investigation of co-worker); *Russ v. Pension Consultants Co.*, 182 Ill. App. 3d 769, 538 N.E.2d 693, 4 IER Cases 509 (1989) (public policy claim recognized for employee's refusal to backdate pension plans in violation of federal tax law).

Indiana: Indiana has recognized the public policy exception. *Frampton v. Central Ind. Gas Co.*, 260 Ind. 249, 297 N.E.2d 425, 115 LRRM 461 (1973) (public policy claim recognized for employee discharged for filing workers' compensation claim); *McClanahan v. Remington Freight Lines, Inc.*, 517 N.E.2d 390, 2 IER Cases 1888 (Ind. 1988) (claim recognized for employee fired for refusing to drive truck exceeding state weight limit). *But see Campbell v. Eli Lilly Co.*, 413 N.E.2d 1054, 115 LRRM 4417 (Ind. App. 1980) (no public policy claim recognized for employee who complained about alleged violations of laws regulating manufacture of drugs).

Iowa: Iowa has recognized a public policy exception. *Abrisz v. Pulley Freight Lines, Inc.*, 270 N.W.2d 454, 115 LRRM 4777 (Iowa 1988) (*dicta* that public policy exception would be created in an appropriate case); *Springer v. Weeks & Leo Co., Inc.*, 429 N.W.2d 558, 3 IER Cases 1345 (Iowa 1988) (claim recognized for wrongful discharge when pursuing workers' compensation).

Kansas: Kansas has recognized the public policy exception and has extended that protection to whistleblowers in limited cases. *Murphy v. City of Topeka*, 6 Kan. App. 2d 488, 630 P.2d 186, 115 LRRM 4433 (1981) (claim recognized for employee who filed workers' compensation claim); *Coleman v. Safeway Stores Inc.*, 242 Kan. 804, 752 P.2d 645, 3 IER Cases 170 (1988) (extending *Murphy* to recognize a public policy claim for employees covered by a collective bargaining agreement); *Pilcher v. Board of County Commissioners*, 14 Kan.2d 206, 787 P.2d 1204, 5 IER Cases 150 (1990) (claim recognized for employee's whistleblowing activities in reporting untenable hiring practices to newspaper).

Kentucky: Kentucky has recognized the public policy exception, and in certain cases it has extended that protection to whistleblowing activity. *Firestone Textile Co. v. Meadows*, 666 S.W.2d 730, 1 IER Cases 800 (Ky. 1983) (claim recognized for employee who filed workers' compensation benefits); *Brown v. Physician's Mut. Ins. Co.*, 679 S.W.2d 836, 1 IER Cases 1132 (Ky. App. 1984) (public policy claim recognized for employee who was allegedly discharged for reporting violations of the insurance code to state authorities).

Louisiana: Louisiana has a very limited public policy exception. *Moore v. McDermott, Inc.*, 481 So.2d 802 (La. 1986) (retaliatory discharge for employee pursuing workers' compensation claim). *But see Guillory v. St. Landry Parish Policy Jury*, 802 F.2d 822, 1 IER Cases 926 (5th Cir. 1986) (no public policy claim stated by at-will employee fired for protesting employer's alleged practice of shipping foreign steel to customers who had ordered domestic steel); *Feemster v. BJ-Titan Servs. Co.*, 873 F.2d 91, 4 IER Cases 643 (5th Cir. 1989) (no public policy exception recognized for employee who refused to violate federal statute since the statute did not provide a private right of action).

Maine: Maine has not clearly recognized the public policy exception. *Larrabee v. Penobscot Frozen Foods, Inc.*, 486 A.2d 97, 118 LRRM 2489 (Me. 1984) (*dicta* that when the discharge of an employee contravenes a strong public policy a cause of action may exist); *Pooler v. Maine Coal Prods.*, 532 A.2d 1026, 3 IER Cases 1007 (Me. 1987) (public policy exception would be recognized if employee could establish that refused conduct would have been a violation of state law).

Maryland: Maryland has recognized the public policy exception and has applied the exception to whistleblowing activity in certain cases. *Adler v. American Standard Corp.*, 291 Md. 31, 432 A.2d 464, 115 LRRM 4130 (1981) (claim recognized for employee who complained about violations of tax and criminal laws); *Kessler v. Equity Mgmt., Inc.*, 82 Md. App. 577, 572 A.2d 1144, 5 IER Cases 545 (1990) (public policy exception recognized for employee who refused to enter tenants' apartments and rummage through personal effects). *But see Beye v. Bureau of National Affairs*, 59 Md. App. 642, 477 A.2d 1197, 2 IER Cases 1893 (1984) (no cause of action for employee who reported to police that co-workers were selling marijuana on the employer's premises).

Massachusetts: Massachusetts has recognized the public policy exception and has extended its protection to whistleblowers in limited circumstances. *Derose v. Putnam Management Co.*, 398 Mass. 205, 496 N.E.2d 428, 1 IER Cases 1672 (1986) (public policy protects an employee who is dismissed for refusing to heed his employer's instructions to give false testimony); *Hobson v. McLean Hosp. Corp.*, 402 Mass. 413, 522 N.E.2d 975, 3 IER Cases 1217 (1988) (public policy claim stated by employee who alleged she was discharged for enforcing safety laws according to her responsibility). *But see Mello v. Stop & Shop*, 402 Mass. 555, 524 N.E.2d 105, 3 IER Cases 1105 (1988) (public policy claim not recognized for employee's internal complaints about false damage reports).

Michigan: Michigan has recognized the public policy exception, and in some cases it has extended that protection to whistleblowers. *Sventko v. Kroger Co.*, 69 Mich. App. 644, 245 N.W.2d 151, 115 LRRM 4613 (1976) (claim recognized for employee discharged for filing workers' compensation claim); *Trombetta v. Detroit, Toledo & Ironton R.R.*, 81 Mich. App. 489, 265 N.W.2d 385, 115 LRRM 4361 (1978) (claim recognized for employee who alleged he was retaliated against for refusing to falsify state required pollution control reports); *Watassek v. Michigan Dep't of Mental Health*, 143 Mich. App. 556, 372 N.W.2d 617 (1985) (claim recognized for employee who was allegedly fired in retaliation for reporting incidents of patient abuse to a supervisor).

Minnesota: Minnesota has recognized the public policy exception and has extended its protection to whistleblowers under limited circumstances. *Phipps v. Clark Oil & Refining Corp.*, 408 N.W.2d 569, 2 IER Cases 341 (Minn. 1987) (claim recognized for discharged employee who refused to dispense leaded gasoline into car using unleaded gasoline); *Friedrichs v. Western Nat'l Mutual Ins. Co.*, 410 N.W.2d 62, 2 IER Cases 660 (Minn. App. 1987) (public policy claim recognized for employee who reported violations of statutory boiler pressure standards). *But see Vonch v. Carlson Cos., Inc.*, 439 N.W.2d 406, 4 IER Cases 789 (Minn. App. 1989) (no public policy claim was recognized for employee's whistleblowing activities when those activities involved reporting theft and fraud to corporate employer).

Mississippi: No public policy claim has been recognized at this time. *Kelly v. Mississippi Valley Gas Co.*, 397 So.2d 874, 115 LRRM 4631 (Miss. 1981) (no public policy claim recognized for employee who was allegedly discharged for filing workers' compensation claim). *But see Laws v. Aetna Finance*, 667 F. Supp. 342, 2 IER Cases 613 (N.D. Miss. 1987) (*dicta* that limited public policy exception to employment at-will doctrine would be recognized).

Missouri: Missouri has recognized a limited public policy exception and has extended its protection to whistleblowers in some cases. *Boyle v. Vista Eyewear, Inc.*, 700 S.W.2d 859, 2 IER Cases 768 (Mo. App. 1985) (employee discharged for threatening to report employer's violation of federal regulations requiring treatment and testing of eyeglass lenses had sufficiently stated claim under public policy exception); *Beasley v. Affiliated Hosp. Prods.*, 713 S.W.2d 557, 1 IER Cases 601 (Mo. App. 1986) (cause of action stated under public policy exception when employee alleged she was discharged for refusing to fix a raffle). *But see Link v. K-Mart Corp.*, 698 F. Supp. 982, 3 IER Cases 979 (W.D.Mo. 1988) (no public policy exception recognized for employee who reported misuses and thefts to employer since employee has not implicated any statute, regulation or constitutional provision).

Montana: Montana has been reluctant to recognize a public policy exception. *Keneally v. Orgain*, 37 Mont. 154, 605 P.2d 127, 115 LRRM 4576 (1980) (*dicta* stating that public policy claim is recognized; however, no cause of action for salesman employee who complained that employer was not properly servicing products sold by employee).

Nebraska: Nebraska has recognized a public policy exception and has indicated that this protection would be extended to whistleblowing activity. *Ambroz v. Cornhusker Square Ltd.*, 226 Neb. 899, 416 N.W.2d 510, 2 IER Cases 1185 (1987) (discharge of an at-will employee for refusing to submit to a polygraph examination violated public policy); *Schriner v. Meginnis Ford Co.*, 228 Neb. 85, 421 N.W.2d 755, 3 IER Cases 129 (1988) (*dicta* that action for wrongful discharge exists when an at-will employee acting in good faith reports to his employer a suspected violation of criminal code; however, in this case employer could not maintain cause of action for wrongful discharge as he did not have reasonable cause to believe that his employer had violated odometer fraud statutes).

Nevada: Nevada has recognized a limited public policy exception. *Hansen v. Harrah's*, 100 Nev. 60, 675 P.2d 394, 115 LRRM 3024 (1984) (public policy exception recognized for employee who filed workers' compensation claim). *But see Wiltsie v. Baby Grand Corp.*, 774 P.2d 432, 4 IER Cases 638 (Nev. 1989) (at-will employee allegedly discharged for reporting illegal activity of his supervisor to his employer could not recover for retaliatory discharge because employee chose to report the activity to his employer rather than to the appropriate authorities).

New Hampshire: New Hampshire has recognized the public policy exception, and under some circumstances it has extended that protection to whistleblowers. *Cloutier v. Great Atl. & Pac. Tea Co.*, 121 N.H. 915, 436 A.2d 1140, 115 LRRM 4329 (1981) (public policy exception recognized for employee allegedly discharged for complaining about lack of security and refusing to jeopardize safety by making nightly cash deposits); *Cilley v. New Hampshire Ball Bearings, Inc.*, 128 N.H. 401, 514 A.2d 818, 1 IER Cases 521 (1986) (claim stated for discharge caused by revenge when plaintiff refused to lie for a company president).

New Jersey: New Jersey has recognized the public policy exception and extended its protection to whistleblowing activity in some cases. *Kalman v. Grand Union Co.*, 183 N.J. Super. 153, 443 A.2d 728, 115 LRRM 4803 (1982) (claim recognized for an employee discharged for refusing to violate state pharmacy regulations); *Potter v. Village Bank of N.J.*, 225 N.J. Super. 547, 543 A.2d 807, 3 IER Cases 1076 (1988) (bank president and CEO who reported bank director's suspected involvement in laundering drug money to law enforcement officials were protected from retaliatory discharge by the public policy exception).

New Mexico: New Mexico has recognized the public policy exception and in certain cases has extended its protection to whistleblowers. *Vigil v. Arzola*, 102 N.M. 682, 699 P.2d 613, 2 IER Cases 377 (1983), *rev'd on other grounds*, 108 N.M. 643, 777 P.2d 371 (1989) (public policy exception recognized for employee who reported unauthorized use of federal monies to employer); *Chavez v. Manville Prods. Corp.*, 108 N.M. 643, 777 P.2d

371, 4 IER Cases 833 (1989) (employee who was allegedly discharged for refusing to lobby for his employer stated a claim under the public policy exception).

New York: No public policy exception has been recognized. *Murphy v. American Home Prods. Corp.*, 58 N.Y.3d 293, 448 N.E.2d 293, 115 LRRM 4953 (1983) (no claim recognized for employee allegedly discharged for complaint of improprieties); *Leibowitz v. Bank Leumi Trust Co.*, 548 N.Y.S.2d 513, 4 IER Cases 1786 (1989) (no public policy exception recognized for employee who reported illegal activities because she failed to allege any violation of laws which presented a "substantial and specific danger to the public health or safety.").

North Carolina: North Carolina has adopted a narrow public policy exception. *Sides v. Duke Hosp.*, 74 N.C. App. 331, 328 S.E.2d 818, 1 IER Cases 512 (1985) (claim recognized for employee allegedly discharged for testifying truthfully in medical malpractice action against employer); *Coman v. Thomas Mfg. Co.*, 325 N.C. 172, 381 S.E.2d 445, 4 IER Cases 987 (1989) (public policy exception stated by employee who refused to comply with employer's instructions to violate federal safety regulations). *But see Guy v. Travenol Laboratories, Inc.*, 812 F.2d 911, 1 IER Cases 1553 (4th Cir. 1987) (no public policy exception is recognized to the at-will employment doctrine unless an employee lost his job for refusing to give perjured testimony).

North Dakota: North Dakota has recognized a limited public policy exception. *Krein v. Marian Manor Nursing Home*, 415 N.W.2d 793, 2 IER Cases 1188 (N.D. 1987) (claim recognized for employee allegedly discharged for seeking workers' compensation).

Ohio: Ohio has recently adopted a narrow public policy exception to the at-will employment doctrine. *Greeley v. Miami Valley Maintenance*, 49 Ohio St.3d 228, 551 N.E.2d 981, 5 IER Cases 257 (1990) (public policy claim recognized for employee who was discharged because child support payments were withheld from wages. The court expressly held that Ohio should recognize the public policy exception to the employment-at-will doctrine, and distinguished *Phung v. Waste Management, Inc*, 23 Ohio St.3d 100, 491 N.E.2d 1114, 2 IER Cases 786 (1986), in which the court held that no public policy exception would be recognized absent a very clear public policy).

Oklahoma: Oklahoma has recognized a limited public policy exception and on occasion has extended its protection to whistleblowers. *Burk v. K-Mart Corp.*, 770 P.2d 24, 4 IER Cases 182 (Okla. 1989) (in response to a certified question, the Oklahoma Supreme Court recognized a limited public policy exception to the employment-at-will doctrine in cases where the discharge was contrary to a clear mandate of public policy); *Rosenfeld v. Thirteenth St. Corp.*, 4 IER Cases 770 (Okla. 1989) (doctor who reported incompetent patient care, gross negligence and fraudulent billing practices to hospital administrator stated a cause of action on public policy grounds).

Oregon: Oregon has recognized the public policy exception and extended its protection to whistleblowers in limited cases. *Nees v. Hocks*, 272 Or. 210, 536 P.2d 512, 115 LRRM 4837 (1975) (claim recognized for employee allegedly discharged for serving on jury); *McQuary v. Bel Air Convalescent Home, Inc.*, 69 Or. App. 107, 684 P.2d 21, 120 LRRM 3129 (1984) (a nursing supervisor stated a cause of action for wrongful discharge when she asserted that she had been terminated for threatening to report patient abuse to state authorities). *But see Sieverson v. Allied Stores Corp.*, 97 Or. App. 315, 776 P.2d 38, 4 IER Cases 785 (1989) (employee who claimed she was terminated in retaliation for reporting employee abuse did not state a claim since reporting suspected wrongdoing within a private corporation does not involve interest of public importance).

Pennsylvania: Pennsylvania has recognized a limited public policy exception which extends to some whistleblowers. *Reuther v. Fowler & Williams, Inc.*, 115 Pa. Super. 28, 386 A.2d 119, 115 LRRM 4690 (1978) (public policy claim recognized for employee allegedly discharged for serving on jury); *Perks v. Firestone Tire & Rubber Co.*, 611 F.2d 1363, 115 LRRM 4592 (3rd Cir. 1979) (claim recognized for employee allegedly discharged for refusing to take lie detector test). *But see McCartney v. Meadowview Manor, Inc.*, 353 Pa. Super. 34, 508 A.2d 1254 (1986) (no public policy claim was recognized for employee who was allegedly fired for seeking employment with competitor of employer).

Rhode Island: Rhode Island has been reluctant to create a public policy exception, but recently has indicated a willingness to apply the exception in certain cases. *Dudzik v. Leesona Corp.*, 473 A.2d 762, 120 LRRM 3452 (R.I. 1984) (employee who complained of an improper assignment had no cause of action because the employment was at-will). *But see Cummins v. E.G. & G. Sealol, Inc.*, 690 F. Supp. 134, 3 IER Cases 705 (D.R.I. 1988) (public policy claim recognized when employee is discharged for exposing employer conduct that is contrary to statutorily enacted public policy).

South Carolina: South Carolina has recognized a public policy exception. *Ludwick v. This Minute of Carolina, Inc.*, 287 S.C. 219, 337 S.E.2d 213, 1 IER Cases 1099 (1985) (claim recognized for an employee allegedly discharged for obeying subpoena to attend state administrative hearing). *But see Smalley v. Fast Fare Inc.*, 4 IER Cases 105 (D.S.C. 1988) (no public policy claim recognized for employee who was allegedly discharged for informing superior of discrepancies in cash inventory because it concerned an internal matter and was not clearly violative of public policy).

South Dakota: South Dakota has recognized a limited public policy exception. *Johnson v. Kreiser's Inc.*, 433 N.W.2d 255, 3 IER Cases 1767 (S.D. 1988) (public policy exception applies to employee who refused to aid employer in illegal conversion of corporate property to his own personal use).

Tennessee: Tennessee has recognized a narrow public policy exception. *Clanton v. Cain-Sloan Co.*, 677 S.W.2d 441, 117 LRRM 2789 (Tenn. 1984) (claim recognized for employee who filed for workers' compensation benefits). *But see Bloom v. General Elec. Supply Co.*, 702 F. Supp. 1364, 3 IER Cases 1842 (M.D.Tenn. 1988) (employee who alleged she was discharged after her husband began work for competitor of employer failed to state a claim under the public policy exception because no public policy was evidenced by constitutional or statutory provision).

Texas: Texas has recognized the public policy exception and extended that protection to whistleblowing activity in certain cases. *Sabine Pilot Serv., Inc. v. Hauck*, 687 S.W.2d 733, 119 LRRM 2187 (Tex. 1985) (claim recognized for sailor allegedly dismissed for refusing to pump bilges of ship in waters where law prohibited such pumping); *Johnston v. Del Mar Distrib. Co., Inc.*, 776 S.W.2d 768 (Tex. App. 1989) (public policy claim recognized for employee who inquired to the federal authorities concerning legality of shipment of firearms by employer).

Utah: Utah has been reluctant to create a public policy exception. *Bihlmier v. Carson*, 603 P.2d 790, 115 LRRM 4305 (Utah 1979) (no public policy claim recognized for employee who sought damages for constructive discharge).

Vermont: Vermont has recognized the public policy exception. *Payne v. Rosendall*, 147 Vt. 488, 520 A.2d 586, 1 IER Cases 800 (1986) (discharge solely on basis of age is contrary to public policy).

Virginia: Virginia has recognized a public policy exception, and on occasion it has applied this protection to whistleblowers. *Bowman v. State Bank of Keysville*, 229 Va. 534, 531 S.E.2d 797, 1 IER Cases 437 (1985) (claim recognized for employees allegedly dismissed for exercising statutory rights as shareholders of employer); *Fielder v. Southco, Inc. of South Carolina*, 699 F. Supp. 577 (W.D.Va. 1988) (public policy claim recognized for employee who was allegedly discharged for reporting incidents of sexual harassment by a supervisor).

Washington: Washington has recognized a public policy exception and has extended that protection to whistleblowers in certain cases. *Thompson v. St. Regis Paper Co.*, 102 Wash.2d 219, 685 P.2d 1081, 1 IER Cases 392 (1984) (claim recognized for employee allegedly dismissed for attempting to ensure compliance with the Foreign Corrupt Practices Act); *Hayes v. Trulock*, 51 Wash. App. 795, 755 P.2d 830 (1988) (employees may maintain a public policy action for discharge after consulting with Department of Labor and Industries concerning right to receive overtime pay).

West Virginia: West Virginia has recognized the public policy exception, and in some cases it has extended that protection to whistleblowers. *Harless v. First Nat'l Bank*, 162 W.Va. 116, 246 S.E.2d 270, 115 LRRM 4380 (1980) (claim recognized for employee allegedly dismissed for voicing concerns over violation of consumer credit laws); *Collins v. Elkay Mining Co.*, 371 S.E.2d 46, 3 IER Cases 801 (W.Va. 1988) (public policy claim recognized for employee who refused to falsify safety reports).

Wisconsin: Wisconsin has recognized a public policy exception. *Brockmeyer v. Dun & Bradstreet*, 113 Wis.2d 561, 355 N.W.2d 834, 115 LRRM 4484 (1983) (court held that an employee has a cause of action for wrongful discharge when the discharge is contrary to a fundamental and well-defined public policy as evidenced by existing law; however, no claim for employee allegedly dismissed for lack of cooperation in defending claim of discrimination by employee's secretary); *Ward v. Frito-Lay, Inc.*, 85 Wis.2d 372, 290 N.W.2d 536, 115 LRRM 4320 (1980) (public policy exception recognized in *dicta*; however, no claim was stated by employee who was discharged for relationship with co-worker); *Bushko v. Miller Brewing Co.*, 134 Wis.2d 136, 396 N.W.2d 167 (1986) (public policy exception exists only if employee is discharged for refusing to violate public policy as established by a statute or a constitutional provision; employee who complained about policies regarding plant safety, hazardous waste did not state a cause of action.)

Wyoming: Wyoming has recently adopted a limited public policy exception. *Griess v. Consolidated Freightways*, 776 P.2d 752, 4 IER Cases 839 (Wyo. 1989) (public policy claim is recognized for employees who file workers' compensation claims). *But see Allen v. Safeway Stores, Inc.*, 669 P.2d 277, 120 LRRM 2987 (Wyo. 1985) (no public policy tort claim recognized for employee allegedly discharged due to discrimination because separate remedies existed); *Horne v. J.W. Gibson Well Serv.*, 894 F.2d 1194, 5 IER Cases 69 (10th Cir. 1990) (court recognized limited public policy exception in *Griess, supra*; however, it declined to apply that exception to employee who refused to submit to a drug test because employers' attempts to ensure a safe workplace did not violate the public policy of Wyoming).

Table of Cases

A

A.J. Foyt Chevrolet, Inc. v. Jacobs, 578 S.W.2d 445 (Tex. Civ. App. 1979) 92
Abrams v. Echlin Corp., 174 Ill. App. 3d 434, 528 N.E.2d 429, 3 IER Cases 1191 (1988) 101
Adler v. American Standard Corp., 538 F. Supp. 572 (D. Md. 1982) 104
Alexander v. Gardner-Denver Co., 415 U.S. 36, 7 FEP Cases 81 (1974) 143
Alexander v. Kay Findlay Jewelers, 208 N.J. Super. 503, 506 A.2d 379 (1986) 101
Allen v. Safeway Stores, 699 P.2d 277, 120 LRRM 2987 (Wyo. 1985) 101
Allis-Chalmers Corp. v. Lueck, 471 U.S. 202, 1 IER Cases 541, 118 LRRM 3345 (1985) 140
Ambroz v. Cornhusker Square, 226 Neb. 899, 416 N.W.2d 510, 2 IER Cases 1185 (1987) 94
Amco Constr. Co. v. Freeman, 236 Kan. 626, 693 P.2d 1183 (1985) 136

B

Barela v. United Nuclear Corp., 462 F.2d 149, 4 FEP Cases 831 (10th Cir. 1972) 126
Barrentine v. Arkansas-Best Freight Sys., 450 U.S. 728, 24 WH Cases 1284 (1981) 143, 144
Beam v. IPCO Corp., 883 F.2d 242, 2 IER Cases 1697 (7th Cir. 1988) 101
Bekhrad; United States v., 672 F. Supp. 1529 (S.D. Iowa 1987) 124
Bellamy v. Mason's Stores, 368 F. Supp. 1025 (E.D. Va. 1973), *aff'd,* 508 F.2d 504 (4th Cir. 1974) 132
Berg v. LaCrosse Cooler Co., 612 F.2d 1041, 21 FEP Cases 1012 (7th Cir. 1980) 128
Bivens v. Six Unknown Named Agents of Fed. Bureau of Narcotics, 403 U.S. 388 (1971) 49
Boisjoly v. Morton Thiokol, Inc., 706 F. Supp. 795 (D. Utah 1988) 123
Bonham v. Dresser Indus., 569 F.2d 187 (3d Cir. 1977) 146
Boniuk v. New York Medical College, 535 F. Supp. 1353, 115 LRRM 4643 (S.D.N.Y. 1982) 114
Bottijliso v. Hutchison Fruit Co., 96 N.M. 789, 635 P.2d 992, 118 LRRM 3095 (1981) 146
Bourque v. Town of Bow, 736 F. Supp. 398 (D.N.H. 1990) 112
Bowman v. State Bank of Keysville, 229 Va. 534, 331 S.E.2d 797, 1 IER Cases 437, 119 LRRM 3095 (1985) 98
Bradford v. Sloan Paper Co., 383 F. Supp. 1157, 8 FEP Cases 634 (N.D. Ala. 1974) 127
Braun v. United States, 707 F.2d 922 (6th Cir. 1983) 49
Brock v. Roadway Express, 481 U.S. 252, 2 IER Cases 1, 125 LRRM 2001 (1987) 78
Brockmeyer v. Dun & Bradstreet, 113 Wis.2d 561, 335 N.W.2d 834, 115 LRRM 4484 (1983) 116, 117
Brown v. General Servs. Admin., 425 U.S. 820, 12 FEP Cases 1361 (1976) 131
Brown v. Transcon Lines, 284 Or. 597, 588 P.2d 1087, 115 LRRM 5072 (1978) 92
Brown & Root v. Donovan, 747 F.2d 1029, 1 IER Cases 413, 118 LRRM 2301 (5th Cir. 1984) 77
Burdick v. American Express Co., 865 F.2d 527 (2d Cir. 1989) 80
Buschi v. Kirven, 775 F.2d 1240, 1 IER Cases 1726, 120 LRRM 3059 (4th Cir. 1985) 132
Bush v. Lucas, 462 U.S. 367 (1983) 49

Buysse v. Paine, Webber, Jackson & Curtis, 623 F.2d 1244 (8th Cir. 1980) 101
Byers v. Follmer Trucking Co., 763 F.2d 599, 37 FEP Cases 1871 (3d Cir. 1985) 130

C

C&D Sportswear Corp., 398 F. Supp. 300 (M.D. Ga. 1975) 128
Callan v. State Chem. Mfg. Co., 584 F. Supp. 619 (E.D. Pa. 1984) 80
Campbell v. Eli Lilly & Co., 413 N.E.2d 1054, 115 LRRM 4417 (1980) 111, 115
Campbell v. Ford Indus., 274 Or. 243, 546 P.2d 141, 115 LRRM 4837 (1976) 98, 99
Carpenters Local 610 v. Scott, 453 U.S. 825, 113 LRRM 3145 (1983) 132
Carson; State v., 274 S.C. 316, 262 S.E.2d 918 (1980) 26
Chance v. Board of Examiners, 458 F.2d 1167, 4 FEP Cases 596 (2d Cir. 1972) 132
Chiaffitelli v. Dettmer Hosp., 437 F.2d 429 (6th Cir. 1971) 132
Chrisman v. Philips Indus., 242 Kan. 772, 751 P.2d 140, 3 IER Cases 181 (1988) 79
Cisco v. United Parcel Serv., 328 Pa. Super. 300, 476 A.2d 1340, 116 LRRM 2514 (1984) 101
Clanton v. Cain-Sloan Co., 677 S.W.2d 441, 117 LRRM 2789 (Tenn. 1984) 92, 118
Clement v. Farmers Ins. Exch., 115 Idaho 298, 766 P.2d 768 (1988) 101
Collins v. Handyman, 341 U.S. 651 (1951) 132
Commonwealth v., see name of opposing party
Conkwright v. Westinghouse Elec. Corp., 739 F. Supp. 1006 (D. Md. 1990) 146
Connick v. Myers, 461 U.S. 138, 1 IER Cases 178 (1983) 47, 48
Consolidated Edison Co. of N.Y. v. Donovan, 673 F.2d 61 (2d Cir. 1982) 156
Coppage v. Kansas, 236 U.S. 1 (1914) 4
Corbin v. Sinclair Mktg., 684 P.2d 265, 116 LRRM 3223 (Colo. App. 1984) 147
Couty v. Dole, 886 F.2d 147 (8th Cir. 1989) 151
Covell v. Spengler, 141 Mich. App. 76, 366 N.W.2d 76 (1985) 67
Crews v. Memorex Corp., 588 F. Supp. 27, 120 LRRM 2679 (D. Mass. 1984) 146
Crosier v. United Parcel Serv., 150 Cal. App. 3d 1132, 198 Cal. Rptr. 361, 115 LRRM 3585 (1983) 102
Croushorn v. Board of Trustees, 518 F. Supp. 9, 30 FEP Cases 168 (M.D. Tenn. 1980) 127
Cullom v. Hibernia Nat'l Bank, 859 F.2d 1211 (5th Cir. 1988) 80

D

Daly-Murphy v. Winston, 820 F.2d 1470 (9th Cir. 1987) 49
Daniel v. Magma Copper Co., 127 Ariz. 320, 620 P.2d 699, 115 LRRM 4326 (1980) 101
Darnell v. Impact Indus., 119 Ill. App.3d 763, 457 N.E.2d 125, 115 LRRM 5012 (1983) 92
Davis v. Louisiana Computing Corp., 394 S.2d 678 (La. App. 1981) 97, 98
Deford v. Secretary of Labor, 700 F.2d 281 (6th Cir. 1983) 78, 151, 152
Delaney v. Taco Time Int'l, 297 Or. 10, 681 P.2d 114, 1 IER Cases 367, 116 LRRM 2168 (1984) 87
DeMarco v. Publix Super Mkts., 360 So.2d 134, 115 LRRM 4784 (Fla. 1980) 101
DeRose v. Putnam Mgmt. Co., 398 Mass. 205, 496 N.E.2d 428, 1 IER Cases 1672 (1986) 83
Dicomes v. Washington, 113 Wash.2d 612, 782 P.2d 1002, 4 IER Cases 1630 (1989) 112
Drew v. Jersey Cent. Power & Light Co., No. 81-ERA-3 (Mar. 5, 1981) 78
Dunham v. Brock, 794 F.2d 1037 (5th Cir. 1986) 154, 155, 163

E

Echard v. Devine, 726 F. Supp. 1045 (N.D. W.Va. 1989) 74
EEOC v., see name of opposing party
Electrical Workers (IBEW) v. Hechler, 481 U.S. 851, 125 LRRM 2353 (1987) 144
Electrical Workers (IBEW) Local 1229 (Jefferson Standard Broadcasting Co.); NLRB v., 346 U.S. 464, 33 LRRM 2183 (1953) 155

Ellis v. Buckley, 720 P.2d 875, 4 IER Cases 1668 (1989) 94
Ellis Fischel State Cancer Hosp. v. Marshall, 629 F.2d 563 (8th Cir. 1980), *cert. denied,* 450 U.S. 1040 (1981) 151, 153
English v. General Elec. Co., ___ U.S. ___, 5 IER Cases 609 (1990) 79
Erickson v. American Inst. of Biological Sciences, 716 F. Supp. 908 (ED. Va. 1989) 122

F

Farmer v. Carpenters, 430 U.S. 290, 94 LRRM 2759 (1977) 137
Felton v. Unisource Corp., 739 F. Supp. 1388 (D. Ariz. 1990) 147
Firestone Textile Co. v. Meadows, 666 S.W.2d 730, 1 IER Cases 1800, 114 LRRM 3559 (Ky. 1983) 92
First Nat'l Bank of Boston v. Bellotti, 435 U.S. 765 (1978) 95
Fitzgerald v. Seamans, 384 F. Supp. 688 (D.D.C. 1974), *rev'd,* 553 F.2d 220 (D.C. Cir. 1977), *rev'd sub nom.* Nixon v. Fitzgerald, 457 U.S. 731 (1982) 13, 15
Foley v. Interactive Data Corp., 47 Cal.3d 654, 254 Cal. Rptr. 211, 765 P.2d 373, 3 IER Cases 1729 (1988) 34, 36, 106, 116
Frampton v. Central Ind. Gas Co., 260 Ind. 249, 297 N.E.2d 425 (1973) 92, 93
Frazier v. Merit Sys. Protection Bd., 672 F.2d 150, 28 FEP Cases 185, 109 LRRM 2959 (D.C. Cir. 1982) 50
Fristoe v. Reynolds Metals Co., 615 F.2d 1209, 104 LRRM 3041 (9th Cir. 1980) 142

G

Gaballah v. PG&E, 711 F. Supp. 988, 4 IER Cases 1039 (N.D. Cal. 1989) 79
Garibaldi v. Lucky Food Stores, 726 F.2d 1367, 1 IER Cases 354, 115 LRRM 3089 (9th Cir. 1984) 142, 143
Garner v. Teamsters Local 776, 346 U.S. 485, 33 LRRM 2218 (1953) 136
Geary v. United States Steel Corp., 456 Pa. 171, 319 A.2d 174, 115 LRRM 4665 (1974) 109, 111
Gifford v. Atchison, Topeka & Santa Fe Ry., 685 F.2d 1149, 29 FEP Cases 1345 and 34 FEP Cases 240 (9th Cir. 1982) 128
Givhan v. Western Line Consol. School Dist., 439 U.S. 410, 18 FEP Cases 1424 (1979) 46
Goff v. Continental Oil Co., 678 F.2d 593, 29 FEP Cases 79 (5th Cir. 1982) 131
Goins v. Ford Motor Co., 131 Mich. App. 185, 347 N.W.2d 184, 116 LRRM 3231 (1983) 92
Gould v. Campbell's Ambulance Serv., 130 Ill.App.3d 598, 474 N.E.2d 740 (1984) 90
Graham v. Scissor-Tail, Inc., 28 Cal.3d 807, 171 Cal. Rptr. 604, 623 P.2d 165 (1981) 176
Gravitt v. General Elec. Co., 580 F. Supp. 1162 (S.D. Ohio), *appeal dismissed,* 848 F.2d 190 (6th Cir.), *cert. denied,* 488 U.S. 901 (1988) 122
Great Am. Fed. Sav. & Loan Ass'n v. Novotny, 442 U.S. 366, 19 FEP Cases 1482 (1979) 126
Greeley v. Miami Valley Maintenance Contractors, 49 Ohio St.3d 228, 551 N.E.2d 981, 5 IER Cases 257 (1990) 98

H

H.J., Inc. v. Northwestern Bell Tel. Co., 57 USLW 4951 (1989) 80
Hall v. United Parcel Serv., 76 N.Y.2d 27, 556 N.Y.S.2d 21, 555 N.E.2d 273, 5 IER Cases 616 (1990) 94
Hallock v. Moses, 731 F.2d 754, 116 LRRM 2407 (11th Cir. 1984) 49
Hansen v. Harrah's, 100 Nev. 60, 675 P.2d 394, 115 LRRM 3024 (1984) 92
Harless v. First Nat'l Bank, 162 W. Va. 116, 246 S.E.2d 270, 115 LRRM 4380 (1978) 103, 104
Harlow v. Fitzgerald, 457 U.S. 800 (1982) 15
Harman v. La Crosse Tribune, 117 Wis.2d 448, 344 N.W.2d 536, 115 LRRM 3252 (1984) 90, 91, 114
Hauck v. Sabine Pilots, 687 S.W.2d 733, 119 LRRM 2187 (Tex. 1985) 85
Hayes Int'l Corp.; United States v., 786 F.2d 1499 (11th Cir. 1986) 30
Hecht v. Commerce Clearing House, 897 F.2d 21 (2d Cir. 1990) 80
Henry v. Intercontinental Radio, 155 Cal.App.3d 707, 202 Cal. Rptr. 328 (1984) 138, 139
Hentzel v. Singer Co., 138 Cal.App.3d 290, 188 Cal. Rptr. 159, 115 LRRM 4036 (1982) 109

Hershberger v. Jersey Shore Steel Co., 575 A.2d 944, 5 IER Cases 710 (Pa. Super. 1990) 100
Hibbert v. Centennial Villas, 56 Wash. App. 889, 786 P.2d 309, 5 IER Cases 161 (1990) 108
Hicks v. Resolution Trust Corp., 736 F. Supp. 812, 5 IER Cases 772 (N.D. Ill. 1990) 108
Hill; United States v., 676 F. Supp. 1158 (N.D. Fla. 1987) 124
Hillenbrand v. City of Evansville, 457 N.E.2d 236, 115 LRRM 2219 (Ind. App. 1983) 112
Hineline v. Stroudsburg Elec. Supply, 384 Pa. Super. 537, 559 A.2d 556, 4 IER Cases 786 (1989) 106
Hobson v. McLean Hosp. Corp., 402 Mass. 413, 522 N.E.2d 975, 3 IER Cases 1217 (1988) 85
Hochstadt v. Worcester Found. for Experimental Biology, 545 F.2d 222, 13 FEP Cases 804 (1st Cir. 1976) 129, 154
Holien v. Sears, Roebuck & Co., 298 Or. 76, 689 P.2d 1292, 36 FEP Cases 137 (1984) 147
Holland v. State, 302 S.2d 806 (Fla. Dist. Ct. App. 1974) 25
Horne v. J.W. Gibson Well Serv., 894 F.2d 1194, 5 IER Cases 69 (10th Cir. 1990) 100
Houck v. Folding Carton Admin., 881 F.2d 494 (7th Cir. 1989) 123
Hubbard v. United States Envtl. Protection Agency, 809 F.2d 1 (D.C. Cir. 1986) 49
Hudson v. Moore Business Forms, 609 F. Supp. 467, 37 FEP Cases 1672 (N.D. Cal. 1985) 162
Hunter v. Port Auth. of Allegheny County, 277 Pa. Super. 4, 419 A.2d 631 (1980) 101, 102

I

Ingersoll-Rand Co. v. McClendon, 59 USLW 4033 (1990), rev'g 779 S.W.2d 69, 4 IER Cases 1515 (1989).

J

Jevic v. Coca Cola, 5 IER Cases 765 (D.N.J. 1990) 99, 100
Johnson v. Louisiana State Employment Serv., 301 F. Supp. 675, 1 FEP Cases 598 (W.D. La. 1968) 132
Johnson v. Railway Express Agency, 421 U.S. 454, 10 FEP Cases 817 (1975) 131
Johnson v. United Parcel Serv., 722 F. Supp. 1282, 4 IER Cases 1513 (1989) 94
Johnston v. Del Mar Distrib. Co., 776 S.W.2d 768 (1989) 114, 115
Jones v. Industrial Elec.-Seattle, 53 Wash. App. 536, 768 P.2d 520 (1989) 109, 147
Jones. v. Memorial Hosp. Sys., 677 S.W.2d 221, 117 LRRM 2915 (Tex. App. 1984) 95
Jones & Laughlin Steel Corp.; NLRB v., 301 U.S. 1, 1 LRRM 703 (1937) 6

K

Kallir, Phillips, Ross, Inc.; EEOC v., 401 F. Supp. 66, 11 FEP Cases 241 (S.D.N.Y. 1975), *aff'd,* 559 F.2d 1203, 15 FEP Cases 1369 (2d Cir.), *cert. denied,* 434 U.S. 920 (1977) 127
Kalman v. Grand Union Co., 183 N.J. Super. 153, 443 A.2d 728, 115 LRRM 4803 (1982) 88, 89
Kansas Gas & Elec. Co. v. Brock, 780 F.2d 1505, 1 IER Cases 1767, 121 LRRM 3133 (10th Cir. 1985), *cert. denied,* 478 U.S. 1011 (1986) 77, 79
Kavanagh v. KLM Royal Dutch Airlines, 566 F. Supp. 242, 115 LRRM 4266 (N.D. Ill. 1983) 100, 101
Kelly v. Western Airlines, 115 LRRM 2110 (D. Utah 1983) 146
Kelsay v. Motorola, 74 Ill.2d 172, 384 N.E.2d 353 (1979) 92
Kessler v. Equity Mgmt., 82 Md. App. 577, 572 A.2d 1144, 5 IER Cases 545 (1989) 87
Khanna v. Microdata Corp., 170 Cal.App.3d 250, 215 Cal. Rptr. 860, 1 IER Cases 1854, 120 LRRM 2152 (1985) 101
Klages v. Sperry Corp., 118 LRRM 2463 (E.D. Pa. 1984) 90, 146
Komm v. McFliker, 662 F. Supp. 924, 2 IER Cases 467 (W.D. Mo. 1987) 80
Kornbluh v. Stearns & Foster Co., 73 F.R.D. 307, 14 FEP Cases 847 (S.D. Ohio 1976) 126
Kotarski v. Cooper, 799 F.2d 1342 (9th Cir. 1986) 49
Kouff v. Bethlehem-Alameda Shipyard, 90 Cal.App.2d 322, 202 P.2d 1059 (1949) 97

L

Lally v. Compugraphics, 85 N.J. 668, 428 A.2d 1317, 115 LRRM 4634 (1981) 92
Lamb v. Briggs Mfg., 700 F.2d 1092 (7th Cir. 1983) 142
Lampe v. Presbyterian Medical Center, 41 Colo. App. 465, 590 P.2d 513, 115 LRRM 4313 (1978) 89
Lanes v. O'Brien, 746 P.2d 1366 (Colo. App. 1987) 54, 55
Lardner v. United States, 216 F.2d 844 (9th Cir. 1954) 26
Leibowitz v. Bank Leumi Trust Co., 152 A.D.2d 169, 548 N.Y.S.2d 513, 4 IER Cases 1786 (1989) 106
Lingle v. Magic Chef, Norge Div., 486 U.S. 399, 3 IER Cases 481, 46 FEP Cases 1553, 128 LRRM 2523 (1988) 144
Littman v. Firestone Tire & Rubber Co., 715 F. Supp. 90, 4 IER Cases 1023 (S.D.N.Y. 1989) 70
Lopes; Commonwealth v., 318 Mass. 453, 61 N.E.2d 849 (1945) 26
Lucas v. Brown & Root, 736 F.2d 1202, 1 IER Cases 388, 35 FEP Cases 1855, 116 LRRM 2744 (8th Cir. 1984) 86

M

Mackowiak v. University Nuclear Sys., 735 F.2d 1159 (9th Cir. 1984) 77, 150
Manzanares v. Safeway Stores, 593 F.2d 968, 19 FEP Cases 191 (10th Cir. 1979) 131
Marbury v. Brooks, 20 U.S. 251 (1822) 25
Maryland-Nat'l Capital Park & Planning Comm'n v. Washington Nat'l Arena, 282 Md. 588, 386 A.2d 1216 (1978) 34
Mayo v. Questech, 727 F. Supp. 1007, 4 IER Cases 1850, 51 FEP Cases 1246 (E.D. Va. 1989) 76
McAuliffe v. Mayor of New Bedford, 155 Mass. 216, 9 N.E. 517 (1892) 46
McCluney v. Jos. Schlitz Brewing Co., 489 F. Supp. 24, 115 LRRM 4227 (E.D. Wis. 1980) 146
McCool v. Hillhaven Corp., 97 Or. App. 536, 777 P.2d 1013, 4 IER Cases 1026 (1989) 108
McDonnell Douglas Corp. v. Green, 411 U.S. 792, 5 FEP Cases 965 (1973) 156
McGonagle v. Union Fidelity Corp., 383 Pa. Super. 223, 556 A.2d 878 (1989) 91
McKinney v. National Dairy Council, 491 F. Supp. 1108, 115 LRRM 4861 (D. Mass. 1980) 147
McLaughlin v. Barclays Am. Corp., 95 N.C. App. 301, 382 S.E.2d 836 (1989) 99
McNulty v. Borden, Inc., 474 F. Supp. 1111, 115 LRRM 4563 (E.D. Pa. 1979) 85
McQuary v. Bel Air Convalescent Home, 69 Or. App. 107, 684 P.2d 21, 120 LRRM 3129 (1984) 108, 115
Melchi v. Burns Int'l Sec. Servs., 597 F. Supp. 575 (E.D. Mich. 1984) 67, 150, 151
Mello v. Stop & Shop Cos., 402 Mass. 555, 524 N.E.2d 105, 3 IER Cases 1105 (1988) 106
Meritor Sav. Bank v. Vinson, 477 U.S. 57, 40 FEP Cases 1822 (1986) 129
Mine Workers v. Gibbs, 383 U.S. 715, 61 LRRM 2561 (1966) 161
Mitsubishi Motors Corp. v. Soler Chrysler-Plymouth, 473 U.S. 614 (1985) 176
Montiero v. Poole Silver Co., 615 F.2d 4, 22 FEP Cases 90 (1st Cir. 1980) 128
Morast v. Lance, 807 F.2d 926, 2 IER Cases 1230 (11th Cir. 1987) 80
Morgan Drive Away v. Brant, 489 N.E.2d 933, 1 IER Cases 961, 122 LRRM 2130 (Ind. 1986) 101
Morris v. Hartford Courant Co., 200 Conn. 676, 513 A.2d 66 (1986) 101
Mount Healthy City School Dist. Bd. of Educ. v. Doyle, 429 U.S. 274, 1 IER Cases 76 (1976) 153
Munsey v. Federal Mine Safety & Health Review Comm'n, 595 F.2d 735 (D.C. Cir. 1978) 73
Murdock v. Pennsylvania, 319 U.S. 105 (1942) 45
Murphy v. City of Topeka, 6 Kan.App.2d 488, 630 P.2d 186, 115 LRRM 4433 (1981) 92

N

Nees v. Hocks, 272 Or. 210, 536 P.2d 512, 115 LRRM 4571 (1975) 96, 97, 118
New York Times Co. v. Sullivan, 376 U.S. 254 (1964) 41
Nicholson v. CPC Int'l, 877 F.2d 221, 49 FEP Cases 1678 (3d Cir. 1989) 176

Nixon v. Fitzgerald, see Fitzgerald v. Seamans
NLRB v., see name of opposing party
Nodine v. Textron, 819 F.2d 347 (1st Cir. 1987) 80
Norman v. Niagara Mohawk Power Corp., 873 F.2d 634 (2d Cir. 1989) 79
Norris v. Lumbermen's Mut. Gas Co., 4 IER Cases 1030 (1st Cir. 1989) 79
Novosel v. Nationwide Ins. Co., 721 F.2d 894, 1 IER Cases 286, 114 LRRM 3105 (3d Cir. 1983) 95, 96

O

Oglesby v. RCA Corp., 752 F.2d 272, 118 LRRM 2203 (7th Cir. 1985) 142
Ohlsen v. DST Indus., 111 Mich. App. 580 (1982) 146
Olguin v. Inspiration Consol. Copper Co., 740 F.2d 1468, 1 IER Cases 399, 117 LRRM 2073 (9th Cir. 1984) 141, 142
Operating Eng'rs Local 926 v. Jones, 460 U.S. 669, 112 LRRM 3272 (1983) 136, 137
O'Sullivan v. Mallon, 160 N.J. Super. 416, 390 A.2d 149, 115 LRRM 5064 (1978) 85, 86

P

Paca v. K-Mart Corp., 108 N.M. 479, 775 P.2d 245, 4 IER Cases 727 (1989) 101
Palmateer v. International Harvester Co., 85 Ill.2d 124, 421 N.E.2d 876, 115 LRRM 4165 (1981) 104, 105
Palmer v. Brown, 242 Kan. 893, 752 P.2d 685 (1988) 104
Parets v. Eaton Corp., 479 F. Supp. 512 (E.D. Mich. 1979) 146
Park; United States v., 421 U.S. 650 (1975) 30
Parker v. Baltimore & Ohio R.R., 652 F.2d 1012, 25 FEP Cases 889 (D.C. Cir. 1981) 128
Parker v. M&T Chems., 236 N.J. Super. 451, 566 A.2d 215, 4 IER Cases 1766 (1989) 70
Patterson v. McLean Credit Union, 491 U.S. __, 49 FEP Cases 1814 (1989) 131
Payne v. McLemore's Wholesale & Retail Stores, 654 F.2d 1130, 26 FEP Cases 1500 (5th Cir. 1981), *cert. denied,* 455 U.S. 100 (1982) 128, 154
Pendleton v. Rumsfeld, 628 F.2d 102, 22 FEP Cases 733 (D.C. Cir. 1980) 154
Peoples Sec. Life Ins. Co. v. Watson, 81 Md. App. 420, 568 A.2d 835, 5 IER Cases 71 (1990) 101
Percival v. General Motors Corp., 400 F. Supp. 1322 (E.D. Mo. 1975), *aff'd,* 539 F.2d 1126 (8th Cir. 1976) 109, 110
Perry v. Hartz Mountain Corp., 537 F. Supp. 1387, 115 LRRM 4934 (S.D. Ind. 1982) 85
Petermann v. Teamsters, 174 Cal.App.2d 184, 344 P.2d 25, 1 IER Cases 5, 44 LRRM 2968 (1959) 17, 18, 82, 83
Petrik v. Monarch Printing Corp., 111 Ill.App.3d 502, 444 N.E.2d 588, 115 LRRM 4520 (1982) 104
Pettway v. American Cast Iron Pipe Co., 411 F.2d 998, 1 FEP Cases 752 (5th Cir. 1969) 126
Pickering v. Board of Educ., Township High School Dist. 205, Will County, Ill., 391 U.S. 563, 1 IER Cases 8 (1968) 46
Pierce v. Ortho Pharmaceutical Corp., 84 N.J. 58, 417 A.2d 505, 1 IER Cases 109, 115 LRRM 3044 (1980) 87, 88
Pilcher v. Board of County Comm'rs, 14 Kan.App.2d 206, 787 P.2d 1204, 5 IER Cases 150 (1990) 113, 114
Plumbers Local 189; EEOC v., 311 F. Supp. 464, 2 FEP Cases 529 (S.D. Ohio 1970) 126
Porter v. Califano, 592 F.2d 770 (5th Cir. 1979) 49
Portley v. Kaiser Found. Hosps., 115 LRRM 2629 (N.D. Cal. 1983) 142
Public Citizen v. Steed, 733 F.2d 93 (D.C. Cir. 1984) 11
Pytlik v. Professional Resources, 887 F.2d 1371 (10th Cir. 1989) 92

R

Rankin v. McPherson, 483 U.S. 378, 2 IER Cases 257 (1987) 47
Read v. City of Lynwood, 173 Cal.App.3d 437, 219 Cal. Rptr. 26 (1985) 106, 107
Reed v. Municipality of Anchorage, 741 P.2d 1181, 4 IER Cases 1613 (1989) 109
Rendell-Baker v. Kohn, 457 U.S. 830 (1982) 132
Republic Steel Corp. v. Maddox, 379 U.S. 650, 58 LRRM 2193 (1965) 141

Reuther v. Fowler & Williams, 255 Pa. Super. 28, 386 A.2d 119, 115 LRRM 4690 (1978) 96
Rockwell Int'l Corp.; United States v., 730 F. Supp. 1031 (D. Colo. 1990) 123, 124
Rodriguez de Quijas v. Shearson/American Express, 490 U.S. 477 (1989) 176
Rollins v. Florida, 868 F.2d 397, 49 FEP Cases 763 (11th Cir. 1989) 154
Rossi v. Pennsylvania State Univ., 340 Pa. Super. 39, 489 A.2d 828 (1985) 112, 113
Rozier v. St. Mary's Hosp., 88 Ill.App.3d 994, 411 N.E.2d 50, 115 LRRM 4391 (1980) 89, 96, 114
Runyon v. McCrary, 427 U.S. 160 (1976) 131

S

San Diego Bldg. Trades Council v. Garmon, 359 U.S. 236, 43 LRRM 2838 (1959) 136
Sarchett v. Blue Shield, 43 Cal.3d 1, 233 Cal. Rptr. 76, 729 P.2d 267 (1987), *modified,* 43 Cal.3d 3166 (1987) 176
Schmidt v. Yardney Elec. Corp., 4 Conn. App. 69, 492 A.2d 512 (1985) 107
Schroeder v. Dayton Hudson Corp., 448 F. Supp. 910, 115 LRRM 4365 (E.D. Mich. 1978) 146
Schroeder v. Trans World Airlines, 702 F.2d 189, 113 LRRM 2051 (9th Cir. 1983) 142
Schultz v. Industrial Coils, 125 Wis.2d 520, 373 N.W.2d 74 (1985) 96, 112, 114
Schwartz v. Michigan Sugar Co., 106 Mich. App. 471, 308 N.W.2d 459, 115 LRRM 4535 (1981) 146
Scroghan v. Kraftco, 551 S.W.2d 811, 115 LRRM 4769 (Ky. App. 1977) 102
Sedima, S.P.R.L. v. Imrex Co., 473 U.S. 479 (1985) 80
Shah v. Mt. Zion Hosp. & Medical Center, 642 F.2d 268, 27 FEP Cases 772 (9th Cir. 1981) 126, 131
Shanholtz v. Monongahela Power Co., 165 W.Va. 305, 270 S.E.2d 178, 115 LRRM 4387 (1980) 92
Shearin v. E.F. Hutton, 885 F.2d 1162 (3d Cir. 1989) 80
Shearson/American Express v. McMahon, 482 U.S. 220 (1987) 176
Sheets v. Teddy's Frosted Foods, 179 Conn. 471, 427 A.2d 385, 115 LRRM 4626 (1980) 83, 84, 103, 115
Shelton v. Tucker, 346 U.S. 479 (1960) 46
Sides v. Duke Hosp., 74 N.C. App. 331, 238 S.E.2d 818, 1 IER Cases 512, 120 LRRM 2091 (1985) 83
Simpson v. Federal Mine Safety & Health Review Comm'n, 842 F.2d 453 (D.C. Cir. 1988) 73
Sitek v. Forest City Enters., 587 F. Supp. 1381 (E.D. Mich. 1984) 138
Skillsky v. Lucky Stores, 893 F.2d 1088 (9th Cir. 1990) 109
Slochower v. Board of Educ., 350 U.S. 551 (1956) 46
Smith v. Columbus Metro. Hous. Auth., 443 F. Supp. 61, 17 FEP Cases 315 (S.D. Ohio 1977) 127
Smith v. Georgia, 684 F.2d 729, 29 FEP Cases 1134 (11th Cir. 1982) 126
Smith v. Greyhound Lines, 614 F. Supp. 558, 117 LRRM 2253 (W.D. Pa. 1984) 142
Smith-Pfeffer v. Superintendent, Fernald School, 404 Mass. 145, 533 N.E.2d 1368, 4 IER Cases 289 (1989) 112
Snow v. Bechtel Constr., 647 F. Supp. 1514, 1 IER Cases 1264, 123 LRRM 3245 (C.D. Cal. 1986) 79
Southwestern Elec. Power Co., 84 LA 743 (1985) 155
St. Anne's Hosp.; EEOC v., 664 F.2d 128, 27 FEP Cases 170 (7th Cir. 1981) 128
State v., see name of opposing party
Steelworkers v. Warrior & Gulf Navigation Co., 363 U.S. 574, 46 LRRM 2416 (1960) 140
Stokes v. Bechtel N. Am. Power Corp., 614 F. Supp. 732 (N.D. Cal. 1985) 79
Strauss v. A.L. Randall Co., 144 Cal. App.3d 514, 194 Cal. Rptr. 520 (1983) 146
Suchodolski v. Michigan Consol. Gas Co., 412 Mich. 692, 316 N.W.2d 710, 115 LRRM 4449 (1982) 89
Sventko v. Kroger Co., 69 Mich. App. 644, 245 N.W.2d 151, 115 LRRM 4613 (1976) 92
Swaaley v. United States, 376 F.2d 857 (Ct. Cl. 1967) 44
Swenson v. Management Recruiters Int'l, 858 F.2d 1304, 47 FEP Cases 1855 (8th Cir. 1988), *reh'g denied,* 872 F.2d 264, 49 FEP Cases 760 (8th Cir.), *cert. denied,* 493 U.S. ___ (1989) 176

Sykes v. DPP, 3 W.L.R. 371, 45 Cr. App. R. 230 (1961) 25

T

Tameny v. Atlantic Richfield Co., 27 Cal.3d 167, 164 Cal. Rptr. 839, 610 P.2d 1330, 1 IER Cases 102, 115 LRRM 3119 (1980) 85
Tarr v. Riberglass, Inc., 115 LRRM 3688 (D. Kan. 1984) 146
Taylor v. Brighton Corp., 616 F.2d 256 (6th Cir. 1980) 74, 132
Teamsters Local 174 v. Lucas Flour Co., 369 U.S. 95, 49 LRRM 2717 (1962) 140
Textile Workers v. Lincoln Mills, 353 U.S. 448, 40 LRRM 2113 (1957) 139
Thompson v. St. Regis Paper Co., 102 Wash.2d 219, 685 P.2d 1081, 1 IER Cases 392, 116 LRRM 3142 (1984) 107
Tidwell v. American Oil Co., 332 F. Supp. 424, 3 FEP Cases 1007 (D. Utah 1971) 128
Todd v. Frank's Tong Serv., 784 P.2d 47, 4 IER Cases 1535 (Okla. 1989) 79
Tonetti v. Shirley, 173 Cal.App.3d 1144, 219 Cal. Rptr. 616 (1985) 176
Townsend v. L.W.M. Mgmt., 64 Md. App. 55, 494 A.2d 239 (1985) 94
Trombetta v. Detroit, Toledo & Ironton R.R., 81 Mich. App. 489, 265 N.W.2d 385, 115 LRRM 4361 (1978) 84

U

United States v., see name of opposing party
United States ex rel. Dick v. Long Island Lighting Co., 710 F. Supp. 1485 (E.D.N.Y. 1989), *aff'd,* 912 F.2d 13, 54 Fed. Contract Cases 391 (2d Cir. 1990) 123
United States ex rel. LaValley v. First Nat'l Bank of Boston, 707 F. Supp. 1351 (D. Mass. 1988) 123, 124
United States ex rel. LeBlanc v. Raytheon Co., 729 F. Supp. 170 (D. Mass.), *acq. in result,* 913 F.2d 17 (1st Cir. 1990) 122
United States ex rel. Newsham v. Lockheed, 722 F. Supp. 607 (N.D. Cal. 1989) 124
United States ex rel. Stillwell v. Hughes Helicopters, 714 F. Supp. 1084 (C.D. Cal. 1989) 124
United States ex rel. Stinson v. Provident Life, 721 F. Supp. 1247 (S.D. Fla. 1989) 123, 124
Utley v. Goldman Sachs & Co., 883 F.2d 184, 50 FEP Cases 1087 (1st Cir. 1989), *cert. denied,* 493 U.S. ___ (1990) 176

V

Vaca v. Sipes, 386 U.S. 171, 64 LRRM 2369 (1967) 141
Vermillion v. AAA Pro Moving & Storage, 146 Ariz. 215, 704 P.2d 1360, 119 LRRM 2337 (1985) 83
Viestenz v. Fleming Cos., 681 F.2d 699, 110 LRRM 2935 (10th Cir.), *cert. denied,* 459 U.S. 972 (1982) 138
Vigil v. Arzola, 102 N.M. 689, 699 P.2d 613, 2 IER Cases 377 (1983) 113
Vonch v. Carlson Cos., 439 N.W.2d 406, 4 IER Cases 789 (Minn. App. 1989) 106

W

Wagenseller v. Scottsdale Memorial Hosp., 147 Ariz. 370, 710 P.2d 1025, 1 IER Cases 526, 119 LRRM 3166 (1985) 86
Walsh v. Consolidated Frieghtways, 278 Or. 347, 563 P.2d 1205, 115 LRRM 5045 (1977) 147
Ward v. Frito-Lay, 95 Wis.2d 372, 290 N.W.2d 536, 115 LRRM 4320 (1980) 102
Warthen v. Toms River Community Memorial Hosp., 199 N.J. Super. 18, 488 A.2d 229, 118 LRRM 3179 (1985) 89, 90
Watson v. Cleveland Chair Co., 789 S.W.2d 538, 4 IER Cases 1779 (Tenn. 1989) 79
Wehr v. Burroughs Corp., 438 F. Supp. 1052, 20 FEP Cases 527 (E.D. Pa. 1977) 146
Wentz v. Maryland Casualty Co., 869 F.2d 1153, 49 FEP Cases 705 (8th Cir. 1989) 130, 150
Weyman v. Updegraff, 344 U.S. 183 (1952) 46
Whatley v. Metropolitan Atlanta Rapid Transit Auth., 632 F.2d 1325, 24 FEP Cases 1148 (5th Cir. 1980) 154

Wheeler v. Caterpillar Tractor Co., 108 Ill.2d 502, 485 N.E.2d 372, 121 LRRM 3186 (1985) 79
Whirlpool Corp. v. Marshall, 445 U.S. 1 (1980) 74
Will v. Michigan Dep't of State Police, ___ U.S. ___, 49 FEP Cases 1664 (1989) 49
Williams v. Hall, 683 F. Supp. 639 (E.D. Ky. 1988) 80
Willy v. Coastal Corp., 855 F.2d 1160, 4 IER Cases 819 (5th Cir. 1988) 79
Wiltsie v. Baby Grand Corp., 744 P.2d 432, 4 IER Cases 638 (Nev. 1989) 106
Winsey v. Pace College, 394 F. Supp. 1324 (S.D.N.Y. 1975) 128
Winters v. Houston Chronicle Publishing Co., ___ S.W.2d ___, ___ IER Cases ___ (Sept. 6, 1990) 106
Wiskotoni v. Michigan Nat'l Bank-West, 716 F.2d 378, 1 IER Cases 250, 114 LRRM 2596 (6th Cir. 1983) 83
Witkowski v. St. Ann's Hosp. of Chicago, 113 Ill.App.3d 745, 447 N.E.2d 1016 (1983) 147
Wolk v. Saks Fifth Ave., 728 F.2d 221, 1 IER Cases 361, 34 FEP Cases 193, 115 LRRM 3064 (3d Cir. 1984) 146
Wulf v. Wichita, 644 F. Supp. 1211, 1 IER Cases 895 (D. Kan. 1986) 49

Y

Yaindl v. Ingersoll-Rand Co., 281 Pa. Super. 560, 422 A.2d 611, 115 LRRM 4738 (1980) 110
Yount v. Hesston Corp., 124 Ill.App.3d 943, 464 N.E.2d 1214 (1984) 146

Z

Zaccardi v. Zale Corp., 856 F.2d 1473, 3 IER Cases 1249 (10th Cir. 1988) 94

Index

P

Y

About the Author

Daniel P. Westman is a partner in the Labor and Employment Relations Group of the law firm of Thelen, Marrin, Johnson & Bridges, and practices in the firm's San Francisco office. Over the last nine years Mr. Westman has been involved in all facets of labor and employment litigation, with extensive trial and appellate experience in whistleblower cases in the federal and state courts, and before various administrative agencies. Mr. Westman has published numerous articles in the labor and employment field.

Mr. Westman received his undergraduate degree from Stanford University in 1978, with distinction, and graduated from the University of Chicago Law School in 1981. Mr. Westman served as a law clerk to the Hon. Barbara B. Crabb, Chief Judge of the U.S. District Court for the Western District of Wisconsin, from 1981–1982.